Recreating Relationships

SUNY Series,
Teacher Preparation and Development
Alan R. Tom, Editor

Edited by
Helen Christiansen, Linda Goulet, Caroline Krentz,
and Mhairi Maeers

Foreword by
D. Jean Clandinin

Recreating Relationships

Collaboration and Educational Reform

STATE UNIVERSITY OF NEW YORK PRESS

Production by Ruth Fisher
Marketing by Fran Keneston

Published by
State University of New York Press, Albany

For information, address State University of New York Press,
State University Plaza, Albany, N.Y., 12246

Library of Congress Cataloging-in-Publication Data
Recreating relationships : collaboration and educational reform /
    edited by Helen Christiansen . . . [et al.].
        p.   cm. — (SUNY series, teacher preparation and development)
    Includes bibliographical references and index.
    ISBN 0-7914-3303-X (hc : alk. paper). — ISBN 0-7914-3304-8 (pbk.
    : alk. paper)
    1. Action research in education—United States.   2. College-school
cooperation—United States.   3. Teachers—Training of—United
States.   4. Educational change—United States.   I. Christiansen,
Helen, 1940–   . II. Series: SUNY series in teacher preparation and
development.
LB1028.24.R447   1997
370'.78—dc20   96-24411
                                                                      CIP

10 9 8 7 6 5 4 3 2 1

CONTENTS

FOREWORD
CONVERSATIONS ABOUT COMMUNITIES

In the spring of 1995 I listened intently while Maxine Greene, a well-known philosopher of education from Teachers College, Columbia University, spoke of her experience in academia. I listened carefully because her stories frequently are, for me, stories to live by. I was caught off guard by what I heard. Rather than telling her story as one with a plot line of support and recognition, she told her story as one lacking community, as one marked by being alone. As Maxine, the external examiner at my doctoral defense some twelve years earlier, told her story, she looked around the audience to catch my eye. When she did, she said, "I'll always remember the community around you, Jean, when we finished your examination." My first reaction was to feel honored, touched that she remembered the occasion. My second reaction was to feel surprised. Was it indeed so memorable in her life? But my surprise has awakened me to consider how rare and precious community was in her academic life and then to realize how central community has been in mine.

As I read this book in the weeks following that spring encounter with Maxine I began to restory community as a narrative thread in my own scholarly life. Maxine's naming of her experience of the celebration following my doctoral examination helped me recollect the experiences of community in my early academic life. My memory is filled with images of research project meetings, proposal writing sessions, long discussions about books and articles, days in project schools, and seminars with other researchers. Memories of all of the work on the personal practical knowledge project were reawakened. As I recollected the images and began to story them I realized that we did not use a language of community. Our words were of collaboration, not of community. But I now realize that those experiences were ones of community.

Michael Connelly and I have recently begun to explore the meanings of community in more focused and thoughtful ways. Not only do we explore ideas of community in our writing but we explore the living out of community in our practices. Our writing and Maxine's naming of the place of community in my life has led me to restory many experiences of community. From the small community created with those in my doctoral studies to the much larger and more diverse Among Teachers Community that Helen Christiansen, Linda Goulet, Caroline Krentz and Mhairi Maeers highlight in their introduction, I now name how community has been central in my academic life. Living in communities is necessary for my work as teacher and researcher.

This recollection and restorying reminds me of the complex and many layered meanings which living in community has for each of us. Frequently researchers lightly toss the word community into dialogues and debates, seeming to assume community is easily understood and easily achieved. Learning communities, research communities, classrooms as communities are terms used to label groups of people working together. But this easy use of the concept belies the complexities of communities. The authors in this book are not among those who take the idea lightly. This is a book that helps all of us understand the struggles of what it means to create, sustain and live in community. It is a book that celebrates community among teacher-researchers in universities, teacher-researchers in schools and universities, and teacher-researchers and children. The book goes beyond a celebration of community to highlight issues related to community. In the chapters I read of the uniqueness of each set of collaborators who struggled for community. I also read of common themes, shared experiences, resonating accounts. I was struck by the ways that issues of trust, mutuality, negotiation, voice and reciprocity were addressed by the authors.

The book reminds me that we do not live our stories outside of cultures and institutions. When we begin relationships intent on forming communities, we are living out those relationships on a storied landscape, a landscape that does not easily nurture collaboration among individuals within institutions nor across institutions.

In this book I read accounts and stories that are hopeful accounts of the struggle for community. They give us stories to live by in at least two ways. First, all the authors who tell their stories in this book are hopeful about their own work and their stories reflect that hope. The plot lines of their stories offer possibility to the authors in their own work. Rarely have researchers told their stories of engaging in research within communities. Telling their stories allows each set of authors to name their sense of possibility and hope in their work. Second, I read the stories as hopeful for in their hopefulness they offer hope to each reader for building communities in our places.

It is a book alive with possibility. It speaks of the authors' sense of imaginative possibility for a new landscape for education. These stories of community become a new set of stories for other researchers to live by, stories of creating and sustaining communities of researchers.

At the book's end, the editors invite readers to join with them in this imaginative task of changing educational landscapes. I know it is a conversation about community in which I want to participate.

D. Jean Clandinin
Centre for Research for
Teacher Education and Development
University of Alberta
Edmonton, Canada

ACKNOWLEDGMENTS

It is a pleasure to acknowledge the people who collaborated behind the scenes in order to make this book possible. First of all, we thank the many students, teachers, administrators, and communities who appear on its pages and between the lines. They are such an important part of the stories that are told. We want to acknowledge Penelope Bailey's early contribution. Penny was an integral part of the book's initial conception. Dean Michael Tymchak of the Faculty of Education at the University of Regina gave encouragement and support to the project from the beginning, as did colleagues in the Faculty and at the Saskatchewan Indian Federated College. We especially want to thank Meredith Cherland for sharing information with us that was particularly useful in the initial phases of the book. For financial support, we need again to thank the Faculty of Education as well as Louis Julé, Director of French Education, for enabling us to make the many photocopies required in such a collaborative endeavor.

We are deeply indebted to Juanita Ingham and Lee Gebhardt of the Saskatchewan Instructional Development Research Unit. To Juanita, a special thank you for your expertise in producing a manuscript of the highest quality. Thank you, Lee, for looking after the many small but important details, not the least of which was making sure that all four of us were available for book meetings!

Beyond the University of Regina, we want to acknowledge some very special people. First among these is Jean Clandinin who organized the preconferences that inspired this book. Thank you for your constant support and encouragement, and for your commitment to write an introduction to a manuscript that was still "becoming." We also owe a great deal to our fellow contributing authors who wrote and revised their chapters, investing much time and energy in this process. We appreciate the trust placed in us as editors.

We want to acknowledge the people at SUNY Press. Lois Patton's enthusiasm for the book proposal gave us the motivation to proceed. We thank her for her ongoing validation as the project progressed. The insightful comments of the reviewers were extremely helpful in turning an earlier manuscript into a more coherent text. We are also grateful for the support of series editor, Alan Tom.

Finally, we wish to thank our families: Bruno, Keith, Koonu, Danis, Art, Nathan, Adrienne, Esther and Stephanie. Thanks for respecting our space when we had to work and for being there when we wanted to share.

PROLOGUE

What This Book is About

This book about collaboration in education focuses on two inter-connected themes: the improvement of teaching practice through collaborative research, and reflection on the role of collaboration in educational change. The authors examine the enigmatic landscape of collaboration and, in so doing, contribute to the theory of collaborative research grounded in the reality of practicing educators. These educators describe their experiences of collaboration, reflect upon the relationships among and between collaborative partners, examine the different roles those partners play during the life of a collaborative undertaking, and discuss the multiple meanings and implications of collaborative research for those who teach in educational institutions.

Collaboration is explored in many sites and in a variety of relationships. It moves from classrooms in schools to those in universities and extends to broader communities. The collaborative partnerships are as varied as the sites. Relationships of many kinds are described and examined: teachers and students; consultants and teachers; teachers and teachers; school staffs and university professors; cooperating teachers, student teachers and faculty advisors; and researchers and participants. Authors reflect on the impact of collaboration on changing those relationships which, in turn, affect teaching practice and educational change.

Peopling the Landscape

This book is a collaborative book. Most of the authors know one another because the book project was the result of a series of critical incidents at conferences sponsored in part by Among Teachers Community (AcT), an association of teachers and teacher educators based in Canada but reaching out internationally. We had accepted Jean Clandinin's invitation to come together to join in conversation about collaborative research in education. Two of the editors attended the AcT inaugural conference in early 1992. There we first met Sharon Abbey, a founding member of the Centre for Collaborative Research (CCR) at Brock University in Ontario. Three of us were at the AcT preconference held prior to the mid-1992 annual meeting of the Canadian Society for Studies in Education (CSSE) where we saw Sharon again and met Helen Stewart, Mary Beattie, Kathie Webb, and Susan Drake. The following year we met many other contributors at the second annual preconference in Ottawa. We attended one another's presentations during the CSSE annual meeting the following week. As we participated in the different sessions, we felt a growing sense of excitement about the knowledge people were sharing. Something important was being said. The conversation needed to be opened up to a wider community.

The actual catalyst that sparked our decision to write this book was a session on stories of collaborative research in education in which we all participated either as presenters or discussants. There were forty of us at one of the last sessions of the conference at 5:00 p.m. on a Saturday afternoon. As the stories were shared and discussed there was a sense of openness. Our views and experiences in collaboration were being validated. We felt ourselves being stretched as we pulled ideas from one another and, in doing so, extended the thinking of the group. The room was charged with excitement. We were breaking new ground in collaborative research.

That evening at our hotel, a small group of conference participants that later became the editorial team, drew up an outline of a book, basing the chapter headings on what we had heard. We drafted a list of possible contributors. By the end of the summer of 1993 a call for submissions had gone out. Everybody who was asked to participate accepted our invitation. Another collaborative endeavor was underway.

Developing our Collaborative Landscape

In a manner similar to the collaborative process that began and sustained its development, the nature of the book evolved over a two-year period while contributing authors and editors got to know one another better. Early on, the four of us had a tentative vision of the book's ultimate shape based on what we knew about the work of the contributors. Later, as we took the various chapters through the revision process and wrote our own contributions to the book, we found ourselves living out a new story of collaboration. We became "connected knowers" (Belenky, Clinchy, Goldberger, and Tarule 1986) with the contributors and with each other.

The "work of talk" (Stewart, this volume) enabled us, as editors, to shape the chapters into a book that would enable multiple voices to be heard and yet still be coherent to readers. Such work helped us make sense of ongoing experience within the collaborative community we had formed to bring the book project to fruition.

In reading the different chapters we found that many of the stories shared a common feature: collaborative partners continually had to reexamine their relationships and often had to renegotiate the parameters of their research. Collaborative endeavors seemed to evolve along with the relationships that sustained them. So it was with us. As the book project evolved, our relationships changed and required renegotiation. We were immersed in collaboration.

Previewing the Landscape

Major themes divide the book into five parts. Part One begins with an examination of the nature of collaboration. The first three chapters explore our evolving understanding of collaboration and provide a conceptual map for what follows. The authors examine the nature of collaboration in different ways: through reflection of past practice viewed in light of recent writing on collaboration; through exploration of the nature of knowing in relation to collaboration; and through examination of metaphors to provide insight into the principles of collaboration. In addition to providing a framework, the first section sets the tone of the book. Each author calls into question past practices and beliefs in education and educational research brought about by involvement in collaboration.

The chapters in Part Two, "Mutuality and Negotiation," continue to question educational practice focusing, in particular, on taken-for-granted assumptions about how to conduct collaborative endeavors. Within their lived experiences the authors strive to redefine and clarify the meaning of mutuality and negotiation in collaboration.

The theme of Part Three, "Collaborative Research Communities," is collaboration in learning and teaching. The authors describe the creation of different collaborative learning communities that build knowledge from within and through interaction with others.

The chapters in Part Four, "Collaborative Partnerships and Projects," continue to reflect on past educational practices. These authors focus on how collaboration can, and does, change traditional roles and power structures in educational practice and research.

The single chapter in Part Five brings the book full circle as we, the editors, rethink the nature of collaboration in light of the collective experience of the authors of this edited book. The final chapter draws out the salient features of collaboration and its impact on educational change.

Part One

$\diamond$

Departure Points

Part One sets the stage for the rest of the book from three very different perspectives as it examines the nature of collaboration as a phenomenon in education and in educational research. Although each chapter, on the surface, appears to distinguish itself from the others in the section, there are common threads. It could be argued that each uses a lens metaphor to examine or reexamine collaborative knowing.

Phyllis Kapuscinski had thought that an earlier study she conducted with student teachers and cooperating (or helping) teachers during the field experience was collaborative. Viewed through her new "collaborative lens," developed as a result of reading and discussion with other colleagues, Kapuscinski realized that those who collaborate need to "rethink professional cultures . . . and their unquestioned values, cherished traditions and comfortable practices."

The second chapter in the section is Margaret Olson's. She explores the nature of knowing and knowledge through two lenses or sacred stories of knowledge: "getting an education" and "becoming more experienced." Olson concludes that "collaboration goes against the grain of traditional beliefs about what counts as knowledge and whose knowledge counts."

In the third and final opening chapter, Helen Stewart tells the ongoing story of the Centre on Collaborative Research at Brock University (Ontario, Canada) and shares metaphors its members developed as "lenses for viewing collaboration." Stewart and her colleagues examine the themes of interrelatedness and connectedness.

The editors chose these three chapters to open the book because they help create a framework for what follows. Subsequent chapters may lead some readers to reexamine their thinking about the nature of collaboration. Others may look upon this opening section as a kind of map. Whatever the case, we recommend that you keep these chapters in mind as you continue reading beyond Part One.

✧ Chapter One

The Collaborative Lens: A New Look at an Old Research Study

Phyllis Kapuscinski

Those who are unfamiliar with collaborative research practices sometimes engage in collaborative undertakings oblivious of the assumptions they bring to such endeavors. Roles and practices considered acceptable in other types of research cannot be transferred uncritically to collaborative research. Ten years ago I conducted a study which, I was certain, was collaborative. After all, it did involve both the Faculty of Education and cooperating teachers who were supervising students during their practice teaching. Today as I reexamine that research I am embarrassed by the inadequacy of my understanding of collaboration. In this chapter I share personal insights I gained from examining that early experience of "collaborative" research. I begin with a description of my original study and then move on to an examination of that study through a new collaborative lens.

3

The Study

Purpose

As a science teacher educator I was interested in the degree to which my secondary science students were able to apply what they had learned in their science education courses to their classrooms during the four-month practice teaching period or internship. I perceived internship as an arena for integrating theory and practice, and for initiating change. The specific facet of science education which I selected was the development of scientific literacy, that is, an understanding of how science, technology, and society influence one another and the ability to use this knowledge in everyday decisions (National Science Teachers Association 1982).

During my school visits I noted that because cooperating teacher-intern pairs were isolated from other science pairs, their efforts at promoting scientific literacy were fragmented and uncritiqued. I thought this situation might be improved through regular meetings of interns, cooperating teachers, and faculty advisors. This idea led to a research project in which interns and cooperating teachers reflected on the development of scientific literacy within the context of the practicum.

Sample

Five science interns, their five cooperating teachers, and I comprised the sample. My main data gathering technique was participant observation (Spradley 1979), in which I was to "engage in activities appropriate to the situation and observe the activities, people and physical aspects of the situation" (p. 54). My procedure was straightforward. I organized monthly meetings, interviewed interns and teachers, made informal observations, and took notes during group discussions. The meetings were usually an hour long, informal in format and hosted by a different cooperating teacher-intern pair each month. During the meetings I attempted to introduce information on scientific literacy into the group discussions as part of the reflection process. At first I tried to audiotape the discussions but found that it inhibited participation. I resorted to listening carefully, then recording what I remembered immediately after the meetings.

Findings

In my analysis I searched the data for patterns and identified three major themes: the significance of perceived goals; the importance of the relationship between intern and cooperating teacher; and the conditions required for effecting change in teacher behavior.

Significance of perceived goals.

The first theme revealed that the interns, cooperating teachers, and I, as faculty advisor, did not share a common perception of the goals of internship. At the university we viewed internship as a time to apply theory to practice and an opportunity to introduce change into the classroom. The interns were ambivalent, their apprehension of the unknown mixed with their anticipation of experiencing the real thing. The cooperating teachers wanted interns to experience classroom reality in a supportive environment.

Significance of relationships.

Three general types of relationships between the cooperating teachers and interns were evident: master-apprentice, idiosyncratic, and interdependent. The majority of pairs were master-apprentice, with the intern perceiving the cooperating teacher as the expert and attempting to emulate his/her teaching behavior. At times the cooperating teacher was responsible for directing the relationship to that end. He or she insisted on setting the pace of the course, dictating the methodology, and determining which resources would be used. Interns in this relationship gained security, acceptance, and a favorable final evaluation but were reluctant to promote scientific literacy beyond the normal practice of the master teacher.

The idiosyncratic relationship was based on the belief that teachers are born, not made, and that each intern would develop his/her own teaching style if given freedom to do so. Cooperating teachers limited the opportunities for interns to observe, encouraged independent planning and evaluation, and gave minimal supervision. Although the interns were free to develop their own teaching styles, they lacked a norm for determining whether they were in fact developing scientific literacy in their classes. Their own feelings became the touchstone for effective teaching. By discounting research findings and the experience of competent professionals, these interns had only a superficial base for their future development.

The ideal, an interdependent relationship, was one in which both intern and cooperating teacher contributed. As a team they explored various instructional strategies and reflected on their effectiveness in promoting scientific literacy. The greatest threat to this relationship was the risk of stunting growth by confusing codependence with interdependence. In the former, both partners are insecure. The intern lacks practical experience, whereas the cooperating teacher is unfamiliar with the underlying theory and the strategies basic to scientific literacy.

Conditions for changing teacher behavior. The most crucial theme emerging from the discussion was the role of attitudes and resources in the promotion of scientific literacy. Cooperating teachers knew that most of their pupils would not continue the study of science at the postsecondary level and those who did would probably remember little of what they had learned. Yet all of the pupils would soon become voting citizens in a society shaped by science and technology. Cooperating teachers struggled with their own reluctance to adapt to this reality. They knew that social issues were not bound to specific academic disciplines, and thus had to be viewed from a variety of perspectives. Relevant science courses needed an interdisciplinary base as well as attention to the nature and limits of science and technology. Because science teachers had not been prepared for this specific curricular and instructional approach, they needed time for sharing insights in a nonthreatening environment.

In the discussion the group appealed for two major considerations: respect for teachers' experience and appropriate in-service. The cooperating teachers felt that faculty rarely recognized the validity of teachers' attempts to cultivate scientific literacy. Activities which the faculty advisor might judge as trivial were in many instances extremely challenging. Moreover, teachers sometimes resisted innovation, not because of the innovation itself but because of faculty's insensitivity to teachers' deeply held convictions. As an example, teachers were convinced that an intern must first master subject matter and basic instructional skills, then proceed to the more sophisticated content and instructional techniques required for teaching scientific literacy. Yet some teacher educators belittled content and skills, even labeling them as obstacles to effective teaching.

The cooperating teachers and interns examined their own understanding of science, technology and society, and their relationships. Because they perceived science as value-free, they had difficulty situating societal issues in a science program. The meaning which the participants ascribed to science and technology influenced their acceptance of scientific literacy-based curricula. When science was perceived primarily as a static body of knowledge, societal issues became illustrations and applications. On the other hand, when science and technology were perceived as humanly created systems of thought, societal issues could readily become the central organizers of science curricula.

The cooperating teachers objected to the manner in which the science-technology-society (STS) curricula had been imposed upon them without adequate consultation, in-service, and resources. They argued that teachers had to comprehend the aims of the new science curricula and consciously accept them before they could overcome their insecurity and personal bias. They suggested that in-service could be provided by practicing teachers who were familiar with the philosophy of the new curricula and who were competent in using the approach.

Conclusions

The study terminated at the end of the internship period. I drew several conclusions related to what I called "the enhancement of professional growth through reflective dialogue." First, cooperating teachers can engage in and benefit from reflection sessions. At the end of the internship semester, participants recommended that the practice be continued with future cooperating teachers and interns. Second, the study reinforced the importance of ongoing dialogue between faculty advisors and cooperating teachers and supported the catalytic role of faculty in supervision as well as implementation of new curricula. Third, there was a strongly expressed need for appropriate in-service. These concluding statements signaled the end of my study. I was pleased with my collaborative project.

Reexamination of the Study

During the past ten years I have become conversant with collaborative research practices through articles, workshops, and participation in a collaborative research group. These experiences gave me an entirely new perspective on my study. Upon rereading the report I was amazed and appalled that I could have perceived the study as collaborative. In fact, I was saddened by the arrogance and insensitivity I had displayed in the planning and conducting of an entire project in which teachers and interns were merely subjects, providers of the information I needed to complete a task. The study had separated me from them, and had fostered an atmosphere that stifled the participatory process.

Collaborative Planning

I had entered the study without examining my assumptions, particularly those related to the processes of collaboration and reflection. I had thought that organizing meetings would ensure participation; that collaboration would occur naturally. Since then, I have learned that collaboration requires practice and generous and sustained mediation to mature (Pallante 1993). If a group is to develop trust, members must be given time to get to know each other on a personal basis. All parties must have the opportunity to demonstrate their knowledge and competence (Yopp, Guillaume, and Savage 1993–94). Reflection, too, demands understanding and effort. I had recognized the need for reflection, but by identifying reflection with discussion, I had denied the group and myself the challenge of probing our assumptions and beliefs, and examining the possible consequences of our actions (Dewey 1933, 9). I had also assumed that discussion was equivalent to collegial talk, not realizing at the time that collegiality is based on trust and that collegial talk develops gradually (Ellis 1993).

The deficiencies in my planning became more obvious when I considered three points raised by Fountain and Evans (1994). They contend that successful restructuring efforts must be situational and problem-based; that successful collaborative activities depend on the extent to which they succeed in transforming independent but interrelated goals into mutually beneficial actions; and that a shift toward collaborative decision making must take place for substantive change to occur in either school or university system. In defining the problem of the study, I had consulted neither the teachers nor the interns to determine whether they had perceived it as a problem. Nor had I inquired about their goals and the benefits for them that could accrue from the study. The decision to implement change in the school system had been made solely by me—the one person who would not be directly affected by the change. My lack of commitment to change and to my subjects was obvious at the end of the project. The project terminated as soon as I had completed my research report. I took no further steps to determine whether the project continued to influence teachers. I perceived the participants merely as sources of data, not as persons deeply committed to improving science education.

Collaborative Relationships

Although I had diligently discussed cooperating teacher-intern relationships within school settings, I had given little thought to roles and relationships within a collaborative project. Recent research reveals a wide variety in the relationships that exist between university researchers and classroom teachers. They range from the teacher playing the role of the subject to be studied, manipulated and probed; to teacher as research assistant aiding in the collection and analysis of data; to that of a teacher being a full member of the educational research community. There has been a shift from viewing teachers as subjects to viewing them as partners in setting the goals of the research and framing or reframing the research questions. This involvement of teachers in university research into teaching is now commonly understood as collaborative research (Clift, Veal, Johnson, and Holland 1990; Kyle and McCutcheon 1984; Lieberman 1992; Tikunoff and Ward 1983; Tikunoff, Ward, and Griffin 1979). Clift and her colleagues have defined collaboration as "the explicit agreement among two or more persons to meet and accomplish a particular goal or goals" (1991, 54).

Establishing roles within a collaborative project is essential. Participants who are inadequately informed will be reluctant and ambivalent (Houser 1990). When collaborative efforts result from a top-down model, those who will be most heavily involved—the classroom teachers—have the least input. Furthermore, such efforts seldom have the desired impact. The teachers who will be involved must understand the nature of the proposed change and must be willing to invest their time and resources into making the project work. By the same token, education faculty must be deeply committed to collaboration, be comfortable working in the field, and must not perceive the expenditure of time as ultimately interfering with tenure and promotion. However, because collaboration takes considerable time and energy, participants must perceive some advantage for their involvement (Yopp et al. 1993–94). This implies an understanding of the perspectives and needs of the other. Then exchange between the two parties can be genuine, not merely action that looks like help (Erickson 1989).

In establishing research relationships we, as university researchers, must respect teachers as knowledgeable educational authorities. There is no reason to place any person in a position in which he or she is subservient to the other (Feldman 1993). In an equitable collaborative project, teachers and researchers work with parity and assume equal responsibility to identify, investigate, and resolve the problems and concerns of classroom teachers. Such collaboration recognizes and utilizes the insights and skills provided by each participant and, at the same time, demands that no set of responsibilities be assigned a superior status (Tikunoff et al. 1979). Feldman (1993) has detected a flaw in Tikunoff's argument, claiming that it harbors within it a hierarchical relationship by forcing university researchers into the role of the benevolent educator who must altruistically serve those who are in need, the school teachers. Although teachers may gain increased prestige among their peers and engage in meaningful professional dialogue with other adults and improve their practice as a result of the research, they are still not in an equitable position. With Goodson (1991), Feldman is concerned about a collaborative mode of research which seeks to give full equality and stature to the teacher but which employs as its initial and predominant focus the practice of the teacher. Both researchers believe that this is a profoundly unpromising point of entry from which to promote a collaborative enterprise. For the university researcher, it may seem unproblematic; for the teacher, it may seem that the starting point for collaboration is focused on the maximum point of vulnerability. The researcher is actually asking the teacher to begin with a public analysis and, at least, an implied evaluation. In a collaborative relationship it is important to make the existence of the hierarchy explicit. If an equitable collaboration is to occur, the relationship between researcher and teacher must be examined in order to unpack complexities, including differences in goals, expectations, and social status.

Collaborative Goals

In my initial study I had noted that the interns, cooperating teachers, and faculty advisors perceived the goals of internship differently. My comments had focused on the priority and validity of my own perception, with little attention to the other participants' goals. As for the research study, I had defined the goals with no consultation. A difficulty arises when one attempts to set common goals in a collaborative project. If university researchers focus solely on the needs and concerns of teachers, they face the uncertainty of not knowing whether the research will aid attainment of goals such as generating propositional knowledge or publishing in refereed journals. If the research is directed toward problems identified by the university researcher alone, then there is no guarantee that any of the findings of the research will be of use to the teachers. Feldman (1993) has suggested that the dilemma could be resolved by proposing one set of goals and one set of research problems. The two parties could share the same ultimate goal, that is, the improvement of schooling and, at the same time, have different immediate goals. The university researcher's aim is to augment the scientific knowledge base for teacher education; the teacher's aim is to improve practice.

The Cultural Gap

Although I had more than ten years experience as a high school teacher, I entered my initial study unaware that a cultural gap exists between the university and the school. The perspectives and cultures of these two institutions differ, particularly in terms of rewards and incentives, organization of task and time, and in assumptions about the needs that will be most served at these sites. Vare (1994) and Clift (1994) contend that there has not been adequate study of the cultural differences between the school and university. Teacher education must bridge two worlds: one of theoretical knowledge, applied science, or technical rationality; and a second of practical competence and the epistemology of reflective practitioners (Evertson 1990; Schön 1983, 1987; Zeichner 1990). Vare (1994) notes that recent proposals for the restructuring of teacher education endorse collaborative activities on the part of practicing teachers and college professors (Goodlad 1990, Levine 1992). However, participants may have fundamentally different views of the activities required of prospective teachers. Collaboration will require discussion of those differences and of the assumptions participants hold regarding the preparation of prospective teachers. If the two real worlds of applied science and reflective practice are to blend, there must be dialogue and discourse beyond their respective borders. Raths, McAninch and Katz (1991) identified five points of tension that differentiate the two cultures: readiness to act, confidence, source of justifications, search for knowledge, and uses of knowledge. These attributes could provide a framework to describe, understand, and cope with the inevitable conflicts arising with the implementation of change. Planning teams could become the negotiating forum for these points of concern and could help improve practice by tapping into new sets of resources and providing a different lens through which to analyze problems. Unity of purpose, decision-making responsibility, and commitment to change and risk taking are three principles which challenge deeply held beliefs and eventually create a shared culture.

Reflections

As I reflected critically on my initial research, I asked myself whether my report would be different now. Obviously, it would present a more equitable research program and process. I hope that it would also allow the participants' voices to emerge, not in statements seeking validation from me, but in questions that would challenge my culture, my goals and my status. I would want all of our voices to be heard in the interpretation of the data. And I would not want the relationship between us to dissolve when I presented the findings.

I was deeply moved by the challenges Clift (1994) issues to teacher educators: "To what degree can we transform (or perhaps set aside) role hierarchies and traditional role relationships?" (p. 31). She relates that challenge to the difficulties encountered in the restorying of traditional conceptions of student teacher, cooperating teacher, and university professor (Clandinin, Davies, Hogan, and Kennard 1993) as well as the role strain, negotiation, and ambiguity inherent in fledgling efforts at school restructuring (e.g., Clift, Johnson, Holland, and Veal, 1992). Clift (1994) asks us to examine the strength of our commitment in the struggle to create new communities. Can we even begin to identify what some of these commitments involve? Vare (1994) applauds those educators who build community by creating pragmatic structures that connect participants from across institutions who cannot separate initial learning for teaching from continual learning for teaching. If we are to create communities of inquiry and practice, we must consider how we are to rethink our professional cultures—our unquestioned values, cherished traditions and comfortable practices. Clift challenges us to move beyond specialization (my students, my school, my research agenda) to create programs of practical research that facilitate an understanding of our community, our children, and of the relations among theories and practices.

Perhaps I have moved to a new level of commitment and integration by examining my initial research through the collaborative lens. If I have moved, I celebrate that success.

✧ Chapter Two

Collaboration: An Epistemological Shift

Margaret Olson

Whereas collaboration shows promise for reshaping the relationship between research and practice as university teachers, classroom teachers, and preservice teachers attempt to integrate and expand their understandings of teachers' professional knowledge, collaborative relationships are relatively new to the educational landscape where formal learning relationships have traditionally been of a very different sort. Developing collaborative relationships calls for a monumental shift in the traditional version of epistemology which is implicitly lived within present social contexts of educational institutions.

Crites (1971) uses the term "sacred stories" to describe the anonymous and communal stories which implicitly underlie the cultural structures that form our consciousness, our taken-for-granted attitudes that we bring to our experience because of the ways in which our world is presented to us by our social contexts. Versions of the "origin, nature, and limits of human knowledge" (Guba and Lincoln 1989, 83) are part of our implicit cultural structures which have developed over time. Thus, I name the epistemological versions lived out in our practice in educational institutions as sacred stories to show they are fundamental and unquestioned in our theory and our practice. Here, I look closely at two conflicting epistemological sacred stories that create tensions and possibilities for collaborative relationships to develop. In the first version, "getting an education" (Gadamer 1975), knowledge is seen as depersonalized, certain, received, and accumulated. In the second version, "becoming more experienced" (Dewey 1938; Gadamer 1975), knowledge is seen as personalized, tentative—constructed and reconstructed through transactions with others. Each version has implications for the methods we choose for becoming knowledgeable as well as for the ways in which we assess the value of what we know. Each version leads to different beliefs about what counts as authorized knowledge, the procedures for constructing knowledge, and the relationship of the knower to the known.

Two university teachers and two classroom teachers (Christiansen, Krentz, Froc, and Adamack 1993), in describing their collaborative relationship, allude to the tension created by these conflicting sacred stories as "something [that] had gotten in our way" (p. 27). They also allude to the possibilities inherent in collaboration for awakening to taken-for-granted epistemological assumptions as they speak of "stirrings beneath the surface" (p. 27). I resonate with these two feelings in my research and my practice as well. I now recognize the first as the implicit dominant version of "getting an education" which tells us how the relationships in our lives as teachers and researchers *should* be lived. The second feeling is that of a newer collaborative version of "becoming more experienced" struggling to emerge to create new stories of educative relationship.

In this chapter I explore some underlying differences in these two epistemological sacred stories and show how collaboration goes against the grain of traditional beliefs about what counts as knowledge and whose knowledge counts. I first describe these two versions. I then discuss the centrality of voice in collaboration. Next, I explore possibilities for creating and maintaining collaborative relationships. I conclude this chapter with thoughts on building strength through collaboration.

Getting an Education: A Body of Professional Knowledge

The first epistemological sacred story is the one we have been born into in our educational institutions. It shapes our beliefs about research, practice, the relationship between the two, and the relationships of the people involved. Here knowledge is believed to take the form of an object separate from the knower making it possible to have objective truth uncontaminated by contextual contingencies and personal biases. As Clandinin and Connelly (1990) state, "it is a view that implies that no matter what any particular person happens to believe about it, there is a correct and true view of the world. It is a depersonalized notion of truth and meaning" (p. 242).

This conception of knowledge is based on the positivistic belief that there are underlying essential objective truths about reality. It leads us to the search for one correct or true version rather than an appreciation of different perspectives developed from individuals' diverse experiences. Bruffee (1986) tells us that in this mode of thought we assume "that there must be a universal foundation, a ground, a base, a framework, a structure of some sort behind knowledge or beneath it, upon which what we know is built, assuring its certainty or truth" (p. 776).

In this version, knowledge is abstracted from experience and knowledge construction is "driven by principled hypotheses" (Bruner 1986, 13). These abstractions become a body of knowledge separate from individual knowers and take on the appearance of being certain, static, and objective. Principles, propositions, and theories become generalizable knowledge which is used to explain, predict, control, and evaluate our world, including the worlds constructed by individual persons. There can be only one correct version. The truth of this knowledge is tested in its replicability enabling us to predict and thus control. Inferior versions are supplemented or replaced by versions which increase our ability to predict and control, that is, by versions which enable us to increase our certainty. The search for certainty is compelling, for if we can know the right way, we can arrive at consensus and thus live in harmony. In this view, rightness is valued as decontextualized truth and perfection seems possible. Anyone wanting to gain certain knowledge would then need to negate the contextual contingencies of personal experience and opinion and trust the certainty of cognitive reason. As Clandinin and Connelly (1990) state, "a disembodied mind permits the certainty needed by technical rationalism" (p. 242).

The methodological split of mind from body, and subject from object, led to the belief that knowledge gained by rational objectivism was superior to that gained by personal experience. This version has left us with a legacy of doubting all things that have not been proven as well as the notion of reductionism where knowledge is built up from a basic truth. Reductionism has led to extensive specialization, compartmentalization, and a hierarchical structure of knowledge. This version provides a pervasive hegemony as the legitimate authority of technical rationalism, shaping our society and education systems and thus our experience. Its pervasiveness in our institutions cannot be overemphasized (Barrett 1979; Bruffee 1986; Crites 1971; Guba and Lincoln 1989; Schön 1983). It is the hegemony of this version that gets in the way as we struggle to enable collaborative relationships to surface.

When getting an education is storied as the accumulation of knowledge, knowing becomes hierarchically structured. Relationships become positional as objective knowledge is transmitted from those who know to those who do not. In this story university professors know more than classroom teachers; classroom teachers know more and better than their students; preservice teachers appear to know very little at all. Knowledge constructed through positivistic research provides a technical rational view of practice (Schön 1983). In this version, empowerment is possible through cooperation as those who already know help those who do not know. It is the premise on which the notion of "theory to practice" is built.

When the truth is known about how things are, correct ways to implement practices through certainty, prediction and control seem possible. Thus, in this version, knowledge already constructed is passed down to others to use in practice. Knowing the truth, and knowing how to practice it, can lead to perfection with enough knowledge and enough practice. Knowing enough enables one to determine what went wrong and, through this process, ways to improve practice are found and future situations are better controlled and closer to the ideal. In this version, questions are asked in order to find correct answers. Individuals strive for perfection as they try to learn the "right way." In this version surprise and unexpectedness are storied as not knowing enough to be able to predict and to be in control. Uncertainty is storied as not yet knowing enough. Unexpected events are storied as "trouble," problems that can be overcome once enough is known. This version leaves teachers (and researchers) feeling vulnerable and incompetent because they can never reach the ideal within the contextual complexities of their practice.

Two approaches to the professional education of teachers based on "getting an education" have historical beginnings which are still prevalent in our taken-for-granted attitudes today. These sacred stories provide the underlying contexts from which collaborative relationships are struggling to emerge.

The apprenticeship approach described by Dewey valued "imitation of model behavior, mastery of essential skills, and acceptance of routine procedures as the basis of action" (Patterson 1983, 6). This approach was prevalent in the normal schools where the focus was on practical issues of how to teach, with academic courses offered "so that teachers would be familiar with what they would be teaching in the schools" (Urban 1990, 61). The intention becomes one in which the novice is expected to learn from the experts who have "more" experience. In this version, experience is seen as a body of practical knowledge which can be transmitted to others to practice. This is a story of practice makes perfect. It is still a prevalent way of constructing knowledge about teaching.

The ways in which emerging universities in America were shaped by the "intellectual hegemony of Positivism" (Schön 1983, 34) during the late nineteenth and early twentieth centuries led to technical rationalism as a sacred story of professional education. Faculties of education soon became part of these institutions, drawing needed clientele to the universities. The tensions between practical relevance and theoretical abstraction are played out in present educational institutions both within universities and between universities and schools. Both are versions of knowledge as hierarchically constructed where getting an education involves the accumulation of theory and practice.

Normal schools, "seeking their proper position in the educational hierarchy" (Urban, 65), became colleges, often hiring their faculty members from the universities. As theoretical knowledge gained status as the measure of competence, knowledge constructed through practical experience was seen as too subjective and nonrigorous to be taken seriously into account.

Moving the focus of teacher education away from schools and teachers created a rift between teacher education institutions and schools that is still pervasive today. The scientific nature of research on teaching split theory from practice. The search for generalizable theories about teaching decontextualized teacher education and technical rationalism became valued over practical knowledge in the training of teachers. The hierarchical nature of the institutional structure reflected the hierarchical epistemology of positivism. The emphasis on scientific rigor as having more status than practical application led to the "denigration of the school classroom as the appropriate focus of educational study" (Urban, 64).

While the sacred story of technical rationalism has been questioned (Schön 1983), the hierarchical organization built up by the epistemology of positivism leaves little space for other stories to be lived or told. This version mitigates against collaboration because the voice of the one who knows is assumed to be dominant. When research is conducted with teachers, researchers' interpretations dominate. Here, researchers appear to know more than teachers, yet the form of knowledge this version provides is too far removed from practice to be useful to teachers and the theory/practice gap is perpetuated. For collaboration to work, all participants must see one another and themselves as knowers whose ideas deserve to be heard. In order for this to occur, an epistemological shift which values the forms of knowledge constructed in practice must take place. All participants can then learn from one another, each strengthening their own knowledge to be used in their own practice, whether that be the practice of teaching or the practice of research, and whether the teaching occurs in school classrooms or university classrooms.

Becoming More Experienced: Knowledgable Professionals

The second version, which Dewey (1938) and Gadamer (1975) describe as "becoming more experienced," is based on a transactional relationship between the knower and the known. In this version, we are all knowers who know the world in different ways. Here knowledge is seen as embodied and personally and socially constructed through the continuous and interactive nature of experience. As individuals in the world, we are each unique and separate beings, isolated in our own continuity of experience with our own unique biographies. At the same time, being part of the world places us in an interactive relationship that constitutes a sharing of experience. Dewey (1938) states that "the two principles of continuity and interaction are not separate from each other. They intercept and unite. They are, so to speak, the longitudinal and lateral aspects of experience" (p. 43). Here, knowledge is socially constructed through transactions with our social and natural environment.

The experiential epistemology of practice is narrative in form (Olson 1995a). Our practice as teachers and researchers takes the form of stories, not the form of theories. Because each of us constructs unique narrative knowledge (Bruner 1986; Olson 1994) based on our individual continuity of experience, infinite ways of knowing are possible. University teachers, classroom teachers, and preservice teachers each express different versions of educative experience, focus on different issues as relevant, and are concerned with different problems of practice. Through interaction, meaning is continually reconstructed as new interactions lead to further understanding. In this version, experience is always open to reconstruction as we tell, live, retell, and relive stories of educative practice. Learning through experience implies being open and staying open to experience—your own experience and the experience of others.

Experience that confirms what we already know, expect, and take for granted, seldom leads to further insights. It allows us to go on "living as usual" (Schutz 1970) and verifies what we already know. As Gadamer (1975) states, "every experience worthy of the name runs counter to our expectations" (p. 319), and thus forces us to question. This unexpected aspect of experience provides opportunities for learning. We can only expect those things which are already in the realm of our experience. Encountering the unexpected opens up new opportunities for adding to or reconstructing what we already know. Bruner (1986) states "surprise is a response to violated presupposition" (p. 46). It is this surprise that can awaken us to reconstructing meaning from our experience. As Connelly and Clandinin (1995) point out:

> The horizons of our knowing shift and change as we awaken to new ways of "seeing" our world, to different ways of seeing ourselves in relation to each other and to the world. We begin to retell our stories with new insights, in new ways. (p. 2)

Narrative knowledge is integral with experience and is continually being constructed and reconstructed through experience. Eisner (1988) tells us "knowledge is rooted in experience and requires a form for its representation" (p. 15). Teachers' stories are one of the most pervasive ways we use to represent our experience. Because stories also reflect the teller's moral stance, stories cannot be correct or incorrect but rather express a moral sense of right or wrong. Stories are told in order to have the teller's stance understood by him or herself, and others as well, and to get validation for having chosen to act in a certain way or to find out what could have been done to make the situation more meaningful and/or useful. Hearing different perspectives gives us new ways to story past experience and imagine future possibilities. Narrative knowledge is constructed and reconstructed as diverse research and teaching stories are told through a collaborative process. In education we try to construct and reconstruct better teaching and research stories. Theories can be used to inform our stories but they do not consume and/or silence the stories. Construction and reconstruction of narrative knowledge is the antithesis of certainty.

When narrative knowledge gained through experience rather than only rational objectivism is taken as the basis for constructing knowledge, a variety of modes of knowing can be explored. We can begin to inquire not only into what we know but how we know, why we choose to know in particular ways, how our knowing changes, and how we experience our knowing. We begin to experience ourselves as dynamic learners and, as such, live rather than only tell a story of lifelong learning. In this way it becomes possible to find integrity as a teacher/learner/researcher in an educational community.

In this version of knowledge construction, each person both shapes his/her own knowledge and is shaped by the knowledge of others. Everyone is a knower whose ideas deserve to be heard, making it possible to learn from and with one another. It is in this second version of becoming educated where collaboration is possible. Here we each become more experienced as we become more able to learn from our own experiences and from the experiences of others. However, this collaborative process requires that participants be able to both tell their own stories and listen carefully to the stories constructed by others, even when these stories express diverse, and perhaps conflicting, versions.

The Centrality of Voice

In the sacred story of "getting an education," there is room for only one voice, one version. The voice of authority (Olson 1993) belongs to the one who knows the most or best. Argument and explanation become the vehicles for arriving at consensus and agreement. In order to transmit this knowledge, one must know enough, that is, more than those who will be receiving the knowledge, and must be able to convey this knowledge clearly so others will understand. One must also be persuasive in order to convince others that the version of knowledge constructed is credible and more worthy of being accepted than alternate versions. This type of communication is pervasive in educational institutions. Telling overshadows listening as individuals compete to have their versions accepted. This voice closes down collaborative relationships.

Narrative authority (Olson 1993; 1995b) speaks in a very different voice—the voice of experience. Here, the stories each individual chooses to author are understood as representations of their experience and thus expressions of their situated or narrative knowledge. When knowledge is viewed as a social construction, "knowing is cooperative and as such is integral with communication" (Dewey and Bentley 1949, vi). We construct knowledge as we represent our experience in ways that express our understanding of the world to others. Collaboration is essential to reconstruction of knowledge as diverse versions of narrative knowledge are shared.

Gadamer (1975) draws parallels between the qualities required to become experienced and the qualities of conversation, describing how inquiry into experience and inquiry in conversation both have a hermeneutic quest for meaning. Collaborative relationships also take the form of conversations. Conversation allows the opening of possibilities and expands the horizons of knowing when ideas and stories are shared providing simultaneous connections between people and ideas. In authentic conversation there is an openness to inquiry. For a conversation to remain open to inquiry, a sense of equality among all participants is essential. Each person in the conversation must be valued as a person in order to feel safe in sharing subjective views. Each conversation is a disclosure not only of ideas but of self. It is the person, not his/her knowledge or status, that must be valued in order for each person to feel free to give voice to his/her own subjective views. Mary Beattie (1993) tells us:

> To be a constructor of meaning requires that the learner has a strong, confident voice to pursue the uncertainty, risk, and tentative process of genuine inquiry, balancing the tensions between the inner, personal voice and the outer, received voices. Thus, meanings can be constructed within the communal conversation, where individual voices are acknowledged, authenticated and integrated, and the imposition of meaning by one or another is replaced by collaborative meaning-making. (p. 110)

The partners in the conversation show both an interest in the topic being discussed as well as an interest in the other person. Thus, conversation is a means of connecting individual views of experience that lead to further understanding both of the topic and of the person. Conversation evolves around objects and situations in the world of the participants and leads to shared meaning. As Gitlin (1990) points out, our questions "reflect an ongoing negotiation among the influences of material conditions or contexts, cultural norms, and self" (p. 454). The sharing of subjective views allows us to hear alternate perspectives that in turn allow us to reshape our sense of meaning "by introducing us to new frames of reference" (Brimfield, Roderick, and Yamamoto 1983, 12).

In order to be part of a community, we shape our voice in relationship with others as we attempt to have our ideas listened to and understood. Brown and Gilligan (1992) tell us "the sounds of one's voice change in resonance depending on the relational acoustics; whether one is heard or not heard, how one is responded to (by oneself and by others)" (p. 20). When relationships are positional, many voices are silenced. Meaning is negotiated by a small minority and the silent majority are oppressed. "Restoring voice requires acknowledging relationships: the individual relationship to the meaning of his or her experience, and hence to language, and the individual's relationship to others, since understanding is a social process" (Britzman 1989, 146). Conversation which is inclusive allows all participants to share in the negotiation of constructed meaning by encouraging the voicing of personal meaning and can consist of both "a good story" and "a good argument" (Bruner 1986). However, it is essential that the partners perceive each other as equal but different persons with different experiences intent on increasing understanding rather than displaying their superiority.

Creating and Maintaining Collaborative Relationships

When we understand knowledge as socially constructed, we need to make spaces for the conversations which are essential in order to tell, hear, and respond to the stories of ourselves and others. Through the opportunity for conversation we can hear a variety of views and experiences which may awaken us to new ways to story our experience. Conversation is not a process of telling what we know in a definitive sense, but rather a collaborative endeavor where each participant brings meaning and questions to the conversation. As stories are told, given back, and retold, "knowledge communities" (Craig 1992) develop in which knowledge is constructed in the transactions between individuals. As Gitlin (1990) states, "the development of voice . . . reshapes roles so that disenfranchised members have the right to tell their stories and the opportunity to examine underlying assumptions" (p. 460). Only when our knowledge is shared can it be open for interpretation and inquiry.

Creating and maintaining safe spaces for people to share diverse ways of knowing is not an easy task. Many factors silence our knowledge as we try to shape ourselves to the canons and authorized versions we may feel compelled to tell. When we construct meaning through collaborative conversation, the reference point exists in the transaction, the space between the individuals involved. This is a "middle ground" (Clandinin, Davies, Hogan, and Kennard 1993) which needs to be a safe space in order for the persons involved to risk making their narrative knowledge public. This middle ground is not possible in the sacred story of certainty, prediction and control where knowledge (and, therefore, the people who hold that knowledge) is hierarchically structured. The middle ground is a collaborative space where each individual struggles to articulate and inquire into his or her own knowing of educative situations. It is the diversity of knowledge expressed in a collaborative situation which makes reconstruction of knowledge possible. This middle ground needs to be a safe space not in the sense of a space where consensus and agreement are possible, but in the sense of a space to risk voicing one's own views as well as hearing divergent views, alternative perspectives, and unauthorized versions. A middle ground develops in relationships built with others over time.

Uncovering taken-for-granted assumptions is risky since these assumptions shape our knowledge about who we are and our relationship to others. Therefore, we need to honor each others' stories as we try to understand them. It is difficult to speak in a voice which does not contain the already authorized versions of knowledge. New ideas are difficult to articulate and need support as they develop. A space where differing views can emerge is a space in which the participants feel safe to voice different and as yet unformed views. New knowledge is constructed as these differing views are shared with those who are willing to take each other seriously. This space is open to infinite possibilities.

Collaboration involves a mutual labor of working together. Knowledge is socially constructed by those who share a community. While we each construct and reconstruct knowledge in different ways, certain authorized versions of what counts as knowledge are constructed as consensus is reached among individual voices. Truth claims are based on agreement among groups of individuals. Bruffee (1986) tells us:

> Knowledge is identical with the symbol system (i.e., the language) in which it is formulated. The community of knowledgeable peers constituted by that symbol system constructs knowledge by justifying it socially, that is, by arriving at a sort of consensus. (p. 779)

Thus, knowledge is negotiated in social situations as people come to agreements about what is the most useful way to think about issues. University teachers and classroom teachers come from different knowledge communities, each developing particular stories of educative practice.

We need to think carefully about the stories we hear and tell, for when communal stories are taken for granted they are accepted as the only right or possible ways to author lives within the community. This can perpetuate our living as usual and work against both collaboration and changes in our research and our practice. However, telling and hearing new or different stories often leads to surprises and, as Bruner (1986) tells us, "The surprises I encounter are most often generated by others violating the usual or doing something 'against the rules' " (p. 47). It is easy to discount other's stories which do not fit with our perceptions of how things ought to be. It is difficult to tell stories which we do not feel will be acceptable within the community. It is crucial to honor all the stories individuals choose to tell if we are going to make changes in our research and our practice. It is only when our experience is represented in public form that we can begin to change our stories and thus our experience. Brown (1991) tells us, "To be an authority on their own experience requires another person who will acknowledge them as such, not simply an audience but a relationship in which they are taken seriously" (p. 84). However, there is a fine line between the validation and confirmation of our own and other's stories and the opportunities to restory our experiences in more educative ways.

Building Strength Through Collaboration

Collaboration involves much more than getting an education. Here, diverse knowledge is shared which takes into account individuals' experiential knowing of situations. As new views are shared, each participant in the collaborative endeavor is provided with new ways to reconstruct past knowledge and imagine future possibilities. New knowledge communities can lead to new communal and individual stories.

Carse (1986) tells us "power is never evident until two or more elements are in opposition" (p. 35). Diverse ways of knowing are the basis of collaborative relationships. Here, rather than defending one's views in opposition to the views of others, collaborators are open to voicing and hearing diverse ways of knowing. This becomes particularly difficult to achieve within the hegemony of hierarchical relationships lived out on the professional knowledge landscape (Clandinin and Connelly 1995). In collaboration we continually strive to understand both the knower and the known from his or her point of view. However, this does not mean that in collaboration agreement and consensus are easily or even necessarily achieved. It is the staying open to different possibilities that increases the strength of each collaborator. As we learn more from and about others, we also learn more from and about ourselves. Strength can only develop with others as each helps the other become stronger. In collaborative relationships there is a strengthening of personal and interpersonal knowledge as well as professional knowledge.

Collaboration implies a "working with" which is mutually beneficial to each participant. This does not mean each participant will leave the collaborative endeavor with the same knowledge. Rather, each will come with his/her own goals, purposes, needs, understandings and through the process of sharing, each will leave having learned from the other. Each will learn more about self, more about other, and more about the topic at hand. Collaborative transactions enable the understanding of different views—each informs and transforms the other.

Collaboration is not easy. The tensions which emerge in collaborative relationships are what keep the relationships alive and dynamic. There are no easy or sure answers. In collaboration, questions become the focus rather than only answers. When it is not assumed there is one correct answer or one right way, questions lead to understanding as we each become researchers of our own personal/professional knowledge and practice. When understandings lead to more questions, learning becomes self-motivated in a version of lifelong learning which is not only focused toward acquiring what is already known, but also inquiring into what is already known and focusing on constructing our own future possibilities. In this version, what is problematic to us provides the impetus for future learning as we try to understand ourselves and others, including the students in our care.

✧ Chapter Three

Metaphors of Interrelatedness: Principles of Collaboration

Helen Stewart

Origins of a Centre on Collaborative Research

The Centre on Collaborative Research at Brock University emerged from the unexpected discovery of connections amongst diverse faculty members. A presentation by a prospective professor during a faculty search process sparked the desire of several established faculty members to explore the possibility of a new association in the Faculty of Education. After the presentation, as professors with varied interests, focuses and backgrounds conferred, we recognized many potentially symbiotic relationships in our research areas and many intersecting strands of interest which we could profitably explore together. One of the professors, Susan Drake, enthusiastically began talking to others about the possibility of forming a group to explore topics concerning education in schools and teacher education. She asked others to accompany her on walks through the tree-lined streets of the lake side community where she lives. During such walks and talks she aroused the interest of almost a dozen faculty members. Several organizational meetings followed. Gradually the seeds of the Brock Faculty of Education Centre on Collaborative Research began to germinate (field notes, July 2–3, 1991).

The Centre's emergence owes much to the generous support of our Dean. Despite such support and the enthusiasm of members of the fledgling group, Susan found herself stymied for a considerable period by the apparent hurdles of traditional university patterns and protocols. Without an operative organization behind her, but committed to seeing the Centre become a reality, she accepted the role of "chief worrier" (Oakes, Hare, and Sirotnik 1986, 550). For some time she struggled valiantly and virtually alone to surmount the hurdles in order to obtain appropriate approval for the Centre.

With such stories as background, it is not surprising that the general image of collaboration as a journey emerged very early in the life of Brock University's Centre on Collaborative Research (Stewart 1993). Our talk, meeting notes, and audiotapes spawned new metaphors as we struggled to articulate our experiences of collaboration.

The Centre's Development

While the specific routes and final destination of the Centre continue to change and evolve, our pivotal goal has always been clear, namely, to investigate the principles and processes of collaborative research. In an era when governing bodies are encouraging and supporting collaboration (Fullan and Connelly 1987; Goodlad 1994; Maudsley 1992; Ontario Royal Commission 1994; Watson and Allison 1992, 1993), the Centre has officially stated that its purposes are: to investigate and study examples of collaborative research in education as they occur in diverse areas; to develop a deeper understanding of the collaborative process and of what collaborative research may entail; and to develop models or frameworks that may provide insights into the collaborative research processes under investigation (Brock Centre on Collaborative Research, pamphlet 1993). Propelling the Centre's forward movement has been our research on the phenomenon of collaboration itself.

At the beginning, guided by methods of inquiry deemed appropriate for grounded theory in process (Glaser and Strauss 1967; Greene 1988; Lincoln and Guba 1985; Woods 1988), we established various research routes, acknowledging as we did so that there would likely be no one methodology. We believed that the research approach should harmonize with the very nature of collaborative inquiry with its ever-new questions. That meant that it should include "self-conscious efforts to continuously document the context and processes" of our collaboration and the "orientations (e.g., sentiments and opinions) of the participants," in other words, "interpretive and reflective methods for making sense" of the data (Oakes et al. 1986, 548). Our approach agrees with Van Manen's (1990) position that the goal in human science research is to explicate "the meaning of human phenomena . . . and . . . [understand] the lived structures of meaning" and that "the preferred method for human science involves description, interpretation, and self-reflective or critical analysis" (p. 4). Thus our ongoing research has included processes such as: discussing and critiquing members' papers; keeping audiotapes, field notes, and detailed minutes of meetings; and maintaining detailed field notes on collaboration with colleagues across the educational continuum.

At several stages during the Centre's development, I asked each participant to capture in an image or metaphor her experiences and resultant notions of collaborative research. The most recent metaphors from seven regular respondents are used here to illuminate emerging notions of principles of collaboration.

While our discovery of these principles has reflected a continuum of clarification and expansion, we were able to articulate a number of central principles when our group was almost a year old and in the throes of analyzing our own early processes. We had already recorded the early metaphors we were using to describe collaboration. Then we also collected straightforward statements encapsulating our notions of the principles of collaborative research statements requested at the end of a meeting particularly rich in talk and dialogue about our collaborative experiences. At that time, I asked my colleagues to submit in sentence form, their statements about what collaboration entails. I received thirty statements which I condensed to six. Several times afterward, the participants submitted metaphors that seemed to convey their developing notions of collaboration. The metaphors and principles have continued to evolve in an intricately interwoven relationship as we have grown in our collaborative experiences. However, articulating our basic principles at an early stage most certainly provided a base from which many of our notions and elaborations of collaboration developed. In this chapter I present the most recent metaphors and then use associations from them to illuminate the six central principles summarized from the Centre's list of thirty.

Metaphors as Lenses for Viewing Collaboration

Northrop Frye's theory of literature can open to us a way of viewing metaphor and story. In narrative, the metaphor is a unit which functions very much like the equation in mathematics (Frye 1963, 11), as a unit of larger structures which cohere and, together, eventually form a unified universe—of mathematics in the one case and literature in the other.

From the time of Aristotle's *Poetics,* metaphor has been considered a powerful tool for viewing and making sense of the world in which we live, for helping us make connections and see new relationships. Theorists in any subject discipline are active synthesizers and constructors of knowledge; for them, a powerful tool of inquiry can be that of metaphor which Linda Olds (1992) calls "an aid to creative theorizing and hypothesis construction." From Olds' psychology perspective, "metaphors and models of interrelatedness can play a vital role in guiding intuitions of wholeness and complexity into responsible dialogue with ongoing theoretical and research traditions" (p. 19). In Schön's (1979) view, metaphor is the central means by which we "think about things, make sense of reality, and set the problems we later try to solve" (p. 254). In diverse fields of knowledge, metaphor can enable us to bring together areas of inquiry in new ways, opening up interdisciplinary dialogue and enabling us to draw out new dimensions of reality. In some instances, according to Schön (1983), when the reflective practitioner may sense or intuit a connection between one phenomenon and another but not know what the connection may be, the metaphor may be a useful aid in generating "new perceptions, explanations, and inventions" (p. 185). New properties can thus be imputed to an entity—properties not normally ascribed to that entity but emerging from reflection on the properties of the other. As "meaning transports," metaphors can "extend our level of understanding by comparison, or . . . by smuggling extra dimensions into our analysis," can enable us to see new connections (Olds 1992, 24, 25).

However, not all metaphors are generative or constructive. In some instances, as Grant (1992) cautions, a metaphor can actually limit perceptions and new insights (p. 434). Despite these and various other caveats, our metaphors seem to be useful lenses through which to view perceptions of the principles underlying collaborative processes.

Collaboration: Recent Observations as Context for Viewing the Centre's Metaphors

Collaboration in education is often understood to be synonymous with partnership or cooperation (Clift and Say 1988, 2). In some instances it certainly may be or, at least, elements of the latter phenomena may be endemic to the processes of collaboration or may represent particular forms of it. But some researchers also distinguish very carefully between the relationships to which the words refer (Gomez, Bissell, Danziger, and Casselman 1990, 3, 4). Also, many terms refer to research that some may describe as collaborative—terms such as *interactive research* and *development, clinical inquiry, collaborative staff development research, collaborative action research*. All such terms refer to the phenomenon of people from differing settings working together to solve classroom and school problems—problems in education (Clift, Veal, Johnson, and Holland 1990).

In light of the multiplicity of terms for and various interpretations of collaboration, it is little wonder that definition has been difficult and tentative. Frymier, Flynn, and Flynn (1992) refer to collaboration as "a relationship involving equal partners working on an ongoing basis to achieve mutually beneficial goals." Gomez et al. (1990) refer to Clark's (1986) definition synthesized from the work of others, as "shared decision-making in governance, planning, delivery and evaluation of programs" (Clark, 40, cited in Gomez et al., 3–4). Collaboration in this sense sees people from different settings and backgrounds working together as equals rather than in a hierarchical relationship wherein one party may utilize another, or at least the setting of another, for a study. Clift and Say (1988) define collaboration as "the joint efforts of university faculty members and public school personnel to design and provide opportunities to improve teaching and teacher education" (p. 2). They identify several models of collaboration. These include the traditional preservice teacher education model organized generally at an institutional level; the inservice model wherein universities provide services such as course or workshops for practicing teachers; the research model in which researchers work with school personnel to develop and implement various programs for schools; and the exchange model which temporarily transfers personnel between the university and the school. Clift and Say's proposed reciprocal model involves mutual and equal engagement of university and school personnel in decision making for curriculum and resource allocation, in curriculum development appropriate to career-long teacher growth, and in research on the collaborative process itself, all centered in a cycle of knowledge production, dissemination and review. Clift and Say make the point that, because there is little research data on collaboration, we tend to operate in terms of hunches and intuition rather than on the basis of empirically grounded theories. These educators emphasize, therefore, the importance of careful documentation of collaborative processes.

For Clandinin (1993), collaborative research projects are "attempts at establishing research relationships founded within conversations" (p. 208). The lacework of such relationships threads itself together through mutual trust in one another; it coheres through shared confidentiality and openness to listening to one another's voices as all participants join in sustaining, developing and renegotiating the conversations, thereby shaping and reshaping shared knowledge and experience. Clandinin's image of collaborative research is that it is flexible, constantly changing and moving, as participants redevelop the research relationships and continue to ask new questions and negotiate and renegotiate in a space where every individual's contributions, backgrounds and roles are deemed equal in value (pp. 208–220).

Metaphors From the Centre on Collaborative Research

Over three years, the following participants faithfully and conscientiously responded to requests for their metaphors of collaborative research: Sharon Abbey, Joyce Castle, Susan Drake, Anne Elliott, Merle Richards, and Alice Schutz. Early statements contained phrases like "working together" and "with others" which suggested a sense of connections and interrelatedness. Respondents saw potential for counteracting isolation. Most envisioned support which could engender, stimulate and encourage individual research, while simultaneously enabling individual members to connect with something larger in the research domain.

The following section sets out the most recent metaphors almost verbatim. Minor organizational and stylistic editing have not altered them significantly. The name of the individual who submitted each metaphor is in parentheses.

I. (a) **Troupe of Travelers (Merle Richards)**
On life's journey, we set goals for ourselves, looking for adventures and new experiences that will
enrich our lives. We support one another as we
trudge along the way, finding something or nothing, but at least enjoying the company. And sometimes one person walks ahead or behind or takes
up with a new group, but the road is still there,
stretching out, and there are still other travelers
to talk to and learn from, still stories to hear and
tell, and another hill and another bend in the
route.

(b) **Sea Anemone (Merle Richards)**
The team or group can be envisioned as an anemone,
a moveable sea creature, with many tentacles wav-
ing in all directions—a creature creating the environment in which it can grow and develop. It
develops itself through testing the environment and
drawing from it what it needs. It is an adaptive
creature or organism as in Piaget's image of intelligent beings who seek to satisfy their needs from
their environment, adapting to it and adapting the
environment to their needs and, in the process,
creating themselves.

II. **The Round Table (Cecilia Reynolds)**
This metaphor emerges from the Arthurian legend of the
Knights of the Round Table, though, at present, all of
the participants from the Faculty of Education happen
to be women. The Centre appears to signal an attempt
at breaking with the traditions and conventions of the
academic setting in which the university members work.
Regular meetings of the large group are customarily held
in a campus building known as "The Tower." Further, it
seems that each individual is in a sense going out to "do
battle" on her own. When they gather together as a group,
the individuals tell "tales" to one another about their
experiences. And although the actual table around which
they gather is not round, the stance of the researchers
has always been to provide an equal voice to all members of the group and to let each have a say in the formation of the Centre.

III. A Web

(a) A Web (Sharon Abbey)

A web connotes natural formation—formation from within. It serves many purposes, all based on nurturing and surviving. If damaged, it can be repaired through reattachment of severed strands or assemblage of new connections. Although invisible in certain lights, the construct displays itself as a very beautiful design when observed in light which catches it at an appropriate angle.

(b) A Web (Susan Drake)

There are many different kinds of webs—those occurring in the natural world and those constructed by human beings. All suggest interconnections. But each web, each construct is different, with the elements intermeshing much more harmoniously and naturally in some instances than in others. In some constructs the coming together of parts is harsh and discordant as in the case where there is an attempt to interlock the fingers of one hand with the fingers of another twisted and backwards-positioned hand with fingers of different shape and size. There is discomfort and meaninglessness in the attempted connection.

IV. The Quilt (Anne Elliott)

Like the quilt, each segment of a collaborative group is complete within itself, but when joined to others, forms a larger, more integrated, complex whole. In some cases the small unit serves as a hologram for, or a microcosm of the larger entity.

V. A Catalyst (Alice Schutz)

A catalyst points to transformation and change. It appears to take the everyday processes, people or interactions and explode their interactions into exciting, often unanticipated outcomes and new approaches. The interaction of various participants uses what each person brings to the enterprise but results in quantitative and qualitative differences which are more than just a sum of the parts. From each other, researchers have been able to learn assorted methods of research, explore diverse subject expertise, interact with different personality types, and promote and accept a variety of views.

VI. The Jazz Dance Ensemble (Helen Stewart)

Viewing collaborative research through the lens of the jazz dance ensemble enables us to see each participant as a significant part of the troupe and of its goal of constructing together a meaningful performance, no matter what the individual's background or customary role may be. Each dancer on an ongoing basis contributes to the whole dance. Each has a part, sometimes in harmony with others, often very different in form, appearance, motion, shape and direction, but always contributing to the growing structure, rhythm, harmony and meaning whether by active involvement or movement away, whether by absence, or even at times by merely taking something for herself from the movement of other individuals and the whole troupe, thereby filling out her own meaning, her own interpretation. The individual's movement continues in and out—altering the shape, form, functioning and meaning of the troupe's actions. When out of harmony or out of step, the individual's or smaller group's roles perhaps prompt the whole troupe to regroup, reexamine or reinterpret the dance with the potential for the development of a further changing, and even an ever-richer movement and meaning, an ever-fuller interpretation and expression of the action of the whole.

A Preliminary View of the Centre Metaphors

At least three primary notions emerge from the participants' metaphors. Most of the images strongly suggest interrelatedness. Many focus on the emergent, evolving, self-constructive nature of collaboration, and many suggest the potential inherent in the give-and-take—the potential for enriched and multilayered perceptions and knowledge development emerging from the convergence of many perspectives and wide diversities. Our group's main inclinations seem to coincide well with the six critical features of collaboration suggested by Gray (1989):

- Collaboration implies interdependence and ongoing give and take

- Solutions emerge through participants' dealing constructively with differences

- Partners must work beyond stereotypes to rethink their views about each other

- Collaboration involves joint ownership of decisions

- Stakeholders assume collective responsibility for future direction of the domain

- Collaboration is an emergent process; through negotiations and interactions, rules for governing future interactions are actually restructured (p. 11).

These features will all emerge in the principles set out in this chapter—principles condensed from our group's early statements about collaboration. However, our experiences and studies also suggest that collaboration's fuller ramifications do not emerge from such basic statements—be they Gray's or ours. Metaphor, by its nature, can enable us to make broader connections and help us to reflect upon and see the principles anew. It enables us to "smuggle" additional dimensions and attributes into our analysis as we attempt to formulate hypotheses about and extend our understanding of collaboration (Olds 1992, 24, 25).

Salient Principles of Collaboration Illuminated By the Metaphors

The next section presents the six principles of collaboration synthesized from our group's original set of thirty and uses the metaphors to elaborate on them. The principles themselves tend to interweave, in that they work intimately together in the complex processes of collaboration.

Principle 1

Collaboration is not a static event nor a formalized route for reaching a specific goal; neither is it an end in itself. It is, rather, an ongoing creative process, one which involves constructing an ever-evolving outcome from within an ever-changing matrix.

Discussion. Our metaphors' vision of collaboration as a dynamic process rather than static structure harmonizes with the conclusions of many other researchers (Auger and Odell 1992, 266; Frymier et al. 1992, 34; Gray, 1989, 11; Watson and Fullan 1992).

At the center of collaboration there is a commonly agreed-upon grail, a journey's destination, a developing harmonious shape or construct which generates actions and further processes (see Gomez et al. 1990, 12). But the formulation of the goal often takes time; moreover, the directions, routes, and even the ultimate goal are constantly under review and negotiation. As in the dance and the quest, active engagement in the process yields energy, empowering participants to move in an agreed-upon direction, continuously constructing new directions and meaning.

The generative power behind collaborative process seems to lie in participants' acceptance of a connecting and connected, genuinely shared goal which they themselves have formulated, and it lies also in the fact that the resulting work appears truly beneficial, lasting and meaningful to all (see Frymier et al. 1992, 10; Gomez et al. 1990, 12; Watson and Fullan 1992, 216). Participants engage and continue of their own accord without an external mandate (see Lasley, Matczynski, and Williams 1992, 261). They need to find meaning in the processes, if only at the level of personal satisfaction.

Our group originally came together to talk about intersecting research interests, to move out of academic isolation, and to construct for ourselves new patterns for living and working meaningfully in the educational community. Only after several meetings could we work out our basic purpose of studying our collaborative processes in schools and in the university. It took many more months to establish a vision of an umbrella project, a several-faceted general study, which would provide a specific route toward our goal. En route, our ways of studying collaboration developed and changed in unforeseeable ways. Even our projected ways of gathering and synthesizing data have continuously evolved with our ongoing experiences. As we pursue different avenues of research, we enable one another to see other ways of working and knowing. And we seem to be savoring the process of looking into the world of research anew, attracted by the grail of discovery. We also recognize that the cohesive and ongoing nature of our collaborative processes has been intricately connected to our ability as a group to enunciate quite early in our formation our own operating procedures.

Although the work towards an ultimate goal in itself may, like a catalyst, be energizing, work with others on the smaller tributary tasks also seems highly empowering and satisfying. Just as the process of constructing a small strand of a web or a section of a quilt, or struggling together to complete a small leg of a compelling journey, or to create a single movement of the dance seems satisfying and sustaining within itself, collaboration on a small research project, a workshop or conference presentation seems to be satisfying for the individuals who connect with one another in varying combinations.

Powerful also, in the ongoing process of collaboration, is its self-generating, self-organizing aspect. Over time, we travelers formulate our destination and our means of getting there. We support each other along the way and share in the challenges and achievements of the journey, the routes and very end of which are under construction. Through the process of socially negotiating and sharing workings in dynamically interconnected, interdependent relationships, we have been able to construct new personally meaningful knowledge about ourselves, about the institutional structures in which we work, about our functions and purposes in education, and certainly about the nature of the collaborative process. Relatively free of external authority or mandates handed down along hierarchical pathways, we have found that the self-organizing, self-generating nature of collaboration has empowered action, responsibility and growth.

Like the sea anemone, the Arthurian knights, and the troupes of travelers or jazz dancers, we in the Centre continue to create the environment in which we grow and develop. We maintain an official office established through the assistance of our Dean; we arrange for a particular windowed room on the top floor of the university's Tower for regular meetings chaired voluntarily by a different member each time; we invite others with varying roles in other sectors of the university to join the group, and in various, ever-changing small groupings we tell the stories of our experiences, talk about issues and work on projects with each other and in association with our colleagues in schools and in other university faculties. At various times at someone's home, we share food, reflect upon and celebrate our collaborative experiences with our school colleagues and, periodically, others in university faculties locally and internationally. Out of these ever-differing sets of collaborations, new understandings of collaboration emerge. We feel that we know what Florio-Ruane (1991) is saying when she suggests that "both the knowledge people have and the ways they represent knowledge are to a great extent shaped by their social places and purposes" (p. 244). Our places and purposes are part of our overall collaborative process and are certainly catalysts for further discoveries.

Principle 2

Ongoing change is essential to collaboration; change itself can be a catalyst in the construction of new knowledge, new patterns, new goals.

Discussion. Most of the metaphors suggest that collaborative routes toward the goal are not fixed. As for the knights, the jazz dancers, the travelers, the quilters, the anemone and even the web spinner, the original goal may develop and change over time; the routes toward both original and evolving goals tend to be emerging ones which progress through many stages, often requiring give-and-take, modification of personal agendas, and compromise (see Watson and Fullan 1992, 227). Because of the ever-changing environment, roles and responsibilities of individuals are also constantly under reconstruction (see Lasley et al. 1992, 257). As Lieberman (1992) suggests, important in creating a collaborative culture is a vision that is broad enough to allow participants room to create meanings, to initiate activities to promote the activities, and to form groups of people with whom to work (p. 152). Collaborative groups and collaborative processes evolve and change (Auger and Odell 1992, 266; Frymier et al. 1992, 34; Gray 1989, 11; Watson and Fullan 1992); the earlier directions and goals become heuristics for new ones (Oakes et al. 1986, 556). And as they change, interactions and relationships also change and evolve along the way. The active moving into and out of various relationships at different times with various combinations of school and university colleagues appears to be liberating in that we continue to refocus and alter our roles and functions. As we undergo our own transformations as individuals, relationships among individuals continuously fluctuate in an ongoing resculpting of the matrix of the whole group.

Other researchers warn of the dangers in collaboration of groupthink—"uncritical conformity to the group, unthinking acceptance of the latest solution, suppression of individual dissent" (Fullan 1993b, 34), or entrapment "within collaborative assumptions" (Miller 1990, 103). Our ongoing new connections, our almost jigsaw-group types of changes in working collaborations seem to have protected us to a certain degree from such dangers. At the same time, such warnings alert us to the necessity to be prepared to change and to learn better how to embrace newcomers and engage in new forms of inquiry their entry offers. As we learn more about collaboration, we also may avoid the pitfall of becoming mere participants rather than the "equitable and consensual" inquirers (Miller 1990, 154) we hope to become.

An appropriate stance for collaborative researchers appears to be one of *becoming*, accompanied by observing, interpreting and setting down layer after layer of meaning, as we attempt to make sense of the experiences which gradually accumulate more substance and value. It is a stance of presence at and engagement in the construction of a new sense of the contours and richness of the terrain, the accretion itself, like the web, luminous and beautiful because of the sense that it possesses within it an inherent worth. The key to our change processes is our active attunement to our environment and our active engagement in collaboration's decision-making processes and leadership roles (see Gomez et al. 1990, 6, 12). The benefits of collaboration for the individual, the group, and the projects occur only over long periods of process and change. Miller (1990), referring to individuals' "finding voices," suggests that various changes emerging through collaboration constitute "not a definitive event but rather a continuous and relational process" (p. xi).

We have learned too that we need to allow change to evolve, that we cannot rush it. We sense that we should examine very carefully pressures to rush changes, as well as pressures to impose traditional structures. We must be astute in eschewing pressures imposed by agendas thrust upon the group either from the larger institutional structures outside or from within the group itself. There is a temptation to yield to such pressures in order to seek the comfort and recognized legitimacy of the established routes for academic research; yielding would likely close down on processes of formation, natural development and essential change. Thus, another emerging recognition important to understanding collaboration is that we must remain *free* and resilient, sustaining a posture which enables us to stand back, observe, and make sense of what is happening. What we see and eventually understand can be a catalyst, propelling us into a new level of experience and new areas of knowledge.

The very changefulness of the collaborative research process seems to be a catalyst for real empowerment and transformation. The recurring lack of equilibrium sets up potentially productive internal tensions. As in the web, the tensions from various points on the outside and even from proddings from within, may keep the whole moving and in an altering state which helps those within view both the whole and the parts in varying lights.

In operative collaboration, each participant actively constructs the environment by both responding to and creating ongoing change, in turn constructing a new environment. The individual, like the anemone, adapts to the environment, moves, and often changes. Sustaining elements are the benefits the individual sees for self and the satisfaction that emerges from contributing to the good of the whole. That satisfaction comes from within each of us in that we have yet to see the reward systems of either the university or the schools recognizing in any significant way our basic collaborative activities. In working with others we have experienced personal benefit, achieved goals and constructed knowledge to a degree unlikely outside collaboration. Working together is a catalyst for discovery. From experience, we in the Centre have augmented our insights into such issues as leadership in educational institutions, the power of narrative to evoke personal knowledge, and the power of interrelatedness in effecting educational change. We have grown to cherish the freedom to choose and to generate goals, means, actions, and the patterns of operation that empower the individual collaborator; we value highly the sense of ownership and shared control over the processes which sustain and develop the operations of the collaborative group.

Through collaboration, we have changed. We have moved hesitantly from a stance of accepting information and knowledge down through a vertically ordered ontology to one in which we have garnered the abilities to construct knowledge ourselves on a flat, equitable plane through story, interaction, and experience. Through our continuing professional and social relationships, we have experienced change in the ways in which we work. We have learned to generate change, rather than merely react to it.

Principle 3

Diversity can be empowering if seen positively and used constructively. Internal differences can be constructive and productive; they can open up altered ways of seeing and living, which are liberating. Internal tensions and diversities may even be essential to the quality and integrity of the whole.

Discussion. During her visit to the Centre on Collaborative Research in July 1992, Patti Lather repeatedly encouraged us to examine our diversities and consider how to use them. At the same time, she warned that foregrounding diversities too soon can be dysfunctional (meeting notes and audiotape, July 22, 1992).

Some researchers, such as Knight, Wiseman, and Smith (1992), have suggested that if collaboration is to work, the participants must be different enough to stimulate change in each other (p. 270). Finding differences is not difficult. Even in one culture, differences can be enormous. Across two or more cultures such as those of the university and the schools, they can take on gigantic proportions. Moreover, the question arises as to who possesses legitimate knowledge and who is the expert (Gitlin, Bringhurst, Burns, Colley, Myers, Price, Russell, and Tiess 1992, 22–23, 179–182). In fact, differences can be too extreme for collaboration to work (see Gomez et al. 1990, 231; Miller 1990, 151). Internal tensions in the web can be sufficiently destructive to cause an irreparable rent.

Largely on others' advice, we in the Centre have struggled with the issue of diversity. In our earliest stages we worked together despite differences. However, we have long been aware that, like Biott and Nias' (1992) collaborating teachers, we can offer each other "new ways of looking at familiar situations, by interpreting evidence in different ways, by airing disagreements or differences of opinion and by sharing aspects of [our] own experience which conflict with those of others" (p. xix). Like the knights, the quests of each of us differ from others', but we continue to press towards the grail in various combinations, bringing our various tales back to the round table for our own and others' edification.

Recently, in a meeting dedicated to reflection and dialogue on the Centre's perceptions of the function of differences, we agreed that for us a powerful factor has been our continuing acceptance of individual differences. We have responsively accommodated differences and varying patterns of participation, allowing individuals to enter, engage, depart and reenter, according to need. In the ongoing rhythm and movement of our particular dance, it appears that a significant feature of what continues to happen is that we accommodate regularly not just one individual, but various individuals at different times. Like sea anemones, we have been exceptionally willing to compromise and adjust in order to promote the good of the entire project or group.

At the heart of accommodation is dialogue which honors each voice, listens to it, and uses it in constructing a larger vision. For example, a subgroup preparing for a conference decided to develop posters visually representing images of various issues. Following a spiral of dialogue, negotiation and consultation processes incorporating many perspectives and differences of opinion, the posters eventually materialized. In meetings, we suggested many images and candidly disagreed with each other on some. One of us synthesized the suggestions following the meetings and consulted with others again before contacting the artist. We asked the artist to translate our many scattered and imprecise suggestions into sketches. One of us again consulted with others both individually and in various combinations, seeking oral and written responses, and then submitted a new synthesis to the artist who agreed to rework any pieces which the group found inappropriate. This collaborative episode exemplifies how we can successfully work through many different positions and genuine disagreement to produce constructive outcomes. We did not achieve consensus, nor did we expect to, inasmuch as consensus is not the goal of collaboration (see Fullan 1993, 82). The goal is to accomplish each movement of the dance, each stage of the journey or quest through our diverse contributions. This means careful attention to processes of connected responsiveness. In all of our experiences, the common goal and sense of interrelatedness have held the web of collaboration intact despite internal differences or tensions from the outside.

Factors engendering accommodation are connected with our stance toward collaboration. Our focus lies in what an individual can contribute to group goals in terms of different expertise, with various spin-off benefits to self. In effect, as in the journey and in the creation of the quilt, there appears to have been an implicit understanding that each participant needs the others in order to accomplish the larger designated tasks and that the reflexivity involved in the collaborative process cannot be limited to one lens but is enriched when filtered through a variety of lenses. The colaboring and contributions of each participant continue to vary in the degree of interrelatedness (amount, kind, and time) but each individual—including the rank newcomer and intermittent participant—has made significant, unique contributions to the reality and shape of the Centre as it is today. The key element is not so much that the differences are evident and we are consciously articulating them in order to use them, but that we implicitly accept and value the varying patterns and work with them. We also acknowledge that enhanced richness may lie in increasing our ability to recognize our own diversity and learn how to use it as a catalyst to transform ourselves and our ways of working. Differences can generate increased understanding, knowledge and productivity.

Principle 4

Processes such as talk and storying, traditionally thought to be unproductive, are deemed meaningful and constructive work in collaboration.

Discussion. On that eventful day of the faculty search, talk, narrative and dialogue, punctuated by energizing and exciting "aha's," sparked our genesis. In our first exchanges we heard ourselves exclaiming, "I did not know that you too were interested in that," and then responding with contributions from related areas of interest and experience. Our first talk surfaced strongly felt needs to join with others in order to learn, share, and experience unprecedented professional and academic interchange and support. Cecilia

Reynolds summarized several participants' earliest notions of collaboration when she spoke of it as an opportunity, not to use one another competitively, but to give to one another constructively. Such talk and conversation provided a sense of the terrain from which each of us was coming and of the directions in which we might travel. It required considerably more talk and dialogue before we were able to formulate our purpose and chart the possible routes toward attaining it (see Senge 1990, 212).

Questioning, reflecting, and talking are central to the knowledge construction and inquiry processes of collaboration. These time-consuming elements sometime seem unproductive in the face of other demands on time and energy. Academia has traditionally omitted or negated talk or tale because they seemed nonproductive. Some collaborative groups may easily abandon these elements in bowing to the pressures of closure and product. Yet, more and more, academics are recognizing that research is "both a social process and a linguistic product" (Florio-Ruane 1991, 236). In the Centre, we have found that, like quilters, it is together that we create and achieve most constructively. Through dialogue and reflective talk we gain a sense of empowerment as we engage in inquiry and knowledge construction. Yet such realizations do not come easily. They are difficult not only for us—university researchers accustomed to reward systems fostering an individualistic need to measure and achieve results within a certain timeframe—but also for teachers whose lives are becoming increasingly complex with the current multiplicity of demands on their time and energy.

Stories of our journeys and various successes and failures in slaying old dragons help us endure the difficult times and celebrate achievements. As we struggle to articulate our own stories and examine them critically, and as we listen to others' experiences, we attempt to make sense of what has been happening and so expand our individual and collective perspectives. Not all collaborative efforts run smoothly. However, self-conscious attention to our stories can help us make sense of patterns and to learn and liberate ourselves perhaps both from them and through them. Our stories form part of our natural data. As we reflect on journeys past, we continue to draw in new details on our rudimentary map, marking the territory we have covered, changing its contours and design, and filling in new projections on the landscape we seek to traverse. We continue to travel and make new discoveries, ever reorienting ourselves to new directions. We continue to develop and change.

While retaining our professional relationships in the business of collaboration, we have also become friends in ways we would not have without our collaborative conversations. Like Senge's (1990) new management teams, we have learned that we talk in different ways as friends than we do as mere associates and we have also learned that "there is a deep hunger to rediscover our capacity to talk with one another" (p. xiii).

Principle 5

Trust and commitment become powerfully constructive factors as collaboration opens participants to vulnerability and the potential stresses of deep change.

Discussion. Though intrigued by Susan Drake's enthusiasm and the excitement of finding connections in our traditionally "cantankerous" academic world (Oakes et al. 1986), our troupe did not enter the dance or embark upon the journey with a sense of commitment or trust. Rather, we gathered together in a spirit of hope, well tempered with skepticism. Merle Richards voiced the anxieties of many, admitting that she was skeptical, wondering whether collaboration would turn out to be merely another fad. And yet she also acknowledged an appeal in the prospect of work with compatible others. Such ambivalence and uncertainty persisted for some time, until we could articulate our shared purpose. Any strands of trust or commitment woven during the early tentative stages were very fragile indeed.

All of us were seeking change and new ways of working together when we embarked upon our collaborative quest, but probably few of us expected that we ourselves would change. We set out with our own belief systems and our own sets of assumptions, and throughout the journey have struggled with how our experiences and new learnings weave into them (see Castle, Drake, and Doak 1995, 256). We began with our own notions of research and the nature of academia. Collaboration has constructively changed these notions and our views of our colleagues in the Faculty and of its leadership and procedural patterns.

Collaboration required and contributed to a shift in stance. We became vulnerable when we committed ourselves to joining this new dance with its unwritten choreography and to undertaking journeys and quests into the unknown with others whom we did not know or trust. At the beginning, we were vulnerable to derision from other university colleagues and to uncertainty created by our own members' honest, doubting questions. In the traditionally isolationist and impersonal realms of academia, we were unaccustomed to the risktaking of self-disclosure and self-commitment.

The very components of collaboration, such as talk and negotiation, change traditional patterns of working, making participants
vulnerable (Hollingsworth 1992; Lather 1991). The processes of
discovery through storying experience also push vulnerability
(Drake, Elliott, and Castle 1993), as do sharing and questioning
our own and others' perceptions and positions. In collaboration we
scrutinize our own experiences; we researchers become the researched, scrutinizing our own work and processes and those of
collaborating team members. Collaborative processes demand new
behavioral patterns, including a willingness to learn how to communicate with others. They demand that we step outside customary patterns of interaction and into broader spaces, forming new
relationships and working at building trust, confidentiality and
confidence. Vulnerability is exacerbated by the stress of personal
change which precipitates a painful questioning of our very identity (see Nias 1992, xvi) and our exposure to opposition, resistance
and devaluation from those others, inside or outside the collaborative group, who do not want to be transformed or who are not ready
to undergo transformation. Only by working and living through
collaborative experience and identifying and grappling with diversity and the discomfiture of perceived vulnerability are participants able to build the kind of trust in the process and in each
other that makes worthwhile the extraordinary commitment of time,
self and energy that collaboration demands. The earliest stages of
our journey were very stressful. We ranged erratically, swinging
individually and collectively between self-doubt and self-encour-
agement, often wondering whether to forge ahead or retreat.

At the beginning there seemed so little to trust or commit
ourselves to. However, as in the jazz dance troupe, we gradually
caught the rhythm and momentum, both individually and in con-
cert, and committed ourselves to working out an ultimate form. We
developed what Senge (1990) calls " 'operational trust' where each
team member remains conscious of other team members and can
be counted on to act in ways that complement each others' actions"
(p. 236). We gradually became more interrelated and more trusting
by acting together. As we began to bond, we began to trust our
processes, purpose, tasks, and one another. Then even our differences of opinion took on a new cast as we began to see their potential for constructing further processes and enriching our purpose.
We realized that we were learning together and gaining access to
larger knowledge constructs than we ever could have done individually. Like the knights of old, we still had our own quests to

fulfill, but we were able to go out and do battle individually with increasing confidence because we had been at the round table and knew we would return again and again to that center.

Trust is central to constructing and sustaining the collaborative process—trust in ourselves individually and collectively, trust in individual others with whom we have gathered (see Clandinin 1993), and trust in our processes and our willingness to step into them and move forward through them. Building such trust accompanies a process of moving out of at least some of the traditional modes and paradigms in order to be able to see those more objectively, to challenge their assumptions and, as a result, develop new perspectives. Appropriate trust depends upon reliability and consistent honesty in the behavior of participants; it relies upon having at heart the interest of each and all of our partners. Trust of such proportions both necessitates and contributes to a strong level of commitment on many levels.

Commitment propels collaboration's forward movement. As in the case of the jazz dance ensemble, the success of collaboration seems dependant on participants' commitment to a common aspiration (see Gomez et al. 1990, xiv; Nias 1987, 149; Senge 1990, 206). That aspiration includes fulfillment of both collective and individual goals. The very process of journeying toward attainment of the shared purpose seems to engender further trust and commitment on several levels. Both desire for the goal and active participation have engendered our group's genuine desire to continue journeying together. As we progress, we accept responsibility for whatever roles we assume. When one of us faces exceptional demands or is absent, others enter the dance, ensuring that the rhythm and developing harmony continue to evolve. Our original skepticism and anxiety about collaboration dissipated as we learned to trust the change processes in our shared commitment to working out the rhythms and patterns together.

As Senge (1990) suggests, we are committed when we genuinely want to achieve a goal and when we are committed we bring energy, excitement, and passion to the task (p. 219). In the Centre, we gradually developed into a troupe more and more attuned to each other, increasingly trusting of one another and committed to our purpose. The movement of each of us tilts the web in different directions, enabling us to see new colors and new patterns in the whole. Our joint ownership of the common vision (see Senge 1990, 206) has contributed powerfully to our becoming more and more a caring community.

Genuine commitment to a purpose seems to engage us also in commitment to the relational processes (Hollingsworth 1992, 399) that are central to collaboration. Participants accept responsibility for carrying out tasks in order to support the others to whom they have committed themselves. Among our shared tasks is commitment to the purpose of constructing the history of the collaborative group (Merle Richards).

Principle 6

A central empowering factor in collaboration is the valuing of each participant's contribution. Co-laboring suggests a shift from vertical patterns of leadership and power to horizontal patterns of shared leadership and symbiotic, supportive relationships.

Discussion. Much has been said about the importance to successful collaboration of conditions of parity and equality (Biott and Nias 1992, xiii; Clift et al. 1990, 53; Gomez et al. 1990, 3, 6; Goodlad 1990, xiv; Hollingsworth 1992, 381; Hunsaker and Johnston 1992, 352; Nias 1987, 142, 149, 150; Oakes et al. 1986, 547). But participants do not simply gather at a round table and begin to collaborate equitably. Parity does not come without hard work (Hunsaker and Johnston 1992, 352), if only because we adults do not change readily or because challenging our positions in the traditional hierarchies of our work places can play havoc with our sense of security and identity (Nias 1987, 141). Thus, a great deal of time-consuming effort and negotiation and a great amount of dialogue must precede the development of parity.

Many researchers also point to shared leadership as a condition integral to successful collaboration (Clift, Johnson, Holland, and Veal 1992, 904; Gomez et al. 1990, 6; Nias 1992, xiii; Oakes et al. 1986, 547, 550). As educators accustomed to the idiosyncratic reward systems and vertical ontologies of our own organizations, we do not move easily into shared or rotating leadership roles. Further, we are accustomed to associating power, status, and responsibility with designated leadership; therefore, we find it unsettling when traditional hierarchical patterns dissipate. But there are many moral issues involved in processes of changing these patterns. We need to address the distrust that emerges when educators traditionally perceived as unequal in status, power, and knowledge come together with a view to breaking down the various barriers. When we alter the contours of the terrain, we must accept responsibility for providing ongoing open dialogue and support; we must be open about our intent and faithful to our evolving role changes.

Successful collaboration requires every participant to accept as part of the task the challenge of exploring the barriers that, in the traditional research model, keep power, authority and voice from being shared. In collaboration, we find ourselves called upon to seek out and do battle with traditional ways of working. We must struggle to deconstruct assumptions and attitudes that hinder and destroy real personal and group growth and progress towards worthwhile educational goals. True collaboration demands that we lay out before us our shadowy assumptions about leadership and working relationships. Once we scrutinize these, as we become a more cohesive group at our round table, we perhaps can gradually garner the resources to slay the dragons that have long stymied our quests for real learning and educational reform.

Shared vision can empower the symbiosis of collaboration because participants, individually and as a group, both own and desire it. This ownership and desire can be energizing, imbuing the work with meaning for all, virtually raising it to the level of vocation (Senge 1990, 148). In the Centre we have experienced much verve and energy in our work together, both inside our university group and with our school partners. Many times, uncertainties about roles or even about the direction or success of our work have caused us to step back and reflect upon what collaboration is, does, and can do. As Schön (1983) suggests, reflection-in-action can raise the intentionality and level of awareness of our practice, enabling us to develop new theory (p. 68). Essential, however, to the development of new knowledge is a quality of interaction and interrelatedness that ensures parity of voice and contribution. As Schön also suggests, there must be "dialogue between reflective researchers and practitioner researchers" and the research must be "of the kind that practitioners can also undertake" (p. 324). Participants must both desire and understand the work.

From the desire for and commitment to a shared purpose, there emerges a very powerful element of successful collaboration—namely, that of essential interrelatedness. Olds (1992) calls it a "sense of ultimate connection" that marks the vision of a larger whole—the notion that "a part of you is always part of me, not only in a sense of reowned projections but in the literal, concrete patterns we share, however distant" (pp. 96–97). In the Centre, we seem to have a sense that the common vision has contributed to a sense of bonding and interrelatedness that differentiates our collaborative group from more traditional organizations. We learned that we share ownership for processes, but that we do not own people. Thus we can all move in and out freely, accepting roles and responsibilities appropriate to time, talent, energy, and desire. Whatever roles we accept, we seem to fulfill to the best of our ability, partly out of a desire not to let others down and partly because we feel responsible to complete the tasks we willingly assumed. As we worked at collaboration and processed the various means to achieving our shared purpose, we seem to have engaged in an "ethics of connection and responsiveness" (p. 127) in a culture of caring and concern.

Through collaboration, as diverse individuals with quite distinct interests, backgrounds, and personalities, both in the university and in the schools, we extended our boundaries, changed our modes of working, and united to attain mutual goals. In varying groupings, we established new programs, curricula, and methodological approaches in various educational contexts. Through our connectedness, we acquired the confidence to question assumptions and pursue answers to recurring and new questions. New participants' questions force us to rethink our positions and ways of working, to ensure that we really are meeting at a round table and are attuned to the dangers of groupthink and acquired assumptions that could be as murky as those traditional ones we set out to examine and free ourselves from.

All dimensions of our collaborative associations continue to operate without a designated leader. Though Susan Drake was originally our chief worrier, in due course she stepped back both intentionally and by necessity as she was very often off campus. Over the years we grappled repeatedly with the issue of leadership in collaboration. Knowing that we needed to learn what leadership is, what it is not, what it can and cannot do (see Oja and Smulyan 1989, chap. 3, 5), we dedicated one strand of our research to studying this issue. In practice our position is one of working out the kind of leadership that frees people to *be*—that frees them to be truly collaborative without the barriers of power struggles.

We understand that egalitarian patterns of leadership have been associated with feminist research and have received encouragement in American educational reform initiatives (Baumann 1992, 6). But we hear Cecilia Reynold's admonition that a number of feminist organizations who attempted to operate without leaders foundered. We have asked ourselves whether the misfortune of such groups resulted from the fact that in traditional university and school settings, to a significant degree "we still lack habit patterns to conceptualize a vision of interrelatedness we can live by" (Olds 1992, 69). We are conscious that, in many quarters, we educators are likely still too deeply set in traditional vertical patterns of leadership to detach ourselves sufficiently to launch powerful new patterns of growth and connection. We recognize that in our own ongoing quest, we must continue to struggle with alternatives suggested by Olds (1992) whose systems metaphors "join feminist perspective not only in a critique of vertical ontology as gendered, but in a powerful concern for introducing alternative metaphors for healing . . . dichotomies, and for founding an ethics of interrelatedness and responsiveness" (p. 127). There is still a tension entangling us in the vertical institutional structures and leadership patterns handed to us. We must continue to heed the tensions within and to seek new ways of seeing which may help us break down barriers that prevent our working together holistically.

Particularly in our earlier stages of development, we reflected upon what might happen in a group with the apparent disappearance of power and control (Joyce Castle). But Alice Schutz also prompted us to consider whether leadership must necessarily be imbued with power. At the same time, we heeded the advice of a representative from an outside grant-awarding foundation who told us that we required a person who would accept responsibility for appropriate handling of projects; thus someone's name always goes on research documents. We remain a leaderless group, but we have realized that we are not a group lacking leadership (Merle Richards). We have effective leadership in many leaders. All of us at various times assumed leadership roles, not merely in meetings and everyday operations, but in larger areas of responsibility such as conference planning. On this journey, at different times, each of us walked at the head of the troupe while continuing to draw upon the resources of others, regularly consulting our fellow travelers as we chart our way. This pattern uses and nurtures leadership styles and abilities where they can be most appropriately applied (see Nias 1992, xviii) and enables all of us to guide various sequences of the dance at appropriate times. Our leadership pattern so far has worked for us. It both manifests and inspires the trust, support, nurturing and empowering of our participants, enabling each of us to grow within a cohort group desirous of moving towards our collective good. Such a pattern bespeaks a sensitivity to the growth of the whole through response to and nurturing of individual development. It frees individuals to make choices about when and how to contribute. It encourages shared responsibility for ongoing procedures and yet at appropriate times foregrounds a spokesperson who acts as a point of contact for the larger community.

Our members acknowledge that there is security in traditional power-endowing vertical leadership models. At times, some have urged the group to reconsider its evolved flat model of mutual empowerment. However, the fact is that the Centre has not only survived but seems to have emerged as a happy, significant composite not dependent upon or associated with any one individual. There are no elections for group leadership; there is no vying for positions perceived as power-endowing. Individuals support one another very richly in many ways. The Centre has indeed brought diverse individuals together in an interconnectedness that is apparently unique in this university.

Conclusion

Our metaphors yield notions of change, process and interrelatedness. Through exploring our metaphors we have journeyed through a deepening experience of discovery and an insight-yielding way of viewing and making sense of what assisted at the birth and ongoing life of the Centre. We are learning what makes collaboration work. Metaphor has enabled us to suggest the complex richness of principles emerging from our experiences of collaborative process. Like Olds (1992), we seem to have a stronger sense that we educators:

> no longer inhabit a universe capable of being represented vertically alone . . . The path of wholeness must take us through and within, rather than leading us upward and outward alone. (p. xii)

As we continue our dialogue and negotiation, our metaphors will likely change. Will they become images of greater immanence? If Olds (1992) is right, our collaborative journey has just begun. For all of us, the understanding of the parameters not only of educational research but of educational relationships may be on the edge of the profound, real transformational change that Eisner (1993) envisions. Where explorations of collaboration will take us is perhaps yet relatively speculative, but like the heuristic of metaphor, it seems to offer us yet unexperienced, expansive powers of interrelatedness and connectedness with tantalizing potential for discovery and construction of new universes of educational knowledge and action.

NOTE

I am grateful for the contributions of all my colleagues at the Centre on Collaborative Research and for permission to use their metaphors in this chapter. The credits below acknowledge members' contributions gleaned from field notes and audiotapes of regular meetings and from various written submissions: Sharon Abbey, May 1995; Joyce Castle, December 1991, 8 July 1992; Susan Drake, 8 July 1992, 22 July 1992; Anne Elliott, 7 May 1992; Judith Parker, February 1993 (metaphor submission); Cecilia Reynolds, 7 May 1992; Merle Richards, 7 May 1992, 17 June 1992, 2 July 1992, 2 June 1995; Alice Schutz, 8 July 1992; Ruth Scott, February 1993 (metaphor submission); Vera Woloshyn, 6 January 1993.

In addition, I have used field notes from a meeting at the Centre with Patti Lather on 22 July 1992.

Part Two

◇

Rethinking Mutuality and Negotiation

The second section of the book challenges us to reconsider common notions about collaboration. Assumptions about the nature of collaborative endeavors usually contain statements about partners agreeing upon goals and the need for some negotiation to fulfill these goals. The chapters in this section cause us to reexamine the meaning and nature of mutuality and negotiation in the unique context of each experience.

"Questioning the conventional" describes the theme that threads its way through each of the chapters. Successful collaboration for these writers depends on more than the mutually derived goals or initial negotiation often noted by observers of collaborative efforts. Instead, these writers speak of living the collaborative experience within differing cultures, with divergent notions of professional growth of contrasting epistemological views. Joyce Castle explicitly challenges the present wisdom that collaborative ventures embrace mutually derived goals when she reminds us how little is known about mutuality and its relationship to collaboration. The complexity of achieving mutuality between diverse cultures for Castle lies, not in the goals, but rather in the responses within the collaborative context. Mary Hookey, Shelley Neal, and Zoe Donoahue echo this need to build a voluntary, collegial relationship in promoting teacher growth through negotiation and recursive consultation. Debra Schroeder and Kathie Webb query the traditional approach to research with its objective view of knowledge that so obviously conflicts with collaborative narrative research. In the two subsequent chapters, Lynn McAlpine and Martha Crago, and Linda Goulet and Brian Aubichon grapple with the responsibility within collaborative endeavors to respect the participants' cultures, worldviews and traditions while realizing mutual benefits. The conventional approaches to working across cultures, differing notions of professional growth and ways of knowing clearly call for other processes.

Each of the chapters offers the reader new ideas and considers approaches that emanate from the writers' own experiences. Hearing the voices of the others in continuing dialogue becomes a part of the fabric of successful negotiation. McAlpine and Crago speak of valuing the perspective of all participants—children and adults—in the social process of understanding that emerges in collaboration. Through active listening, a process that Goulet and Aubichon say challenges us to examine our beliefs and assumptions, we learn about ourselves and the context of the collaboration. To Hookey, Neal and Donoahue the unhurried nature of the consultation encourages resolution of differing viewpoints and allows the listeners to set tasks for their collaborative and personal growth and development. Castle tells us that collaboration must allow room for us to attend to the multiple voices in our dialogue to negotiate new meanings.

Adaptation and flexibility in collaboration enhance the growth of understanding in collaborative relationships. Schroeder and Webb speak of the need to change the customary power relationship, in which the researcher is expert, to one of collaborative effort that recognizes strength in the mutual creation of data and knowledge. Working in crosscultural contexts has, for McAlpine and Crago, expanded the ethical considerations usually accepted by the dominant culture. Change is both procedural and ethical according to Castle. Reexamination of long-held beliefs and building on the experiential wisdom of these writers will enhance our understanding of the complexity of mutuality and negotiation in collaboration.

✧ Chapter Four

Rethinking Mutual Goals in School-University Collaboration

Joyce Castle

Driving much of the current reform movement in education is a belief in the value of collaborative ventures between schools and universities. The ultimate goal is always held to be the same: better schools and better teachers. The more specific goals driving each venture are not as readily identifiable, and are expected to vary according to the different contexts. Nevertheless, present wisdom holds that it is essential in any collaborative partnership that these specific goals be mutually derived and central to the relationship (Lasley, Matczynski, and Williams 1992; Patterson and Stansell 1987; Sirotnik and Goodlad 1988). Gone are earlier research and development models which viewed universities as knowledge producers and schools as simply sites for research; the newer model sees school-university cooperation as a jointly owned venture aimed at achieving mutually beneficial change.

59

While this newer rhetoric is welcome and promising, it is not yet characterized by a shared understanding of what it means to set, work toward, and achieve mutual goals. We really know very little about what constitutes mutuality and how it relates to collaboration. Just what is involved in sharing a common purpose? What issues impact on mutual goal setting and achievement? And when mutual goals do drive a partnership, does this mean all outcomes are mutually beneficial? These are the sorts of questions I explore in this chapter. I begin by focusing on the complex nature of collaborative relationships and the issues related to achieving mutuality. In the next section, I call upon my own and others' experiences of collaboration to illustrate what I see as the emerging reality in collaborative ventures: mutuality is rarely achieved. In the final section, I conclude that perhaps much of the current emphasis on the centrality of mutual goals in collaborative relationships is misguided. I suggest instead that the key to collaboration does not lie in goals, but rather in responses, that is, in the ways in which those involved respond to each other, learn from each other, and negotiate a relationship.

The Complexity of School-University Collaboration

At the conceptual level, school-university collaboration for change seems straightforward, but clearly, the concept is easier to articulate than to act upon. According to Valli (1994), if the parties involved in these partnerships wish to collaborate in any meaningful way, they must get beyond hollow statements about school improvement, achievement gains, and collaborative relations and reexamine their fundamental beliefs about educational change. The questions underlying this reexamination include, What are we collaborating for? and What types of changes do we want to achieve? and How do we want to achieve this? All are questions which call for collaborative partners to look closely at what they take for granted.

This point of Valli's deserves attention, for it suggests that mutual goals and tasks and outcomes do not emerge in a collaborative partnership unless those involved achieve some consensus on issues foundational to the partnership. To achieve mutually beneficial change, then, school-university collaborators would need to be constantly reexamining and articulating their own and each other's notions about change as process and product. This makes change itself a conceptual, procedural, and ethical issue in collaboration, for the way in which the partners frame change colors the models they create, and the degree of similarity in their views fuels or dampens the joint effort, affecting how individuals interact.

Jackson (1992) presents a framework for educational change that proves helpful in understanding possible differences in views. Jackson holds that change is not synonymous with development and that what is really sought in education is development—those changes which are desirable and positive in quality. He then outlines four strategies available for promoting desired change, at least in teachers. The first three are somewhat traditional routes: (a) provide teachers with greater know how (tell or show them how to teach better), (b) provide teachers with greater independence (improve their working conditions and increase their power), and (c) provide support to help teachers alleviate stress (use mentor programs, support groups, journals). Jackson's fourth strategy is newer and less structured: deepen and broaden teachers' insights by promoting prolonged reflection on teaching. This last strategy means choosing materials and arranging experiences that promote understanding from a variety of perspectives and allow teachers to see themselves and their own teaching differently.

These strategies of Jackson's illustrate different viewpoints about change and the role of collaborative partners in the process. Some important differences characterize each strategy, and questions such as, What is the collaboration aiming to change? and Which party is the change directed at? and Who will control this change? are important to consider. Jackson's strategies become progressively more teacher centered in that each focuses more on empowering the teacher. But all these strategies can still be seen as driven by underlying notions that development is something directed *at* teachers *by* outside experts, and that teachers are more passive than active when it comes to development. This contrasts with Clark's (1992) portrait of teachers as active, knowledgeable, and ready to take charge of their own development. Jackson's fourth strategy is directed toward helping teachers become the kind of teacher portrayed by Clark, but the question of who initiates the activities and what role each partner plays in these activities is not clear. If Valli's point is taken seriously, *both* parties in the collaboration should engage in the reflection and deepen their insights and expand their perspectives. But these are conceptual and procedural issues in collaboration which can prove difficult for both parties to agree upon.

When school and university partners are searching for common ground, the gap between theory and practice can loom large, and institutional differences can keep interaction minimal. The Holmes Group (1986) acknowledged this difficulty when they called for increased interaction and holistic, long-term efforts by both parties. Both parties are not always prepared for this, however. They can experience difficulty moving from more familiar cooperative arrangements where they simply work side by side, to newer collaborative arrangements which call for shared decision making. Clift and Say (1988) hold that schools and universities seldom engage in meaningful conversations, so agreeing upon concerns and goals and courses of action does not come readily. Two cultures and two systems of meaning come into operation at the same time, with university faculty and teachers holding different goals and values and language systems. Goodlad (1988) suggests that this duality holds the promise of shaking up both and bringing about change. Stacey (1992) goes further to suggest that this conflict is essential to successful change. Others such as Lasley, Matczynski and Williams (1992) are not as optimistic, claiming that most school-university partners simply continue on their independent courses, never achieving a status characterized by collective decisions.

What affects the likelihood of both parties' achieving mutuality is whether or not they experience collaboration within their own institutions. Universities are known for traditionally promoting and reflecting pluralism and autonomy among members (Clark 1987). Teacher cultures are considered more diverse, but they are still rarely portrayed as collaborative. According to Hargreaves (1992), what passes in some institutions as true collaboration is only "bounded collaboration" which he sees as restricted in depth, scope, frequency or persistence. Without some experience of collaboration in their own institution, however, it proves difficult for both parties to achieve any degree of mutuality. What often results is one or more of the traditional problems identified by collaboratives. These include the emergence of power and status issues, the failure of one party to appreciate the other, and the reference to time, or rather lack of time, as the reason for failure. But often the problem is deeper and stems from the absence of an ethic of care. Fullan (1994) argues that without this ethic of care, true collaboration will not come about and productive change will not occur. To Fullan, this care ethic involves much more than personal caring and interpersonal sharing; it is linked to broader social purpose that acknowledges moral responsibilities. Schools and universities alike must grapple with this ethical aspect of change, for consensus on this moral responsibility issue is perhaps the most critical of all to mutuality.

This characterization of school-university collaboration as a collective of individuals working for educational change has given rise to the conceptual, procedural and ethical issues noted here. These issues relate to mutuality in that they suggest what needs to be dealt with at the outset as well as throughout the relationship.

School-University Partnerships in Action

While the previous section focused on the complexity in school-university relationships, this section is concerned with what actually tends to happen when both institutions come together on a collaborative venture. I touch briefly on my own and others' experiences here to point out patterns and themes which when taken together illustrate that mutual goal setting rarely occurs, and that even when the stated goals are truly shared, it does not often follow that the end result is mutually beneficial.

In my own case, my experiences with collaboration began several years ago when I opted to work with a number of my colleagues at the university on three separate reflective research projects aimed at understanding ourselves better as professors and researchers and colleagues (Castle, Drake, and Boak, 1995; Castle and Giblin 1992; Drake, Elliott, and Castle 1993). All were positive and productive experiences, leaving me assured that collaborative ventures, while demanding, resulted in feelings of fulfillment. When I graduated to collaborative projects with others in the school system, however, everything changed; both process and end product were vastly different. To date, differences have continued to emerge with each new project I live. Some of my efforts have met with what appears to be considerable success (Castle and Shuttler 1993; Field and Castle 1992), while others have been only moderately successful, and still others have failed, sometimes never getting beyond the initial opening stage. Other researchers and educators tell similar stories. These as well as my own experiences have advanced my understanding about collaborative relationships.

One thing I learned early on is that school-university collaboration is distinct from other sorts of collaborative relationships. When I moved from collaborating with university peers to collaborating with individuals in school systems, I struggled to understand the difference. Stepping back and observing the major collaborative processes as specified by Oja and Smulyan (1989) proved helpful here. They suggest studying the group dynamics process because "how the group negotiates various aspects of interaction ultimately affects both goals and results" (p. 55). This explained why my collaborative experiences with university colleagues seemed more fulfilling initially than my experiences with school groups. With my university peers, all norms, decision making processes, roles and interpersonal structures were already well established, whereas in school projects, these shared understandings did not exist initially, and we had to work through phases to establish a level of rapport to open up communication.

I have also learned, however, that communicating well with those in the school system differs depending on whether the project involves a one-on-one relationship or larger groups of individuals. While it is rare to find the university side of a partnership consisting of more than two or three individuals, it is not uncommon to find the school side including entire staffs and even system administrators and directors. In such cases where large groups are involved, collaborative ventures seem less successful. Shulha and Wilson's (1993) story of their efforts to establish a collaborative project with a school staff point out clearly how difficult it is even to get started. They relate how even after a lengthy negotiation of one and a half years, the school they were involved with opted not to undertake the project. This was difficult for me to understand when I first heard it, given that my own experience with a school system at that time seemed in sharp contrast to theirs. But upon reflection I came to concede that my relationship was not really with the larger school system as much as it was with one or two specific individuals in that system. I was resonating with and working closely with one highly committed principal and one dynamic curriculum consultant, rather than directly with the whole staff itself. I forced myself to admit that it was most likely the case that the receptive environment I constantly experienced in the school itself was not my doing at all.

Further proof of this same point was driven home to me last year when a first-year principal in another school approached a university colleague and me to speak with his staff about a collaborative venture they were considering which would link our preservice science majors with his experienced classroom teachers for the purpose of enhancing the science curriculum in that school. It was somewhat shocking to learn the day after our visit with them that the teachers had decided not to pursue the project after all. Even though they had apparently agreed with the value of the project earlier with the principal, then considered with us how we could both benefit from this, and how we might work together to accomplish this, they concluded that the demands on them would be too great. The principal had turned control over to the teachers in order to empower them and give them the opportunity to establish all details of the partnership themselves; instead, however, what the teachers did was opt to not even begin. This principal now questions whether teachers can be expected to perform in ways that will reform education. I still wonder what would have happened if I had begun working directly with the principal, or with only one or two of his teachers, rather than agreeing to meet with the whole staff. Fullan (1992) warns against "visions that blind," and advises principals first to establish a collaborative culture in the school before moving to larger collaborative projects. How a particular idea is initially represented no doubt directly affects the future agenda. As such, the importance of one or two key leaders in each party who can get a project going has taken on a new meaning to me. I see collaboration now as more person driven than institution driven.

The stories recounted here connect with points made earlier about the need for agreement between school and university partners on conceptual and procedural issues related to educational change. It seems that in practice this consensus is indeed difficult to achieve and that key leaders in each institution are needed to help bring this about. While most collaborative efforts between schools and universities appear to be initiated by the university community (Boyer 1982), it seems that the right connections have to be made with the right individuals, and that this is best done on a small scale initially.

Despite such potential difficulties, school-university projects do get off the ground, with both parties voicing common goals. But even in such cases, what constitutes mutuality needs to be considered seriously. Grimmett (1994) recounts what he calls a particularly difficult experience of collaboration. From his perspective, the problem arose because of incorrect assumptions: since he and the teachers shared a common set of progressive educational terms, they would have many things in common. Grimmett discovered that even though he and the teachers shared these terms and appeared to possess a common goal, they in reality had very different notions of the processes to which these terms referred. As a result, misunderstanding and vacuous discourse and action were great. Grimmett felt neither valued nor appreciated in his attempts to work with the teachers, and any sense of shared negotiation of task disappeared. Knowles (Cole and Knowles 1993) also tells of a personal experience in which he and a student teacher worked on a research project aimed at understanding teacher development.

What Knowles discovered as he continued to work with the student was that all their earlier work had not been collaborative at all; the agenda had been Knowles' alone. Change occurred only after continuous ongoing discussion and reflection between the two of them.

The realities encountered by both Grimmett and Knowles are no doubt more common experiences than we may wish to admit. It is perhaps time to accept the reality that stated mutual goals are often pursued in ways that maximize one party's needs. In other words, the actual behavior of those involved often comes to contravene what were supposedly agreed upon commitments. One of the reasons this occurs in school-university partnerships is that both cultures hold different sets of needs, norms and values. Huberman (1990) calls this the "chronic two communities problem" and Cuban (1990) adds that this embodies a whole series of value conflicts. Perhaps the greatest dilemma to be overcome, however, is the incongruity of the reward systems in each institution. Schools continue to be rewarded most for implementing programs and practices that increase student performance. They are not rewarded for engaging in inquiry as university faculty are. In universities it is still traditional research that is valued over applied research. Both the school and the university templates are incongruous with the newer vision of restructuring which calls for both institutions to work together in innovative, creative, and nontraditional ways. Without a new set of rules, however, it continues to be difficult for schools and universities to set and work toward goals and outcomes which are truly mutual.

I am not saying here that schools and universities never share a common goal or mission; rather, I am suggesting that even when a goal is shared, institutions will have different expectations around that mission (Green, Baldini, and Stack 1993). This is proving to be the case in a project that I am currently involved in. This is a Professional Development School operation which has seen the entire staff in a kindergarten to Grade Eight school mentor a new group of approximately twenty-five preservice teachers each year for the past three years. I have come to know the staff and administrators quite well, and we have discussed the perceived purpose and outcomes of this collaborative venture many times. All of us voice the same broad goal, and all of us are driven by a vision of better teachers. Beyond this, however, I have come to accept that our notions of what constitutes "better teacher" or "good mentoring" or "adequate instruction" or "meaningful professional development" all differ. And yet, the project in my mind is very successful. Data gathered at the close of the second year revealed that all involved thought the project was successful as well. The reasons given were not the same, but all parties voiced a sense of achievement and reward. The outcomes were not perceived as beneficial by all, but all reported that they benefitted from the project in some way. I have learned that on this journey toward a larger common goal, it is not essential that all of us share identical specific purposes or that we all participate equally in the same activities, or that we all benefit equally from each outcome. This would be the ideal, but it is not proving to be essential to the success of this project. I have come to understand that what is more important is the nature of the interaction among all of us. How we respond to each other, how we deal with issues, and how we negotiate our own understandings has emerged as central to our collaborative effort.

Revisiting Mutual Goals

The point I want to stress in concluding is that our efforts to understand and to promote collaborative relationships between schools and universities have perhaps focused too much on the extent to which mutual goals are the key to collaboration. It is time for the rules of collaboration to shift and acknowledge the reality. The focus is better placed on the ways in which those involved in collaborative relationships interact and respond to the broad common goal and to one another.

Relationships between schools and universities must leave room for a multiplicity of voices as participants come together to engage in a new dialogue and negotiate new meaning. The learning occurring in this new arena is constructed and reconstructed by each individual throughout each new phase of the collaboration. This necessitates that our present narrowly conceived notion of what constitutes collaboration be expanded to include personal learning and personal growth. Without attention to the individual and the ways in which individuals grow and learn from one another, collaboration remains more form than content.

✧ Chapter Five

Negotiating Collaboration for Professional Growth: A Case of Consultation

Mary Hookey, Shelley Neal, and Zoe Donoahue

Teachers are always calling on colleagues for professional advice. Teachers next door, in another school, or in an administrative position all may provide ongoing assistance with, and feedback on classroom programming. During the last decade, there has been a shift in the literature on ways of supporting teacher growth. Supervisory models that formerly sent mixed messages of support and evaluation to teachers have been redefined. The newer professional roles that placed teachers as observers and advisors in colleagues' classrooms (Little 1985) removed the formal power differential, but still were structured by administrators.

But what are the issues for teachers themselves as they seek the support of other teachers for their professional growth voluntarily? What is the nature of the process that teachers use to find professional support? What helps them collaboratively define their problems and engage in action research on their practice? As we found in our own joint work, building a voluntary relationship that supports professional growth requires ongoing negotiation (Hookey 1993).

Negotiation can be defined several ways. Probably the most familiar definition describes negotiation as the process for arriving at a solution to a problem or conflict. Fisher and Brown (1988) and others associated with the Harvard Negotiation Project have provided us with many examples of the place of negotiation in conflict resolution. In contrast, negotiation may also be described as a process occurring "in the ordinary social interactions of everyday life" (Martin 1976, 3). In this chapter, negotiation fits the latter definition. Our story highlights the negotiations we undertook as we explored, not the problems, but the *possibilities* in our professional collaboration. It provides an example of how three teachers, two working in their own classrooms and one in a resource role, each benefit professionally by documenting and examining their ongoing joint work (Somekh 1991). In this chapter, we consider the role that negotiation played in our professional relationship. We also discuss how the process of negotiation and the decisions made, provided us with further insights into our work as a case of consultation.

Some educational researchers have already documented the interpersonal negotiation in both professional development programs and collaborative school settings. Wallace and Louden (1990), for example, inquired into the nature of collaboration between two teachers involved in a professional development program. Both they and the teachers described this collaboration as a successful professional growth experience. Wallace and Louden concluded that the preconditions for successful professional growth were to be found, not in the qualities of the program, but in the qualities of collaboration. These qualities included similarity in terms of understanding the importance of the problem; symmetry or balance of power; preparedness to take risks; trust; emergence in terms of a naturally occurring growth in the relationship; humility; and, fair exchange among the participants in terms of the rewards of the relationship. While not directly mentioning negotiation, they talk about "how well the participants managed the delicate balance between individual freedom, mutual respect and a desire to extend the horizons of their professional practice" (ibid, 3). While we also examine the qualities and nature of our collaborative relationship, we take a closer look at the ways we managed, or negotiated, our joint work.

Nias and her colleagues found that, in schools that were moving from individualistic to collaborative cultures, staff members were "continuously involved in negotiating their relationships in response to the forces of change acting upon them" (Nias, Southworth, and Yeomans 1989, 76). These researchers describe several types of negotiation used by school staffs to reach what they call "working compromises": explicit negotiation, implicit negotiation, and truces. Both explicit and implicit negotiation were evident in our work as well. However, we also use the framework developed by Martin (1976) as another lens on our joint work.

Martin (1976) studied teachers involved in team teaching situations and compared the negotiations they engaged in with their colleagues to those with their students. Martin's framework has five major elements (p.10): (a) the preconditions that lead to negotiation, (b) the extent of the negotiation in terms of its content, on who asserts influence on whom, and on the degree to which changes are made as result of negotiation, (c) the stages, including the time spent defining goals, the process of defining and redefining the situation, the use of persuasive techniques, and the arrival at a working agreement, (d) the strategies designed to influence the outcomes, and (e) the outcomes of the negotiation process.

To give a sense of our project, we begin by sharing the ideas that brought us together, then describe how we negotiated our joint work, creating an opportunity for professional growth through a more consultative relationship (Knoff 1988). Because we found that our joint work on this project contributed to a continuing interest in collaborative work, we conclude the chapter by individually setting this project into the context of our ongoing professional lives.

Why Did We Begin Our Project?

At the time our project began, Shelley and Zoe taught in two different schools, one at the kindergarten and the other at the grade one level. Mary was a music resource teacher working with elementary classroom teachers in eighteen schools. A change in Mary's resource assignment provided an opportunity for a different kind of joint work. Previously, resource teacher time was spent providing service to schools and teachers during biweekly scheduled visits. With the change in the resource role, resource and classroom teachers were given some flexibility to arrange joint work at times that were more convenient to the teacher. In this context, resource teachers could address individual teacher questions about program more directly.

Each of us had our own motivations for becoming involved. Since Mary had argued strongly for the benefits of increased flexible time, she had an interest in how this would affect her work. Zoe was keenly interested both in child-centered learning and in sharing ideas with colleagues with the same philosophy. Shelley was one of those colleagues. The two had met several years earlier during teacher in-service sessions. They had set up days when they could make short visits to each other's classroom during lunch hours to share ideas. Both classroom teachers saw the project as an opportunity to see the actions behind the talk, to consider how to communicate their ideas to other colleagues, and to explore something new.

Designing Our Project

As we began, our question was, How might we build a collegial relationship to support our professional growth? Data were collected in several contexts: two audiotaped planning sessions, two videotapes of classroom teaching, videotaped conferences and audiotaped reflections. Transcripts were made of the conferences and reviewed for patterns in our work and interaction. Our analysis illustrates "how teachers and support teachers use talk to form the inter-subjectivity of their roles and so to make sense and meaning of their work together" (Gronn cited in Biott 1991, 19).

How We Negotiated Our Joint Work

Our negotiations clustered around five tasks involved in facilitating our joint work: initiating a working relationship; determining worthwhile purposes; establishing supportive contexts; maintaining a working relationship; and, expanding worthwhile purposes.

Our initial challenges were to negotiate a working relationship, find a focus that would meet our individual needs, and gain administrative support for our joint work. The time we took to deal with these three aspects made our ongoing negotiations possible.

Initiating a Working Relationship

Since we were breaking new interpersonal ground, we took the time to negotiate both *how* to work together, and *why*. The first stage and easiest task in our joint work was coming to an understanding of how we might interact in the two classrooms on our projected visits. Since neither Shelley nor Zoe had observed in each other's classrooms, and Mary had never visited the classrooms solely to observe and conference, we talked about what this experience might be like and how our different roles might be accommodated. Initially, we focused our discussions by looking at Kagan's (1985) guides for peer coaching. The guides served as a foil for stating what might feel appropriate and what might not. These guides served not as models, but as a stimulus for clarifying what was important in our own work and for designing a process that felt right to us. We negotiated why, when, and where to conference in a new and potentially intimidating situation. We wrote down examples of questions that would feel supportive and mapped the whole process in graphic form.

We agreed that we should all be involved in any joint planning discussion. We also agreed that when a teacher was being observed in her own classroom, she should lead the conference and hear ideas and comments from the other teacher before the interaction opened up to include Mary acting in her resource role.

What was the outcome of this negotiation process? We never referred to the alternative questions or process which we had developed. However, the boundaries which we had established shaped our conferences. The result of these negotiations was a working agreement in which teacher interactions were foregrounded and where resource work was dependent on the directions established by the two classroom teachers.

Determining Worthwhile Purposes

Determining a worthwhile purpose for joint work was just as critical as establishing ways to work together. It involved time and careful listening. The overall challenge depended on building stronger bridges between a child-centred, literature-based classroom curriculum and the music program.

This was developed through a number of activities: the sharing of stories of past practice; brainstorming practical classroom applications for untried ideas; building on ideas from a workshop which we all had attended; and, identifying resources that would help one or more of us build images (Clandinin 1986) of new ideas-in-use. Developing these images of joint work was an implicit form of negotiation. Thinking about storying and building joint images as negotiation strategies is a case of making the familiar strange. Listening to our three voices, the question of whether any idea could serve as a focus sounded more like an invitation than negotiation.

Do you have some things you would like to work on like. . . ?

I'd have to think about it a little more and talk more.

When one of us could not picture ourselves as a participant in a suggested activity, the idea was set aside for the moment or rejected. As we moved closer to our focus, the sound of cautious possibility was heard in our voices.

If I was going to do this, I would be very hesitant to deal with music other than singing. I would like someone to help me plan this instead of doing it on my own . . . and I think that's the whole idea of teaming . . . just to allow us to use some of these ideas and build together.

When an image finally seemed possible to all of us, the words of agreement with the focus tumbled quickly over each other.

So maybe the two of us together could. . . .

And we could tape it.

YES, UH HUH. I DON'T MIND DOING THAT TOO.

The topics we considered in our initial discussions ranged from sound exploration and creative music to more teacher-directed activities for exploring elements of music, such as rhythm pattern and dynamics, in songs and instrumental pieces. The focus that we finally chose was the integration of music and language.

Establishing Supportive Contexts

Our collaboration across schools and the school system required that we negotiate the support of principals and administrators. To obtain permission and release time for work across two schools, we drafted a letter outlining the proposed project. We were successful in convincing the principals in each of the two schools of the need for release time for one or two visits to the other school. The resource teacher's time was limited so that time on this work did not affect service to other teachers. Since we valued the time that we would have together, we accommodated our limitations by negotiating changes to our initial plan: visitations would take place at the end of the day; conferencing would be after school, if a visit could not be arranged, we would tape teaching episodes and then conference while watching the tape. These broad parameters shaped the time available to us and the number of contacts that we would make during our joint work.

Maintaining a Working Relationship

According to Martin (1976), preconditions for negotiation include the presence of an ambiguity or disagreement and one or more of the following: a lack of, or unwillingness to use power to achieve personal ends, or an unwillingness to remove oneself from the situation. Unlike a confrontational or problem solving situation, we mainly faced ambiguities, not disagreements, as we worked together. We had talked through a number of the uncertainties surrounding our behavior during observations and conferences during the initial planning meetings. However, particular issues emerged at the end of each conference which needed negotiation. These included practical matters such as the time of the next observation or conference and the setting of the agenda.

Sometimes the reasons behind certain teaching activities were ambiguous. By playing back the videotapes after school, we had the opportunity to focus on the underlying rationale. The usefulness of our joint work meant that *disagreement* was too strong a word for the philosophical questions that arose. Instead, the questions provided opportunities for negotiating shared meaning. Sometimes these ambiguities in understanding were addressed directly through our questions.

Do you sit down at some point and say you are going to cover this, this, and this in your lesson?

I find with this gang they say so much when we sing and read together. They always make observations about patterns and about what they notice or how things have developed. It just happens, so I don't guide them. I just go where they go, and pick up on them.

Did you have to guide them last year?

No. I think it's mostly if you provide them with an opportunity to speak afterwards. . . . I usually sit and look expectantly at them after something finishes. Once they get the idea that you are open, they just volunteer naturally. It ties in the math, the reading, the writing, the repeated patterns—as long as they know that you don't have something [specific] that you want. I think if I was waiting for them to say certain things, I wouldn't get such a variety of responses.

At other times, ambiguities in understanding emerged in response to a comment.

I like your pattern of reading the whole thing before going to the skill—and before you went to the skill you always allowed them to talk.

Its funny when you say "skill" because I don't think about it that way.

What would you call it?

I think it's starting with the whole and then looking at the parts more closely.

That's exactly what the pattern was. . . . I think what I do is get right into the nitty-gritty of the text . . . instead of just enjoying it, [and] letting them respond to it. That's the first thing I learned. Sit back and let them respond and see what they do.

There was also an element of ambiguity in projecting how music and language would be integrated in the classroom. Many commercial and school system documents offered suggestions for the integration of specific songs and pieces within broad thematic units. There were also similar materials available for integrated arts. However, there were few descriptions available of this type of cross curricular practice. We were actively seeking to describe the curriculum integration (Hookey 1994/1995).

Expanding Worthwhile Purposes

In addition, part of our willingness to continue to work together might be attributed to the fact that we were able to expand the purposes for our work. The extent of our negotiations was not limited to a curricular focus. Certainly, as the months progressed, our conferences focused more intently on the integration of music and language. However, our original concern about how to work together was also broad enough to allow three very different possibilities for individual professional growth. For one of us, it would be a chance to refine current practice. For another, it would be an opportunity to enrich current classroom practice through imagining and implementing new learning opportunities in the classroom. For the third, it would mean stepping outside a familiar disciplinary framework to see more holistic connections across the curriculum. For all of us, it offered new ways of thinking about ourselves as professionals. We talked about the potential for professional growth in the alternative administrative and curriculum leadership routes open to teachers. Increasingly, the talk in our conferences shifted back and forth between classroom work and the links that this had with our wider roles as professionals. We were negotiating not only the curriculum, but the images of the educators we might become (Foote cited in Martin 1976, 8).

Qualities of Negotiation

What were the underlying qualities of our negotiations? The negotiations were recursive. Certain issues, such as the notion of the classroom as a community and the importance of balancing depth of knowledge with integration across several subject areas, were continually at the center of our discussion. We were continually widening our understanding of the importance of community gatherings for experiencing a range of activities beyond the learner's individualized or small group classroom work and for making connections within and beyond the traditional school subjects.

The negotiations were asymmetrical, revealing different types and levels of input from each of us depending on the topic under discussion and the point we were at in the process. Mary's subject matter expertise was drawn on more widely in the initial planning stages. In later stages, more specific questions were asked, but less frequently, as the teachers themselves shared observations on their ongoing practice. We benefitted from Zoe's ability to link our discussions to the ideas of Piaget, Vygotsky and the place of play in the classroom program. Shelley's frequent probing questions led us to articulate our underlying assumptions about teaching, learning and professional growth.

The negotiations were unhurried. As we have described, we took time to develop a wide range of ideas before we selected a focus for classroom observations. Our conferences and observations unfolded over several months.

The quality of most interest to us, however, was the consultative nature of the relationship.

Collaboration as Consultation

At the beginning of this chapter, we described our joint professional work as an example of teacher-driven collaboration and contrasted it to supervisory and advisory relationships. We used the concept of negotiation as developed by Martin (1976) to examine the five tasks we encountered in facilitating our joint work.

How did our negotiations reveal our work as a case of consultation? Our decisions supported an underlying premise of consultation—that the person responsible for the actual work should both identify a work-related question, concern or interest, and decide if, and how, to use the shared knowledge in their own work setting (Gallessich 1982; Knoff 1988). Teacher purposes were central to our work, making it an example of professional development, not of implementation (Biott 1991).

Interpreting collaboration as consultation provides an alternative to supervisory and advisory frameworks for thinking about collaborative relationships. The decisions that are reached through negotiation reveal much about the nature of collaboration. One decision, such as the attempt to exercise unwarranted authority over another's work, may be enough to alter the character of the relationship.

Seeing our work as consultation leads us to a whole set of ideas in the consultation literature about the issues and dilemmas of serving as a resource. Although our curriculum work was central to our joint work, our consultative collaboration was both an occasion for professional growth and part of the larger web of our individual professional lives. We began our chapter by sharing how we came to work together; we finish by sharing how we are reaching out to new professional partnerships.

Zoe: Working with Mary and Shelley on this project was the beginning of a way of working with other teachers as equals, seeking the answers to our questions and supporting one another in our daily work. This project gave me glimpses of the power of working with colleagues, the importance of negotiation, trust and talking about roles, and how this could help me effect change in my teaching practices. Since then, I have looked for further opportunities to work in this type of supportive situation. Four years ago, a change in teaching assignments from primary to junior caused me to seek out colleagues who were changing divisions. We formed a support group and have been meeting monthly since then. Another result of this project has been an interest in doing my own research. I have pursued this through course work toward my Master of Education degree, conducting inquiries about support groups and design technology. I am currently working with a group of colleagues to design a school-wide model for teaching spelling. I have presented my findings at conferences hosted by the Ontario Educational Research Council, the International Reading Association and the Science Teachers' Association of Ontario. A final result of this project has been an ongoing dialogue with Mary about our current projects and with Shelley about our day to day experiences in the classroom.

Mary: My joint work with Zoe and Shelly has been a critical incident in my ongoing professional development. One reason for this has to do with the value of collaborative action research. There is a heightened edge to one's work when you are a participating observer. Your words are immediately challenged by your actions and bring double loop learning into play (Argyris 1982) For example, this project raised questions about current arguments surrounding the nature and quality of music education provided by classroom teachers (Bresler 1993). Our joint work helped me see how music might be integrated within the primary program in ways that respected both music as a way of knowing and the holistic way that a child approaches his or her experience. It revealed how two skillful primary teachers could draw on the big ideas in a variety of curriculum areas to help students integrate their knowledge (Hookey 1994/1995). What seemed like very open-ended teaching strategies were more like improvisations over an underlying structure. Because there were strong challenges to some of my basic assumptions about music education, it convinced me of the importance of research on one's own work for professional development. I have tried to put myself in a similar situation through research on my own work in the pre-service classroom and in a school featuring an arts-based integrated curriculum. My only regret is that I did not learn to take these opportunities much earlier in my career.

Shelley: My mother always told me never to gossip. So like eating a forbidden fruit, it became something I like to do. Put that together with my passion for the craft of teaching and I could talk for hours. When I began teaching, there was a certain fear that I didn't know enough about what I was doing to be a valid teacher. Meeting Zoe gave me a partner and a resource for my professional growth. When Mary approached Zoe and me to undertake such an interesting collaborative effort, we quickly agreed and the process began.

Our gossip turned into purposive talk—the true beginning of growth for my learning style. After working with the team, I realized the importance of talk—sometimes directed and sometimes in the form of a brainstorming session—as the basis for planning, consulting, reflecting and refining as one evaluates and evolves his or her teaching practices. Time to talk was a time to reflect, a time to orally practice a new idea and a time to develop a support system. The groundwork was laid during those early talking meetings. We had developed a sense of trust to share and evaluate our attempts, as well as a common language and perspective about change. The next step was to start the classroom aspect of the cycle.

The ramifications of this collaborative process did not stop with my music lessons, but continued in terms of working together with other colleagues within my school setting as well as at the graduate level. I now value the time for talk and encourage it to occur whenever I can with a group of teachers interested in growing and changing. I plan time for this talk to occur and when the groundwork is solid, we, as a group of teachers, can move along the cycle into action and reflection. I am also continuing to study the importance of teacher talk and collaboration during my graduate studies. Presently, I am involved with a panel of professors and colleagues studying the implementation of science programs within the classroom. This study group is looking at the importance of talk among colleagues as they undertake the process of working in the sciences with their students. Again, we talk, plan, implement and reflect on our experiences in this new domain.

Teaching can be an isolating career as we become engrossed in the daily demands within the walls of our classrooms. However, the powerful resource of collaborating, planning and talking together makes our work richer and exciting. So, if you are ever interested in some good school gossip, a cup of tea and box of cookies are waiting for us as we begin.

◇ Chapter Six

Practitioner and Researcher Perspectives in Teacher Research and the Construction of Knowledge[1]

Janet Blond and Kathie Webb

New ways of thinking about knowledge have relevance not only for conceptions of curriculum and, hence, teaching and learning, but also for educational research—in particular teacher research—that is, research by and with teachers. In this chapter we describe how *shared responsibility* in the research process and *the relationship between the practitioner and the researcher* are central to the collaborative research design and to the kind of information that the research yields.

Our research is concerned with who produces knowledge about teaching and with the nature of that knowledge. We question what counts as knowledge. Our findings have implications for research on teaching, in particular the design of research methodologies which are meaningful to, and include, teachers. In this chapter we describe how our research relationship works *and* how the findings are dependent on, and emerge from, that relationship. We share research stories in order to make explicit the way in which we collect information and interpret our findings. These stories reflect our narrative knowing (Bruner 1990; Connelly and Clandinin 1990; Polkinghorne 1988) and the ways in which we story and restory our experiences and our knowing.

Collaborative Narrative Inquiry

We are two teachers who first met in March 1992 and started to talk about negotiating a collaborative study on teacher knowledge. We were both active in our development and shared a common interest in wanting to understand more about our own knowing as teachers. Janet is a junior high teacher of language arts/math and has been teaching for nine years in Edmonton, Alberta. She sees herself as knowledgeable about teaching twelve- and thirteen-year-olds. Our study is concerned with exploring her teaching practices as expressions of her teacher knowledge. Kathie is completing her fourth year as a doctoral candidate at a Canadian university. She taught grades seven to twelve in Australian schools for seventeen years, including ten years as a department head in a large secondary school before coming to Canada to pursue doctoral studies. Her long experience of working in a team with fellow teachers at department and whole school levels resulted in a commitment to collaboration for teacher development.

A commitment to collaborative teacher development is reflected in the research design we negotiated. Part of our commitment to each other involves respecting each other's voice. We continuously renegotiated the study in order to include and honor Janet's meanings, Kathie's meanings, as well as new meanings we have come to jointly as a consequence of collaboration. We have different experiences in and of the study and we tell different stories about the same event. Hence, in writing about our collaboration we have chosen to use a format which allows us to represent both our voices.

In early November 1992 Kathie commenced fieldwork, visiting Janet's classroom at first two days per week and later, four days per week. With Janet's consent, she wanted to be both a researcher and a co-teacher in Janet's classroom over the remainder of the school year. At that time, both co-researchers agreed that Kathie would assume the major responsibility for writing the final report of the study and that Janet's major responsibility was to be the teacher in the classroom. Though we were unsure as to how we would interpret *collaboration*, we had established very early in our relationship that we wanted to share in decisions about what constituted data for the study and the meanings/interpretation of the data. We discussed the philosophy underpinning narrative inquiry (Connelly and Clandinin 1990) and shared our common belief in the importance of teachers' stories about their practices. We both felt confident that our stories would teach us and be a source of our learning, even though we were unsure as to how this research methodology would unfold for us.

Our intent was (and is) to tell and understand practitioner and researcher stories of teaching practice and to make educational research meaningful for teachers and researchers by grounding it in everyday classroom realities. The need to pay attention to the stories teachers are living and telling in their classrooms has been addressed by Carter (1993), Cochran-Smith and Lytle (1990), Connelly and Clandinin (1990), and Florio-Ruane (1991). These authors describe teachers' stories as a largely untapped source of information about teaching. Florio-Ruane is critical of much educational research saying that it often loses sight of the insider perspective—it fails to ring true to the experiences of teachers. Further, Cochran-Smith and Lytle (1993) make a strong case for why teachers should participate in research on teaching. With specific reference to the *Handbook of Research on Teaching* (Wittrock 1986), these authors state that missing from this knowledge base for teaching "are the voices of teachers themselves, questions teachers ask, and the interpretive frames teachers use to understand and improve their own classroom practices" (p. 7).

We interpret our research as collaborative, in that it is research *with* rather than *on* a teacher. The analysis of data, constructing the meanings of the stories, has been a joint process where a researcher-teacher and a teacher-researcher have worked together to understand the meanings of the stories. In the three and a half years we have worked together, inside and outside of Janet's classroom, we have helped each other with *what we know* and *how we know what we know* about teaching and learning. It has been a two-way sharing of information and ideas. Our research relationship and the ways in which we have shared responsibility in and for the research have influenced the findings—what we know and what we can help others to know.

We share stories from early in our study that describe our continuous negotiation and our vulnerabilities in order to show how the methodology hinges on relationship in collaborative research. We draw attention to the multiple perspectives of events and multiple tellings and interpretations of stories that occurred in our study. We suggest these various tellings and retellings are "multiple truths" (Rorty 1991). With Cole and Knowles (1993), we argue for recognition of the epistemological perspective in which collaborative research into teacher development is situated. In telling stories from the research and how we are making sense of them, we are describing how we are authoring our development as teachers. We are showing how collaborative teacher research has the potential to change conceptions of teacher development.

Practitioner-Researcher Relationship as Central to Collaborative Research

On November 11, 1993 we met to talk about and start writing this chapter concerning relationship and shared responsibility as emergent themes in our collaborative methodology. We tossed around ideas about how we should start and what to include, and asked each other questions about what we thought was important. Janet suggested the "parent-visitor story"[2] should be included. Kathie agreed that she thought it was important to the chapter's focus but was surprised that Janet seemed positive about the story. Janet said the parent-visitor story created a turning point in the research for her. She explained that up to that point she had felt relatively insecure in the research and the research relationship. When she read the parent-visitor story she realized that Kathie was supportive of her. She said to Kathie, "Knowing that changed things. I knew then that I could trust you."

Janet: At first, it was a bit stressful having someone in my room that didn't know the kids or me that well. I was worried about what she'd think. Were my lesson plans okay? How would she judge me? What would parents think about all these people in my classroom? (I also had two student teachers for five weeks during the first term of the study.) Would she write about my messy desk? What about those days when I wasn't the perfect teacher, or when the lesson didn't turn out the way I expected? Would she understand? I also worried about how I could help her to feel comfortable in the classroom. Some of these anxieties were not verbal-

---

ized at the time. I wasn't sure what it was I felt unsure about.

Teachers often feel uneasy about someone coming into our classrooms. We know the newcomer does not know the full context of our situation—the kids, the school climate, our extracurricular and supervision duties, parental support. All impact on the job we do in the classroom. I worried about the effect of another person in the classroom. How would that affect my relationship with the kids, the way that I teach, and the behavior of the kids? This mish mash of questions tumbled around in my mind and mixed with the excitement of having a colleague to share and exchange ideas with, and the opportunity to showcase some of the things that I thought I was doing right as a junior high teacher. I thought of myself as a Grade Seven specialist, having taught that grade for some years. I was looking forward to the opportunity to discuss the reasons for doing some of the things that I do somewhat intuitively.

I guess the first time I realized that Kathie was appreciative of some of the things I was doing in the classroom was when she had been there for a couple of weeks and a parent-visitor came to the class. Kathie later told me (orally and in a story she had written) that the parent had made derogatory comments to her about the lesson. The parent said that our class on geometric shapes and three-dimensional objects looked more like an art lesson than a math lesson. She thought it was of no academic value and a waste of time. Kathie explained to the parent some of the philosophy behind the lesson, how it connected with other lessons we had been doing on measurement, the rationale for working in groups, and the importance of a creative-design component. Kathie explained the logic involved in relating a two-dimensional template to a three-dimensional object. I was relieved when I heard this.

Kathie: I was extremely surprised by Janet's revelation a year later that the parent-visitor story had been the turning point in the research for her. I thought she had not given the story much credence. When I wrote the parent-visitor story in early December 1992, it was only four weeks after I had started coming to her classroom. Though I knew I wanted to use a narrative approach to the research and had read widely on this, I was very unsure of how to *do* it. When Janet told me stories about her teaching, it was relatively easy to record them by making notes about them. But I knew that her stories were not the only stories, and I was not sure how to pull together the many threads that were already appearing in the research. I did not feel confident that I could do this in a meaningful way. When I wrote the parent-visitor story it was an experiment—a first attempt—to pull together a number of incidents that I saw happening in her classroom and which I thought were relevant to the research. I tried to tell these as a story.

As I was writing the story, I felt like it almost wrote itself. The story was about multiple perspectives of what was happening in a classroom—the teacher's, the parent's, the student teachers', the students' and mine. I realized this was an important story for me because telling it caused me to ask questions about how research is done, what counts as data, the interpretation of data, and the accepted norm of the researcher's perspective as the right one or the only one. In telling this story I also questioned my own role as researcher. I realized that the story exposed my initial dilemma about defending Janet's practice to the parent-visitor. In becoming involved in the research, I felt I had breached the requirement for objectivity. In telling this story I began to understand that it would be impossible to do this research and maintain an objective stance as the researcher.

Writing the story resulted in contradictions for me as researcher. It was rich. I knew I had told a story of the many things going on in Janet's classroom and had begun to raise important methodological issues. It concerned me, however, that I had constructed the story on my own. The research was supposed to be collaborative. The thought that I was writing, pulling together events and interpretations on my own, nagged at me. How could we do narrative research and be collaborative when Janet held a full-time job teaching? While I realized it was my responsibility to write, I struggled with the question: How does one do this and still allow the other person space to decide what is important and what it means? I didn't know and hoped that I was on the right track with my first attempt.

I took the story to Janet at school and waited eagerly for her to read it. I wanted her to say it was good. She read it but did not make a comment. I was desperate to know what she thought, but tried not to show it. When I got a chance to talk to her at the end of the day I asked her what she thought about the story. She said, "Mmmm." I asked her if it was how she saw things had been happening. She said, "It's close." I took her comment to mean that all I had was *my* story, and, though it was an interesting story, it was only "close" to, but not, *her* story. I thought I had failed and was very critical of myself. I decided this was not the way to do collaborative narrative research. I resolved to not try anymore to pull events together into a story on my own. In the future I would concentrate on compiling field notes and then talk with Janet about the meanings. Somehow we would construct the research stories together.

A year later, at our November 1993 meeting when Janet told me that the parent-visitor story was a turning point in the research for her, I shared with her my reaction to her comment "It's close." I told her I realized later, after working in her classroom for about three months, that I had been foolish. By then I had realized no matter how hard I tried or how well I wrote I would never be able to capture someone else's story. I recognized the unrealistic task I had set myself when I wrote the parent-visitor story and when I had waited for Janet to affirm it. I was learning to relate my life, and my learning from life, to doing research. We tell many stories of an event in our lives; so too in research. By this time I had also come to know Janet a lot better. I had come to know that "It's close" is high praise from Janet. She is critical of her reticence to give praise and says she has modeled herself on her mother in this regard. Frequently she has told me stories of doing something very, very well as a child and how her mother would only say, "Mmmm."

We both laughed when we found out how the other felt and when we realized we had kept our stories private for so long. It was a year before we shared with each other what the story and our responses to it had meant for each of us. Why did it take so long? We had a positive research relationship and had become friends. Why didn't we tell each other? Our stories emphasize the need to allow for time to develop trust in a research relationship.

Shared Responsibility in Collaborative Research

We took time to break free of the traditional division of labor when one person is designated "researcher" and the other "participant." At first Kathie assumed responsibility for data collection: writing field notes, conducting interviews, collecting documentation. In her classroom Janet was busy with teaching so it was unrealistic for her to write in a research journal. She took the research journal home each week or each month and, on occasion, the day Kathie's notes had been done. On evenings and weekends she responded to Kathie's notes, wrote her observations in the journal, and indicated what she considered confidential information. Janet retained the right of veto. As the days spent together in Janet's classroom passed into months, we became friends. In our talks after class, on weekends, in our many phone calls, and on the odd occasion that Janet got a lunch break, we told each other about our lives and what is important to each of us. Our relationships (in our families and in our teaching) figured heavily in these talks. As we came to know each other better, we felt more comfortable sharing our roles and responsibilities in the research. Janet often took on the researcher role, reflecting on Kathie's stories and experiences, retelling those stories and sharing her interpretations. Janet also collected data about her students. Negotiating responsibility for teaching in Janet's classroom, however, caused us to confront very early in the study what we meant by collaboration.

Janet: At first, when Kathie was giving the kids instructions on tessellations (repeating graphical designs) in a math class, I had mixed feelings. On the one hand, I felt a bit defensive. I thought she was filling in the gaps where she thought I had missed the boat. At the same time, I was glad the kids were getting some added attention that's impossible for one teacher to provide in a class of twenty-eight students. Kathie broke the sequence of design formation into nine squares. She showed how to complete a miniature version of the complete design so the kids could get the pattern and see the whole concept on a small scale. I thought that strategy was quite good and decided to teach it that way next time. I learned from watching her and noticing what the kids were doing, that I probably should do more demonstrations and practice. Most kids did not understand the concept of a sliding tessellation. One thing bothered me somewhat. It seemed as if she was telling them too much and not allowing them to discover the patterns for themselves. At the time I didn't say anything to Kathie. I wasn't able to verbalize what bothered me. I thought Kathie was the expert because she was doing the Ph.D. Thinking about it now, if Kathie had not been there, and if it had not been so early in the partnership we were developing, I would have stopped the whole class and given a mini-lesson on the sliding part. It was clear the kids didn't get it. But I had made a commitment to the exercise and because I didn't know what Kathie would think if I stopped in the middle, I continued on as if that was the way I had planned it. It was the first time I had taught the unit. I have quite a few modifications for next time based on our classroom observations and experiences. I take a lot of risks with my teaching. I have brilliant lessons and I have duds. Sometimes what works well with one class doesn't work with another. I felt it was important for Kathie to know this, but I wasn't sure at the time if she did.

Kathie: In the math tessellations lesson, I attempted to help students when I observed that a large number of kids were just not "getting it." At first I wasn't sure what to do to help them as I had never heard of a tessellation before and did not know how to construct one. The next time I was in the class I experienced the same difficulty trying to help a lot of kids get started on something most of them did not seem to understand how to do. I still had not "got it." There was the concept of a sliding tessellation to be understood and I had tried to "pick it up" from Janet's demonstration. For the kids, getting started seemed the main problem. I watched Janet give a demonstration on the blackboard as well as individual demonstrations with small groups of students. Suddenly the process of tessellations made sense to me and I felt able to be a teacher in the classroom. I began showing groups of students in twos and threes, how to do a tessellation in a six-step process. I adapted Janet's methodology and developed a new one of my own which made sense to me. For the kids who had trouble thinking up a pattern to start off the tessellation, I drew a template to get them started.

Reflecting on this lesson and Janet's story of this lesson, I realize a number of factors came into play for me: I saw that kids were not "getting it" (the concepts involved in doing a tessellation); time was passing, the material had to be covered; I thought there needed to be a result to prove learning had occurred. I believed the result was important. In terms of the conduit metaphor for teaching and learning (Clandinin and Connelly 1992), I achieved what I now recognize as a problematic view of teaching. Further, I did not know how to "be" in another teacher's classroom for the purpose of doing research. In my previous school I had regularly been in other teachers' classrooms, but I always carried with me the authority of my roles as a teacher and department head in that school. In Janet's classroom, however, I was just another adult in the room. I had none of the authority that goes with being known as a teacher in that school. I had no legal responsibility to teach, discipline students, assign homework, or to make any of what I thought were the important decisions concerning the classroom.

Though I was competent at math, I had never taught math as a course. It had seemed quite realistic when negotiating this research with Janet to assume that I could be a researcher in her classroom, take notes about what was happening, and also be a co-teacher. I was busy keeping up with my commitments on campus, including teaching, and did not have the time to also plan with Janet the content or teaching strategies for her seven classes. I did not imagine this would be a problem, as teaching was mostly her responsibility. However, when I tried to be a co-teacher, which we thought was a good way for me to be integrated into her classroom, it immediately became evident that I needed to know the content she was attempting to teach. I also needed to develop strategies for teaching that content which made sense to me. Very quickly, I also realized I needed to get to *know* her students. There was much to know about each of them that Janet was aware of, and I was not, at this early stage in the research—knowledge that made a difference whether the students learned or not. The curriculum that I saw being lived out (Clandinin and Connelly 1992; Eisner 1988) in her classroom drew heavily on her relationships with the students and her knowledge of each student as a person. Even though I knew myself to be an intelligent and experienced teacher, I found I could only be a teacher in limited ways in her classroom when I focused on teaching as knowing the content. I needed to know her students if I really wanted to participate in the curriculum they were living out.

We resolved the dilemmas raised in these stories by writing to each other in the research journal about our feelings of discomfort and by talking to each other about how at risk each of us felt. We found it reassuring to learn that we both felt vulnerable in the research. We began to trust each other more and expand our conceptions and practices of shared responsibility in the research. Toward the end of the school year we presented together at a national conference, describing our methodology and early findings.

Kathie: There were risks for both of us in this venture. As a classroom teacher addressing a conference of university researchers, Janet knew she was telling a new story of educational research. There were few teachers from schools there. Going public as co-researchers in this study felt risky for me as a doctoral candidate. The university expected me to be responsible for "my study." But Janet and I were sharing the responsibility and some of the work in the study—"our study"—and we wanted to talk with other researchers about how this was changing the research. Being willing to take some risks, while at all times caring for the other, has developed our commitment to each other as professionals and as friends.

When I ended fieldwork in Janet's classroom in late June 1993, we were unsure how the ensuing writing process would enable both our voices to emerge. In the fall we renegotiated our responsibilities in the study. Though we maintained our initial agreement that Janet's major responsibility was teaching with research secondary, we began to change our original plans concerning writing the research reports. Janet began to be a co-author of the research papers.

Janet: Why did I accept more responsibility in this study? Why did I start to write? It is important to think about why, as a teacher, I would involve myself in writing about our collaborative study. Throughout the study Kathie continued to ask me if I was comfortable with my role in the research. She asked how I felt about each aspect. I was flattered to be asked to speak at an educational conference because hardly anybody cares what a teacher thinks. She gave me the message over and over again that what I had to say was important. I started to believe that I had something important to say.

Knowledge Construction in Collaborative Research

In a January 1994 doctoral research committee meeting, Kathie was asked how she planned to link the stories on "shared responsibility" that Janet and she had written to "teacher knowledge" (the thesis focus). Good question, but she did not know the answer. She did know that shared responsibility was important to this research. Janet had shown her that. The most she could say was that Janet used responsibility as an interpretive frame for her teaching. Kathie had borrowed this term from Cochran-Smith and Lytle (1993). It sounded good—but what did she mean? What was it she was trying to say? One of her advisors pushed her a little further and asked, "How are you going to get out of the stories? How are you going to make connections to knowledge?" Kathie answered as honestly as she could. She said she didn't know yet. Part of her felt confident that she and Janet were on their way to answering this difficult question, but another part felt little pangs of worry that they might not find an answer.

Kathie turned her advisor's questions over and over in her mind trying to find a clue. A question had been framed that was integral to the study and she could not think clearly about a possible answer until she understood why the question felt so important to her. She was involved in the stories and found it hard to get past them. The research stories were rich, full of numerous threads, and they told her so much. Though she had earlier viewed some of the stories as able to speak for themselves, she started thinking about the meanings of the stories and retelling as a way of accessing the multiple meanings of the stories. Her advisor's question helped her to think further. The research texts needed to say *why* the stories were important.

Kathie: In a weekend meeting with Janet, to work on a paper on themes of responsibility and relationships in the research data, I shared the questions raised in my doctoral committee meeting. In response, Janet did what I had done—returned to the stories. At first we focused on her strategies for sharing decision making in her classroom and the ways she had given her students choices. But this only answered "how" and not "why" Janet shared responsibility for learning in her classroom. I said, "In your classroom you shared responsibility with your students because you wanted them to see themselves as constructors of knowledge. Our stories about you allowing students to make decisions and have choices in their learning describe the strategies you used in your practice to live out your philosophy." Janet agreed. We could both see that shared responsibility was important to her teaching, and to teaching and learning broadly conceived. But we could not explain *why*.

We sat in her kitchen struggling with what we knew and trying to name it. I continued to think aloud saying, "We know shared responsibility for learning is important because it works. It seems like common sense and yet if it is, then why doesn't everyone know it? This is like a jigsaw and we have a piece missing." Janet started to draw a conceptual map made of jigsaw shapes. She drew two separate shapes and listed responsibility and teacher knowledge inside each one. Then she connected them with another shape labeled "effective teaching and learning." She drew a fourth puzzle shape linked to teacher knowledge and labeled it "research." Beside the effective teaching and learning shape she wrote, "If I choose I learn it better." She was trying to answer the question: Why is shared responsibility important? I responded verbally to her notes, "Yes, but what does that tell us about teacher knowledge?" She drew a box beside teacher knowledge and wrote "interactive knowing." Then she started talking about her own learning and how she constructs knowledge. She said, "If I can base my future knowledge on my past knowledge, it's like a step from one to the other. It's a link."

I knew she was moving our thinking in a positive direction and that we were helping each other answer an important question in the research. Her explanation of past and future knowledge, building upon knowledge one already has, helped my thinking on this issue. I remembered the work of Belenky, Clinchy, Goldberger, and Tarule (1986), particularly their concepts of "received knowledge" and "constructed knowledge." A received knower is someone who sees that she can learn from others but views all knowledge as constructed outside of herself. A received knower does not perceive that she can construct knowledge. Though the research of Belenky and her colleagues was with women, their findings have relevance for learners in general. Their epistemological basis interested us. Janet and I began to interpret the implications of these findings in terms of teaching and learning. We saw that the concepts of received and constructed knowing opened up possibilities for thinking about how knowledge is constructed in classrooms and in research. We recognized we were constructing knowledge together.

We started to talk about how shared responsibility for learning fits with a conception of constructed knowledge, drawing on the stories we had shared and written that described how shared responsibility was lived out in Janet's teaching. We realized shared responsibility for learning was a central theme in our research on teacher knowledge. We began to talk about the importance of assuming responsibility for constructing your own knowledge, for students, and for teachers. We began to see that by sharing responsibility in this inquiry into teaching we were taking responsibility for our own development.

Why Are We Telling These Stories?

These stories demonstrate how our research relationship and our sharing of responsibility in a collaborative narrative study influence construction of the research knowledge. We tell our stories in order to draw attention to methodological and epistemological issues inherent in this type of research.

In telling our initial responses to the parent-visitor story we show how our research relationship formed over time and how the research changed when trust developed between us. It took time for Janet to be comfortable that her meanings and teaching emphases would be respected and included. It took time for Kathie to be able to critique a conception of truth that conflicted with her experiences in the study. It took time for both of us to reach a point in our relationship where we felt safe enough to question aloud each other's ideas, values, and developing (as well as entrenched) philosophies. Once we were able to trust each other, we shared insights and gave each other information that we were not prepared to share without the trust. Our stories demonstrate the importance of the research relationship to collaborative research on teacher development. Knowing the person is crucial.

A central issue in our stories concerns the need for both the teacher and the researcher to know the context for teaching (and research) and how this knowledge fits with developing a research relationship. When Kathie wrote the parent-visitor story, she emphasized that a visitor to Janet's classroom needed to be aware of the continuity the teacher was striving for—how and why an individual lesson commonly fits in a sequence of lessons. Janet's emphasis on continuity in her teaching and the time it takes her students to learn influenced Kathie's writing of the story. Seeing her meanings of the importance of knowing classroom context and the context in which a lesson is set referred to in the story helped Janet trust Kathie as a co-researcher and trust the research process. Janet's realization that the research would support her development as a teacher rather than judge her as a "good" or "bad" teacher increased her commitment to the inquiry.

For us, articulating the importance of knowing the context for Janet's teaching, and knowing the context in which our study is set, led us into numerous discussions about subjectivity and objectivity in educational research. When Janet began the research, she exclaimed, "There's no such thing as objective research!" Kathie's background in science and the overwhelming messages of the need for "reliable data" in graduate research methods courses, caused her initially to worry about subjectivity as a researcher. Even so, at the beginning she had many questions about truth and the assumptions about what constitutes "good research." Despite Kathie's early recognition that the parent-visitor story revealed multiple perspectives of what was happening in Janet's classroom, at the time of writing the story she still had not completely let go of the notion of a single truth. Later she saw the contradiction inherent in writing a story about multiple perspectives of what was happening in a classroom and wanting Janet to say it was exactly as things had happened. The transition in her thinking about knowledge and truth is part of her story and signifies her ongoing development as a consequence of inquiry into practice. Both our stories speak to the transition in our thinking: how we were learning to be collaborative, to research our meanings of the relationship between theory and practice, and, how we were learning about ourselves. We show that collaborative teacher research can be transformative research.

Our intent in telling the tessellations stories is to show that collaboration is not easy or simple. The tessellations lesson provides an example early in the study where we began to problematize our roles and responsibilities. When we told each other the dilemma we experienced in this lesson, we began to question our prior assumptions about what it means to be collaborative in a study of teaching. Our different experiences in this lesson also caused us to confront our conceptions of curriculum. Kathie's initial attempts to "deliver" curriculum were challenged by her realization that in Janet's classroom curriculum was a dynamic enacted and lived out with students. She learned that she needed to develop relationships with Janet's students for knowledge construction to occur. Through reflective conversations and writing with Janet, Kathie saw her practices in this lesson as problematic—her teaching as "delivery" of information. She felt in conflict with the constructivist teaching she espoused and believed she had practiced in her teaching of Textiles and Design. Reading Clandinin and Connelly's (1992) criticism of the influence of a "conduit metaphor" in curriculum reform (ideas are reduced to objects and teachers' work is minimized to delivery of ideas along the conduit) helped her articulate her conflict. Both co-researchers moved on to new levels of understanding curriculum as a consequence of discussion and reflection on their different experiences of shared responsibility for teaching.

In Janet's classroom, and later in our writing together, we were exposed to each other's weaknesses and strengths. We learned each of us had to give and to assert if this collaborative relationship was going to work. The ways we have shared responsibility have required two-way trust and, in turn, trust has developed our research relationship. We continued to renegotiate our responsibilities to meet our requirement that this work be useful to each of us. Our view supports Cole and Knowles' argument that collaboration requires not *"equal* involvement in all aspects of the research, but rather for *negotiated and mutually agreed upon* involvement" (1993, 486). We did not share responsibility in ways that were equal. Janet was always responsible for her students in legal and professional ways that Kathie was not. It was Kathie's responsibility to prepare a dissertation that would meet the university's requirements for award of a doctorate.

Shared responsibility is a central issue in collaborative research, demanding a shared vulnerability. In our view, the importance of shared vulnerability in collaborative research is not widely understood. Persons who have not engaged in collaborative studies with teachers may find it difficult to understand how shared experience of risk significantly alters the research. LaRocque (1995) reminds us that collaborative research between teachers in schools and persons located at the university involves risk taking and vulnerability by *both* parties. This is a profound change from an old story of research done *on* teachers. Being "observed" in educational research (but not included in interpretation of their practices), teachers have commonly been positioned in ways that placed them at risk. Researchers, by not addressing their own stories or practices in studies of teaching, have avoided the vulnerable positions

in which participating teachers have often been placed. Our tessellations stories describe how shared responsibility in our collaborative study involved each co-researcher taking risk and feeling
vulnerable.

Our stories describe figuring out how "to be" and how to share
responsibility and authority in the research. At first, as Janet tried
to be the expert teacher who never made a mistake or changed her
mind about a lesson plan, and as Kathie tried to be the expert
researcher and co-teacher who could step into Janet's class and
simply "be a teacher," we tried to mask our vulnerability, not even
admitting it to ourselves. In our research conversations and in the
research journal we shared with each other how much we felt at
risk. We began to see that shared vulnerability was necessary for
collaboration and was strengthening our relationship. We were able
to see ourselves as collaborative researchers. Acknowledging our
different vulnerabilities allowed us to talk about and discard our
earlier expectations. The pressure we felt to be experts was contradictory to our reality of "figuring out" how to be collaborative. We
thought about where this pressure had come from and why.

Britzman's (1986, 1991) critique of the cultural myth of the
"teacher as expert" in teacher education is relevant to our dilemma
with the notion of "expert" in this study. Britzman's criticism has
an epistemological basis. In her view, the myth that the teacher
has to know the answers reduces knowledge to a set of discrete and
isolated units to be acquired, and "not knowing" is perceived as a
threat to the teacher's authority. She argues that the myth of the
teacher as expert denies the problems of how teacher education
students come to know, learn, and teach. We suggest that the negative effects and pervasiveness of the myth of the expert for other
aspects of education remain to be made public. The myth of the
expert is active in educational research in a number of subtle and
not so subtle ways and, as Britzman points out, how we think
about knowledge is part of the problem.

Our purpose in telling the story of data analysis in Janet's
kitchen is to show the social process of knowledge construction and
reconstruction in our collaborative study—a process which involves
both of us as co-researchers. Our story of questioning why shared
responsibility in Janet's classroom is important provides an example
of how we worked collaboratively in determining *what* is important
and *why* in this research. This story of how we work together to
construct the research knowledge challenges conceptions of the researcher as the determiner of research findings, and the researcher
as "the expert." Such a conception structures a research relationship

as hierarchical and impedes collaboration. When models of research on teaching assume that the researcher decides what constitutes data, decides the meanings of that data, and informs teachers of the meanings, then teachers are placed in the position of received knowers and the researcher is positioned as the expert. We describe how we negotiated a collaborative narrative methodology which allowed us to challenge the notion of the researcher as "the expert." We learned in the process that the research methodology and findings are altered when trust develops in the researcher-participant relationship. When responsibility for construction of the research knowledge is shared, both persons share responsibility for the research design, decisions about what constitutes data, and the meanings of that data. In an article that also explores issues of relationship and shared responsibility in collaborative teacher development research, Cole and Knowles (1993) argue that epistemological and methodological changes are demanded when teachers are included as co-researchers in all phases of research.

When we both assumed roles of teacher and researcher, we were able to go beyond the expert-received-knower model and gain insights not otherwise available to us. The implications of our story concern recognition of teachers as knowledge constructors in educational research. In acknowledging data collection and data analysis in our study as mutually constructed knowledge, we are changing not only *how* research is done, but what has been traditionally defined as research. Our intent is to advocate that educational research should be developmental for *both* teacher and researcher. In this regard, we are attempting to redefine the purposes of teacher research and argue for recognition by school systems and universities of the development possibilities for teachers and researchers engaged in collaborative research.

The stories shared in this chapter also demonstrate that our teacher research is not located solely within the confines of Janet's classroom. Our collaborative study is set within a broader educational and research context in which there are powerful meta-narratives at work. One such powerful story assumes that the university researcher should decide the research questions and focus, as well as be the person responsible for (have the authority) educational research. There are other stories that are similarly contradictory if we begin to deconstruct their meanings in terms of teacher development. The conduit metaphor critiqued by Clandinin and Connelly (1992) in relation to curriculum reform also has relevance for much of the research that has been done *on* teachers and teaching. Teachers have been treated as the eventual receivers of the knowledge of university researchers (Cochran-Smith and Lytle 1993). We are critical of claims to knowledge about teaching by research that does not include the voices and meanings of teachers.

Implications For Teacher Research and Epistemology

In educational research the researcher has traditionally been considered "the expert," deciding the research focus, findings, and meanings of the data. This view derives from an objective view of knowledge (Code 1991) and assumptions that are problematic for a study of teacher knowledge. Those assumptions are that knowledge is fixed, acontextual, and transferred from the "one knowing" to the "one not-knowing." In our research we have been concerned with expanding what counts as knowledge. We negotiated a methodology that allowed us to challenge the assumptions underpinning the objective view of knowledge. Our teacher researcher stories of practice reveal that the ways we use and construct knowledge in the research are: dynamic and not fixed, highly contextual and interactive (rather than a one-way transfer of knowledge from one person to the other), and relational, that is, dependent on the knowing that comes from being "in-relationship" (Hollingsworth, Dybdahl, and Minarik 1993; Hollingsworth, Cody, Davis-Smallwood, Dybdahl, Gallagher, Gallego, Maestre, Minarik, Raffel, Standerford, and Teel 1994). We are beginning to describe our personal practical knowledge (Clandinin 1986; Connelly and Clandinin 1985; Connelly and Clandinin 1988; Elbaz 1983) as teachers. Research on teachers' personal practical knowledge describes the ways teachers construct and reconstruct their knowledge—how teachers' practices express their knowledge. The knowledge being constructed in our work together is influenced by our research relationship and sharing responsibility in and for the study.

Conclusion

Our engagement in collaborative narrative research about teacher knowledge and curriculum has helped us challenge assumptions about knowledge construction within classrooms *and* within university-school research. We see parallels between teaching and learning in a classroom, and research on teachers' knowledge. The same themes of shared responsibility and relationship that influence a teacher's knowledge construction with students (Webb and Blond 1995) also influence knowledge construction in collaborative research about teaching. In the same way that our knowledge in this research has developed step-by-step, so too, our relationship has moved forward. As we began to share responsibility in the study we came to trust each other more and found that the research relationship was being reinforced by sharing responsibility and knowledge.

In doing this research we moved into uncharted territory and adopted an openness to working it out. We knew from our teaching experiences that we might make mistakes, but these could be part of our learning. Our stories show that we influence each other's thinking and our knowing is influenced by the contexts in which we work and live: knowing each other, knowing the students, knowing the school, influences the knowledge we construct together. Flexibility in the ways we shared responsibility enabled us to access information that would not otherwise have been revealed. The research methodology, findings, and interpretations of data, hinge on our research relationship.

A further rationale for describing our methodology and what we have learned as co-researchers in a collaborative narrative study concerns making a case for the multiple perspectives of persons engaged in educational research. Our work challenges an objective view of knowledge based on the notion of a single truth concerning research findings and researcher objectivity (as in an uninvolved impersonal stance) as the criteria for "good" research. The promotion of objectivity in research is based on the idea that a single truth exists and can be determined. Such a stance limits the findings of research in teacher development. We do not claim to have presented a complete picture in our research findings, but by working as co-researchers, we help others understand there is more than one perspective on what happens in a classroom or research project. We asked questions of each other and came to new questions together. If we had only asked Kathie's questions it would have been a very different piece of research.

Our experience is that when the researcher and practitioner share personal stories and meanings of the data, being in relationship with each other and drawing knowledge from that relationship, then not only is the research methodology changed, but different findings are yielded than would be if only the researcher interprets the data. We suggest that collaborative narrative research, by and with teachers, offers the opportunity for a richer, more detailed and more meaningful research base for teacher knowledge—one which will ring true to the experiences of teachers.

Finally, we stress the need to think about how teachers learn, and question whether the role for teachers in research on teaching acknowledges teachers as constructors of knowledge or implies that teachers be the receivers and eventual implementers of university researchers' findings. Our research stories provide support for reconceptualized views of knowledge and research and demonstrate that collaborative teacher research has the potential to transform how we think about teacher development.

NOTES

1. This co-authored paper is Chapter Two of a doctoral dissertation on Teacher Knowledge submitted by K. M. Webb to the Faculty of Graduate Studies and Research, University of Alberta, Edmonton, Fall 1995.

2. This story has since been published in *Among Teachers, 14*, Summer 1994.

◇ Chapter Seven

Who's Important... Here Anyway?: Co-Constructing Research Across Cultures[1]

Lynn McAlpine and Martha Crago

Introduction

This is the story of how we, two mainstream academics privileged to be doing classroom research in aboriginal communities, are learning to be more respectful and useful researchers. We do not claim to have succeeded; rather, we wish to report on our progress at an early way station on the journey. We describe what we have learned about doing collaborative inquiry across cultures. In this case, the cultures are the academic culture with its mainstream values in contact with the schools and the traditional cultures of different aboriginal communities. We describe our evolving understanding of the ways in which different and sometimes competing voices and world views of researchers and research participants may be heard, acknowledged, respected, and incorporated. Since this is our story, the voices of other participants in the research process are only rarely heard.

Lynn: I have twenty years experience in the classroom, as an elementary school teacher, second language teacher of adults, and teacher trainer. When I first conducted formal classroom research it was in the school in which I worked. I struggled with the tension between my wish to carry out the study and the shift this brought to the relationships I had with colleagues. I came to understand that the tension was rooted in the different perspectives that teachers and academics have regarding what we each recognize as problems and how we structure solutions. Now, as an academic doing research that I believe is useful and contributes to better learning environments for students, I still find myself struggling with the tension between my interests and those of other participants in any studies in which I'm involved. This has been particularly the case in the research[2] that Martha and I are doing in a number of aboriginal schools.

Martha: I am a university educator, having taught for twenty-five years in teacher education and communication disorders departments. Ten years ago I began work as a consultant in aboriginal communities. My first research project grew out of my need for information on child rearing and language development relevant to the aboriginal teachers I worked with. It involved living with aboriginal families and documenting their interactions with their children. In fact, my own parenting and the families' comments on it became important in the study. That experience served to remind me that all people involved in research are in fact participants in the process. I also learned that the times when I feel most uncomfortable living with people of other cultures—the "pinch points"—are the times to learn most about myself and the assumptions of my own culture.

Lessons For Us

Coyote is a trickster or magical figure in the oral traditions of a number of aboriginal cultures in North America. Terry Tafoya (1982) of the Pueblo Nation has transformed one of Coyote's stories from the oral form into a literate version. We tell part of the oral form of Coyote's story because it speaks to us of the need to rethink how we do research if we want it to be a truly collaborative process.

At the point where we take up this story, Coyote has lost his eyesight. He's very unhappy, and stumbles along, bewailing his fate. Mouse hears him and asks him what is wrong. He tells his story and Mouse says: "I have two eyes; I'll give you one". Coyote takes Mouse's eye and puts it in his eye socket. Now, of course, it doesn't fit; it's much too small. Only a little bit of light comes in and Coyote can only see up close, only see things in great detail. He doesn't like that, so he continues on his way, still very unhappy. Shortly, Buffalo hears him and asks what the matter is. Coyote again tells his story and Buffalo, who is also generous, says: "I have two eyes; I'll give you one". Buffalo's eye is much bigger than Coyote's eye socket and it's hard to make it fit. But when Coyote succeeds, so much light comes in that Coyote sees everything very big, magnified. He doesn't like seeing like this, so he continues on. This time, he meets Eagle. Eagle, when he hears Coyote's story, also offers to give up one of his eyes. Coyote tries to see with Eagle's eye and everything is far away, seen from a great distance.

What does this story about Coyote's eyes say to those of us involved in research in aboriginal communities or in any community rooted in a culture different from our own? First, participants in inquiry have many different perspectives. Second, such perspectives are not all equally powerful. As academics, often from dominant cultures, we need to find ways not only to represent diverse perspectives but to balance the needs, goals, and values of the different participants. Inquiry is not a neutral activity: it's filled with the hopes, values and unresolved questions about the social affairs of all of the participants, including researchers.

Others before us have ably documented some of the very pressing issues surrounding research conducted by mainstream academics in aboriginal communities: differences in aboriginal and non-aboriginal visions of the nature of human beings as actors within the universe (Wax 1991); past failures of the research processes in aboriginal communities (LaFramboise and Plake 1983); concerns relating to the relationship between academics and funding agencies involved in conducting research in cultures other than our own (Deloria 1991; Wax 1991). In this chapter, we respond to the idea that construction of knowledge is a social process (Haig-Brown 1992) as well as to the challenge of negotiating a covenantal ethic among research participants (Wax 1991). We bear in mind the words of Verna Kirkness (Haig-Brown 1992, 96): "Every time a white person gets up to talk about Indians, I get knots in my stomach," and reiterate that this is our story, not those of other participants in the journey.

Events Leading to the Research

Our research program on various aspects of schooling in aboriginal communities grew out of our involvement with a university unit that works in partnership with aboriginal communities to deliver field-based teacher education programs preparing qualified aboriginal teachers for schools in aboriginal communities. Working and teaching in this program[3], we came to recognize the lack of empirically-based knowledge of what happens in aboriginal classrooms in which aboriginal students and aboriginal teachers work together. We often ended up using mainstream knowledge and negotiating with trainees the ways in which this information approximated the reality of the aboriginal classroom. We came to believe it was important to document the interaction and practices in aboriginal classrooms where trainees were being placed, not just to validate these pedagogies but also to develop a body of knowledge which could be used in both aboriginal and mainstream teacher education programs.

A Guiding Structure

Ethical Guidelines for Research (1993), a document published by the Royal Commission on Aboriginal Peoples, has provided us with a framework for analyzing and discussing some of the tensions we have experienced doing research. The *Guidelines* identify four critical elements of the research process from the perspective of aboriginal communities: consent, data collection, dissemination, and benefits. Overlaid on these elements is our recognition of the multiple perspectives or cultures of all the participants.

Teachers have their own culture[4] based on their experiences in the classroom. They have particular notions of what warrants study, what constitutes inquiry, how best to carry it out, and what constitutes evidence. These ideas vary (in some cases, quite dramatically) from the culture of the academic world. Teachers also live within communities, in this case, aboriginal communities in which parents, educational administrators, and others, may share nonmainstream world views. In contrast, many academics have grown up in mainstream North American cultures. The cultures we, as academics, represent are seen to be more powerful. In our attempt to redress imbalances of power and account for the range of perspectives of research participants, we envisage the research process as iterative and recursive. Each of the elements (consent, data collection, dissemination and benefits) is revisited many times

in the ongoing interaction between researchers and others participating in the research in order to co-construct a process with pro-
tection and benefits for all. As we discuss each of the elements we
highlight what we have learned, as well as the dilemmas we face,
and try to respond to in ways that are respectful of all participants.

Consent

A key aspect of our conception of the research process has been
to see consent as entailing two structures—formal and informal.
The informal structure of consent is an ongoing process of negotiating participation from the time the research is envisaged until
it ends. It is marked at different points by formal consent which
involves obtaining signatures from individuals regarding their
willingness to participate after being informed in writing of the
goals of the research, their roles, and how the information obtained
will be used. The formal process meets the legal requirements of
our culture, whereas the informal structure helps us to co-construct
the direction of the research and to reaffirm or renegotiate earlier
decisions. By incorporating the informal notion of consent, we
move beyond the ethics of obligation to the ethics of aspiration
(Wax 1991), the intention to fulfill the true spirit of an ethical
relationship.

Participation entails some proprietary issues. The information provided belongs to the person who gave it. Thus, in accord
with the legal or formal consent our culture requires, we ask the
potential participant in their preferred language to designate who
may use the information, and how credit will be given for its use.
We outline and request consent for specific uses to which videotapes of classroom interaction might be put (e.g., Can your video
tape be used: by only these researchers? by other researchers? for
teacher training? only outside of your community? only in your own
community?). We are also in the process of modifying the consent
form to assure participants that anything submitted for publication that concerns them will first be verified by them. We were
informally negotiating issues such as this before, but did not specify
them at the legal consent stage.

The preceding deals with the formal ritualization of our mainstream notions of informed consent. We have also learned the importance of understanding and incorporating the formal rituals of those
from other cultures who are willing to work with us. In some communities, for instance, we have learned giving and receiving tobacco

is a way of marking an agreement to participate. We try to be attentive to these values and incorporate them into the process, just as we ask participants to be accepting of our cultural imperatives.

Another aspect of formalizing consent we have learned to negotiate is differences in cultural perspective about the age at which an individual is deemed able to give consent. In some communities even a five-year-old child makes the decision whether or not to attend school. Thus, from the perspective of local educators, seeking formal consent from parents is inappropriate. Given the requirements of our academic and mainstream cultures this view reinforced for us as researchers how important it is for us to openly negotiate whether to and how to involve participants in the research. In one situation, although we received consent from the band council, we chose not to conduct our research at the primary level and to work only in classes made up of young adolescents since, from our perspective, we felt that these individuals could decide whether to participate after the research was explained to them.

The different rituals which mark commitment to the research are interwoven with the informal consent process which goes on throughout the research. In our research, we first discussed our ideas informally with the community representatives we work with in the teacher education program. Those who expressed interest helped us make contact with whomever they felt was appropriate (band council or school committee) for gaining formal community approval. At this point, the research focus and objectives were specified in writing. After receiving letters of consent at the community level, we approached school administrations about the possibilities for research. With their informal consent, we then were able to enter schools and talk to potential teacher participants. For those interested, we spent time describing in more detail what participation involved. We were particularly happy when, during this process, some teachers defined very specific goals they wished us to incorporate into the research, for example, to track their interactions with a particular student. After these individuals signed legal consents, we negotiated the participation of the children in the teachers' classrooms. Again, this involved an informal negotiation with parents either through meetings at the schools or visits to homes by a local person working on the research team. In many instances, teachers themselves were very active in reaching the stage where formal consent was gained from parents. At this point the research could actually begin. However, since we wanted to intentionally sustain the covenant that had been established between us and the participants, we have worked to develop a policy used throughout the time that we work in the communities.

At each contact with a participating teacher we reestablish consent. We restate the goals of the research and explain what has happened to the data they provided. In addition, we clarify who will have access to the data and in what form it will be returned to them. We find this process of confirmation and clarification useful for participants and ourselves. First, participants often ask us questions which force us to rethink what we are doing. Secondly, as we carry out the research, we realize that our respective ideas (academics and teachers) about the research change as our knowledge of it becomes more sophisticated. We force ourselves to be explicit about these ongoing changes by talking about them with the participants.

As we see it, the primary issue in consent is that it not be restricted to a legally signed piece of paper. We believe that people may legally and formally consent without truly being informed. The informed nature of the consent develops as people participate in the research process and then reflect on what they have said or done.

Data Collection

Data collection is done at the teachers' convenience. It includes: a videotape of a class, a stimulated recall interview where the teacher watches the videotape and provides us with her/his own interpretations, and a life history. After the videotaping and before the stimulated recall interview, teachers are asked if they are happy with the tape or if they want to be revideotaped. Teachers receive copies of the videotapes of their classrooms and transcriptions of their interviews. We ask them to read over the transcripts and tell us if they want to add or change anything; we also reaffirm that they are still in agreement with our using the videotape. Much later, when the analysis for all of the teachers is complete, we ask them to assess the validity of the findings from their own perspective. After any necessary adjustments are made, these become the final versions used in any reporting.

Time lines of programmatic research can be rather lengthy as data are collected from multiple sites, then transcribed or otherwise treated before being analyzed. Thus, in this research program, teachers may have to wait more than a year from the time data are collected until a summary is available for them to review and critique. One of the things we have learned is to contact participants regularly about the progress of the study so they are assured we will be returning to visit them.

An overall concern we always have is not disrupting the social fabric of the school and community. Most communities where we work are small, from 350 to 800 inhabitants, and when we travel there we often board with school staff members. An inadvertent comment about a research participant, perhaps misinterpreted, is easily communicated to a large segment of the population and can create hurt and misunderstanding. We have learned to think of ourselves as always "on," even in the evening when sitting in the living room of the individual who has agreed to board us. This helps keep us vigilant and protects the interests of participants.

Finally, although we have not done this consistently, we have found it valuable to turn the spotlight on us: to document participants' reflections on what we do as well as the impact of the research on them. This enables us to learn more about what we should and should not be doing, and it provides an occasion for teachers and researchers to reflect on changes that may be occurring as a result of intervention.

Dissemination

As with the previous sections, we describe where we are now in our journey toward developing responsible, ethical, respectful ways of disseminating results in these cross-cultural contexts. Three principles guide our conception. First, we are responsible for reporting back to the different individuals from whom we received consent— the individual teacher, the school, parents (and students), the board or community, as well as the university. Second, different modes of discourse are required for different audiences (e.g., teachers, parents, academics) since each has particular interests. Third, we undertake to reconfirm the validity of the contents of all written and oral reports with participants. In doing this, we are recognizing knowledge is a social process and that no individual can accurately represent the experience of any other (Haig-Brown 1992).

We conceive of two types of dissemination: informal oral presentations often directed toward local audiences (teachers, school and community), and formal or written submissions to provide a permanent record. An important aspect of dissemination is co-constructing with local educators an appropriate plan for informing all those who might be interested. Informally, we try to use channels of communication that are part of ordinary discourse patterns in the community, e.g., local radio shows, parent committee meetings, or workshops at the school. Written reports may be one-page documents written for general interest and posted in locations that most community members visit regularly (e.g., the local post office and stores). Written reports may also take the form of five- to ten-page summaries designed for teachers which can be deposited in the school library and used in the course work of the field-based teacher education program referred to earlier.

The third principle of dissemination—to reconfirm with participants what will be reported each time a new presentation/publication is planned—is an essential but sometimes problematic aspect of the research. Here's an instance of the kind of dilemma that can occur: an individual in the community reviews a potential publication and feels his or her standing in the community is at risk because of something documented in it. On the one hand, we feel a responsibility to remove the aspect of the story that puts the individual at risk. However, with omissions and modifications come questions: do we let readers know that part of the story is missing, and if so, how? At what point do we decide not to go ahead with any publication because the story no longer represents what we believe happened? Such dilemmas surrounding dissemination are intimately linked to how we ensure benefits and most important avoid psychic or social harm to participants.

Benefits

"Among many questions I ask myself as a community aboriginal person is why should I be involved in this kind of research?" (personal communication, May 1, 1993). As mainstream academics, we ponder this question constantly. We initiate classroom research because we believe there is potential long-term benefit: future aboriginal teachers will learn about classroom interaction in aboriginal classrooms rather than mainstream ones. However, we also want to show respect toward those taking the risk to work with us by ensuring they have some benefit. So, what can we do? We spend time listening to their stories. We respond to requests for feedback on students or for published information on particular topics. We solicit and incorporate the teacher's interpretation of events. We sometimes collect data and discuss topics that are only tangentially related to our own goals as researchers, but are central to the lives of particular teachers. Just as teachers show their willingness to engage in work around issues that may not be of interest to them, we bear the responsibility to reciprocate.

Those who choose to participate are placing their trust in us as researchers, believing us when we say that their contribution to the larger program of research will ultimately benefit the future teachers and children of their community. This places great responsibility on us: the duty to ensure that these long-term benefits we have promised are eventually realized.

Conclusion

"We're being studied the heck out of, and we don't know what the study is about" (Wax 1991, 431). If individuals in aboriginal communities feel this way about research then it is not surprising that May described the relationship between academic researchers and aboriginal participants this way: "Research is a dirty word among (and irrelevant to) Native communities" (1989, 71). As researchers we are striving to overcome this view by our struggle to minimize our feelings of proprietary claim and by more highly valuing the perspective of others. We hope and believe we are learning how to conduct research in ways more respectful of all participants. We know we have to keep asking ourselves the question: "Who's important . . . here anyway?"

NOTES

1. The title comes from a mainstream educator's tale (Aitken 1993) about incorporating critical pedagogy into her teaching in an aboriginal classroom. The students did not necessarily share her interest and one day in an altercation with two students, one boy said to her, "Who's important in here anyway?"

2. The research referred to was funded in part by the Social Sciences and Humanities Research Council and the Fonds pour la Recherche et l'Aide aux Rechercheurs.

3. For more information on this program, see McAlphine, Cross, Whiteduck, and Wolforth (1990).

4. Culture represents shared-but-frequently-unnoticed speech and interaction patterns, biographies, assumptions and attitudes (Rothe 1982), which can be based on gender, ethnicity, training.

✧ Chapter Eight

Learning Collaboration: Research in a First Nations Teacher Education Program

Linda Goulet and Brian Aubichon

This chapter focuses on the collaborative component of a research project undertaken by a university-based research team. The research examined a developing First Nations[1] teacher education program (TEP). Although the TEP participants were not part of the initial decision to conduct the research, the commitment to be collaborative enabled the participants and the researchers to respond to, and engage one another in the collaborative process. Through the process, participants came to share the power in the research. The story of this process is told by one of the program participants and one of the members of the research team who share our perspectives on some of the critical experiences in the research. These incidents highlight for us what we came to identify as key issues for collaborative research in cross-cultural situations.

115

The Context: Beginning a First Nations Teacher Education Program

The First Nations Teacher Education Program (TEP) where the project took place is located in a territory in Northern Canada. The TEP program began as a result of recommendations made in several education studies in which the territorial and First Nations governments emphasized the need for First Nations teachers in the school system. In the spring of 1989 an agreement between the territorial government, the territory's college and a southern university allowed the establishment of a four-year degree in elementary teacher education. However, funding for the program was ensured for five years only. The Education Department and the university had discussions regarding an evaluation of the program to record the growth and development of the TEP and provide a rationale for possible future funding. A university- based research unit from the south was contracted to conduct the research project (Hart, Robottom, and Taylor 1993). The research unit set up a team that included the director of the unit, the associate dean of the faculty of education, a visiting scholar, and a graduate student. A fifth member, the co-writer of this chapter, was later added to the research team.

In early discussions among the research team about methodology, three guiding principles emerged: the research had to be participatory, collaborative, and emancipatory. A more detailed description of the research project and all three guiding principles are detailed elsewhere (Taylor, Goulet, Hart, Robottom, and Sykes 1993). For the purpose of this chapter the principle of collaboration is examined in depth to see how it shaped the research process, especially when participants were not party to the initial decision to conduct collaborative research, particularly in a cross-cultural context.

The Writers: Participant and Researcher

Brian writes from the perspective of a program participant. He is the Executive Director of the First Nations teacher education program involved in the research project. Brian is a Cree Metis who spent many years as a senior administrator in First Nations teacher education programs.

Linda shares her perspective as a member of the research team. She is a non-First Nations person on faculty with a southern based First Nations teacher education program. She has many years of experience in First Nations teacher education programs elsewhere in Canada.

Beginnings: Brian Questions How But Sees Potential

As with most new government funded programs, our teacher education program required an evaluation to determine whether it would be funded beyond the initial five years. When faced with the choice of a one-shot summative evaluation after the initial five years or an ongoing three-year research project, I saw the long-term research as a more suitable approach to meet the program's needs. At the same time, I had a number of reservations about the implementation of the research project. I was concerned about how the research would impact on my role within the program and the relationship the program was trying to establish with the college, educators, First Nations peoples, and the university. I questioned how I could participate in a research project when the program implementation required my full attention. I felt that the question of how to capitalize on this situation needed to be asked and answers needed to be provided to faculty and students.

I did think that the collaborative aspect of the research was a positive one. Since the associate dean from the university was on the research team, I saw the research as an opportunity for her to become more aware of our program and the challenges we faced. The opportunity to set the direction for the research was exciting. Equally exciting was the opportunity to have the university monitor our development and assist with a written rationale and record of what the program is and why it should continue to exist beyond the initial five-year funding. Even though I had thought through the benefits and had accepted the idea of the research project, the reality of the research was not as easy to deal with.

Linda: Can Collaboration Address Cross-Cultural Issues?

When I was approached to become involved in the research project, I was both hesitant and interested. I saw it as an opportunity to gain understandings about the beginnings of a First Nations teacher education program. At the same time, I was reluctant to become involved because there was no First Nations representation on the research team. Without meaningful input from First Nations peoples, research in First Nations communities can be misinterpreted by non-First Nations researchers (St. Denis 1992; Royal Commission on Aboriginal Peoples 1993). I hoped that this concern could be addressed to some extent by the research team's effort to make the research collaborative.

Brian's Initial Participation: Reluctance to Trust

St. Denis (1992) cautions that even though the research is planned to be participatory, the reality of participation is not always easily achieved, especially in cross-cultural situations. Effort and time are needed to convince potential collaborators that the invitation for involvement is sincere. Participants also want to know the practicalities of how the project will be useful to them.

The most difficult challenge at the outset of the research was trusting and establishing trust with non-First Nations academics with whom I had no prior relationship. As faculty and as a First Nations person, I wasn't sure how the researchers would interpret what we were saying and doing, particularly since none of them had previous experience in First Nations teacher education. Trust is the first step in collaboration and, in this case, trust took some time to achieve with the different members of the research team.

Establishing Trust: Linda Gives the Outsider's View

As a member of the research group, I noticed on our visits, although we didn't have much free time, that our group tended to socialize with the non-First Nations instructors from the college. Since I knew the TEP director from past association in TEP's, I began to socialize with him, his family and colleagues. On reflection, I came to realize how important this socializing was in establishing trust with the participants. Visiting is an important aspect of cultural life in northern communities. Time spent visiting by outsiders shows respect for people, that you are interested in them, their way of life, and their way of seeing the world. If we expected Northerners to be interested in working with us, we needed to show that we were interested in them as people, not just as research participants.

Research Design: Brian Raises Questions

Early in the research we, as TEP faculty, raised concerns over the logistics of the research project. The research team was scheduled to visit the site three times a year for one week each time. To us, this wasn't enough. We would try to participate in the project but we were working in very demanding full-time jobs, adapting classes to meet the needs of our context, and creating a new program. We strongly suggested an on-site researcher, preferably a First Nations person. The research team's initial response to this suggestion was to add my co-writer, Linda, to the team. She was a non-First Nations person and from the south, but since she had experience in First Nations teacher education in a northern setting, I felt she would know many of the issues we faced. I expected that she would be better able to understand why we acted the way we did in our situation. She was also known by all the faculty, so at least we had a basis for establishing trust.

Research Process: Linda Encounters Barriers

We as researchers planned our data gathering in a way we hoped would foster collaboration. In the project, data was gathered, validated, and disseminated following a research process similar to that outlined by Rizvi and Kemmis (1987). In brief, team members gathered their own notes from observations, meetings, and interviews on a daily basis. Summaries of oral interviews were written out and returned to the informant for validation. At the close of each day, the team gathered to share field notes from which we compiled a "Working Notes" report. The "Working Notes" would then be shared with the program participants for the purpose of providing an initial interpretation of events. We hoped the "Working Notes" would promote interactive dialogue about issues of interest and concern to participants and thus promote collaboration.

At the outset, these proposed reporting methods seemed like they would work well. On reflection, it is clear they were our methods more than the methods of the participants. In planning the research process, we had consulted the literature but had failed to consult with the participants, so had not taken into consideration the Northerners' preferred way of knowing, participating and communicating. Because we were coming from a university environment, we tended to use academic language to describe our reality. Besides using academic language, our "Working Notes" were in written form which we distributed expecting written feedback from participants. It was not forthcoming. We were trying to communicate with busy TEP faculty and students who came from cultures that valued the oral tradition.

The written communication we did was still valuable to the research project. Our "Working Notes" helped us as researchers organize and reflect on the massive amounts of data we were collecting. The written documentation served as one means of sharing ideas and communicating with the program participants. It also allowed participants to check our recordings and tentative analysis.

Linda: The Need to Negotiate

I had some previous experience with collaborative evaluation in a TEP program, where we, as First Nations and non-First Nations program participants, sought to create a common vision of our teacher education program through the incorporation of a multitude of perspectives that included First Nations Elders, students, and academics in our program review (Goulet, Beaudin, Fietz, Heit, and Tarasoff 1991). Despite this experience I was not prepared for the level of negotiation required as we "outsiders" struggled to collaborate with participants. Collaborative research took a different form when it was initiated by outsiders. In the project, it seemed we were in a continual state of negotiation (Hookey 1994). Our meetings with program participants were frequent and seemed to— and often did—go on for hours. Negotiation became a dominant feature of our relationship with the TEP faculty and students. Sorting out issues often felt like a "confusing and agonizing journey" (Goodman 1992 as quoted in Hookey 1994, 57).

Although negotiation is an essential feature in collaboration, in our case I think it was even more dominant. On reflection, I believe there were two main reasons for the need for so much negotiation. First, we were in a cross-cultural situation and so much of the meeting time was time spent getting to know about one another, trying to adapt to the others' ways of knowing, valuing, and communicating. Secondly, although we as researchers invited the participants to collaborate, the parameters of the research were already set by us and we had expectations established as to how the participants would collaborate. We had ideals of the participants being engaged in the research, but we didn't realize that meant the participants would be engaged with us, the researchers. In the beginning we had ownership of the process. We had defined how the process of collaboration would take place without including those we wanted to collaborate with even though they primarily came from a culture different than ours. Long negotiation sessions were needed as participants clarified what the research focus needed to be and how they were prepared to contribute. We as researchers had to learn how to listen, how to adapt to different cultural norms and to share power.

Negotiation: Brian and Other Participants Assert Their View

To us as faculty, negotiation was an important part of the collaborative process. It was in our meetings with the research team that we expressed, clarified, and justified the direction we thought the research should take. We also had to sort out our role and the role of others in the project. As participants in the research, we also reacted strongly when something happened that we disagreed with and let our opinions be known.

For example, the TEP faculty continued to reiterate the need for a First Nations, on-site researcher. One of the members of the research team had moved to the territory for personal reasons, so she was asked by the research team to fulfill that role. Since she was not a First Nations person, the appointment was not well received by the faculty. The faculty view was further compounded when informal discussions were noted by the on-site researcher and returned to faculty for verification. The faculty were upset by this since they considered their interaction as a social one. This incident precipitated the need for negotiation to clarify what constituted research data and what did not. Faculty didn't want to have to think about everything they said in informal conversation as becoming recorded, public knowledge. They would participate in the research only if they were informed when the conversation was being viewed as research data.

This incident precipitated several discussions that on reflection should have taken place at the beginning of the project. We clarified what counted as data and the processes of verification and interpretation of data. We identified stakeholder groups whose views were important to the program participants. We wanted the research to prioritize contact with First Nations peoples. Faculty also asked the researchers to examine the ownership of the program by the students and the role of the student body, the largest single group of professionals in the First Nations community. The use of First Nations professionals had been seen by First Nations governments as playing a crucial role in the development and implementation of strategies contributing to self-determination (National Indian Brotherhood 1988, 92). We wanted our First Nations professionals to be an integral part of the research.

Brian: First Nations Participants as Researchers

As faculty, we always felt that the students were very much an under utilized resource to the researchers. At the urging of the TEP faculty, a summer student job program was put into place so that the students could become principal researchers within the First Nations community. The students designed ways to gather information in specific areas and prepared to do informal oral interviews with members of their own and other communities.

As they became an integral part of the collaborative research students widened the conversation and the voices of their own communities were heard directly by them. Students reported that people told them they were more comfortable with someone they knew coming to the community to talk about the program. This process had a profound effect on the students who were a part of the research. One student described the impact of interviewing people from her own community:

> One person was telling me how wonderful it was to think that I would be graduating next year. I got a real sense of energy from the community support. Before this summer I felt like I was trudging through the program day to day. I didn't realize how I was viewed. I saw myself just like any other student. Now I've come to realize how important my becoming a teacher is to the people of my community, not just high [important] people but parents and single young people too. It motivates me. (Interview, October 30, 1992)

Being a part of the collaborative research project had changed this student, both in her view of herself and the way she interacted with the program. The potential of collaborative research to transform people and their lives was realized for her.

Linda: Participants' Actions Determine Roles

Sometimes participants didn't negotiate verbally. Students and faculty defined how they would collaborate by their actions. For example when the researchers suggested to students and faculty that they keep written journals of events between our visits, they didn't. We had also envisioned faculty and students engaging in interpretation of data through written response to our "Working Notes", but this did not happen to the extent we had hoped for. However, when we used our written work as a basis for an oral discussion with the student body, they responded with the rich, complex, articulate, diverse voices we had been looking for in written form.

For example, one of the researchers had prepared a paper on the community view of the program based on interviews conducted by the researcher with people in three different communities. In the paper she used strong words of a community member that described the racist nature of the schools in dealing with First Nations children. The research team had seen racism as one of the important issues of power that the research needed to deal with openly.

In a meeting to discuss this paper the TEP students reacted to this description. They were concerned that making the statement about racism so blatantly and judgmentally regarding the teachers would invite a backlash from non-First Nations teachers. They felt the idea could be conveyed in an indirect manner using statistics that showed that the school system was not being successful with First Nations children. The TEP students didn't see themselves as the people to expose racism in the schools. They felt First Nations people were aware the schools were not serving their children well. They saw themselves as entering the schools and making the change from within. They wanted the truth about racism in the report to be stated in a way that would not put more barriers between themselves and the teachers who were their future colleagues.

The discussion evolved into an examination of their role as First Nations peoples in the classroom and how they brought First Nations culture into the schools. Different students voiced different views as to how each of them would do this. Through this discussion students reflected on their role in changing the power structures in the schools and how they could appropriately change the curriculum from their cultural perspective.

So rather than written responses, students and faculty engaged us as researchers in rich oral discussions. Their actions defined their role, thus determining how they would collaborate with us. As they made decisions about how they would participate they took ownership of the research process, making the power relationship much more equitable.

Linda: Participants Move Us, the Researchers, Into Their World

The collaborative nature of the research challenged us as researchers. Interactions, such as the above discussion, clarified the view of the participants and when contrasted with our view, enabled us to see the ethnocentrism of our views regarding the research situation. We had thought it was important to expose institutional racism in the school system, whereas the students wanted access to the system so they could change it from within.

Collaboration forced us to examine our taken-for-granted assumptions. Too often First Nations peoples are seen by non-First Nations peoples as passive recipients of unequal power relationships. Although it is true that First Nations peoples historically, and in present times, do not have the same level of economic power as others in North American society, they are certainly not just passive recipients of the will of the majority (Goulet 1986). First Nations peoples are active participants who are aware of and can assess power relations, then act to create their own history, to shape it from their own perspective and, in the process, shift power. Although we, as researchers, were aware of the issues of power in the research project, ours was a generalized view of power relations. We were focused on issues of power in the context, but did not examine and reflect on issues of power in the collaborative relationships we were trying to develop. Therefore, we did not specifically look for the ways First Nations peoples exercised power, or recognize in ourselves how our own beliefs, actions, and behavior continued to reinforce hierarchical relationships rather than create equitable ones. Issues of power in our relationships were dealt with only implicitly, primarily through the process of negotiation.

The ongoing negotiations necessary in collaboration forced us to reflect and change our vision of the research process. We had to change our expectations and question the way we communicated with others, as well as our use of coercion and power in our style of communication. We were led to examine our own cultural beliefs and views of the program. As a member of the research team, I came to see myself being changed through interaction with the participants. The research process was changing me.

Speaking With One Voice: Brian and Linda in the Middle Ground

There were other occasions when students made presentations to which we were invited where they shared their lived experience in the program. These presentations often dealt with the reality of First Nations culture, its history and struggle for survival, healing, and the implementation of self-determination. The presentations were followed by a discussion where all spoke from the heart— researchers and participants alike. These were significant moments that went beyond the research project—we became fellow human beings and shared an understanding of our lives. Sometimes our cultural differences were brought into sharp focus and became very clear. At other times, we simply shared a common sense of human struggle. These were moments of deep emotion and clarity of vision that had a profound effect on all of us.

Finally . . .

Reflection on this research project validated the use of collaborative research in cross- cultural situations. It has the potential for participants to take ownership of the research and become equal participants in the process. However, the roles of participants and researchers and the question of ownership of the process has to be negotiated at the outset of collaborative research. Focus in negotiation could then turn to how that ownership will be exercised. Research on First Nations teacher education requires previous knowledge of the First Nations community and of First Nations teacher education programs. If it is not a part of the researcher's background, then how to address questions of culture need to be dealt with at the beginning of the project. The ability to build and maintain trust is critical to the success of the research. Equally critical is the input of First Nations researchers to address concerns about how much First Nations people communicate to non-First nations researchers and, more importantly, whether that communication is heard, how it is heard, and through whose values and cultural context it is being heard.

Cross-cultural situations are too often characterized by un-equal power relations. Attention needs to be paid to issues of power in both the context and in the collaborative relationships because both affect the other. Power relations and issues need to be dealt with explicitly but in an honest and culturally appropriate manner. Through negotiation, collaboration can provide for more equitable power sharing and decision making if all are willing to become aware of and make explicit their different ways of exercising power—ways that reinforce hierarchical relationships or facilitate power sharing. All engaged in collaboration need to be prepared to change how they exercise power and to negotiate its use in the different roles of the collaborators, so that power is used in a way that empowers all and is conducive to the collaborative process.

The strength of collaboration is to encourage different voices to speak. This research project demonstrated the importance of including students, the often overlooked source in research, as key participants. Students had much to say about the program in their lives. They made a significant contribution to clarifying the TEP program's place in the broader context of schooling and First Nations peoples. Student voice was essential in this project to clarify how educational change was taking place and would take place in the future. The importance of student voice in program change and educational reform has been documented (Goulet 1996; Nieto 1994). Collaborative research needs to include not just those delivering the program, but the recipients of the program as well, for effective change to take place. "In order to reflect critically on school reform, students need to be included in the dialogue" (Nieto 1994, 392).

As different perspectives and views come to light, the ongoing process of negotiation is essential. In cross-cultural collaborative research, when we as researchers ask participants to be reflective we also have to be open and reflective about our own taken-for-granted assumptions. We need to be prepared to negotiate and listen to participants about the way research will be conducted: how we build relations and communicate with others; who is capable of gathering primary data; how the data is organized, prioritized and analyzed; and how the findings are shared. As we ask participants to reflect about their place in the context we need to reflect on our place in the context and our role within it. In collaborative research both researchers and participants are an integral part of the process. If we as participants and researchers are open in collaboration we not only learn about the context, we learn about ourselves.

NOTE

1. In this paper the term "First Nations" is used to denote Indian or Native peoples primarily because it is the term that the participants in the study used to name themselves collectively. Generally, the term First Nations is used because it acknowledges the primacy of the people's presence in North America, their diversity as peoples, as well as their definition of themselves politically.

Part Three

✧

Communities of Reflective Practice

Part Three, as its title indicates, is about communities of reflective practice or, in the words of Mary Beattie whose chapter opens the section, about "collaboration in the construction of professional knowledge." In each of the stories told in these chapters individuals engage in collaborative inquiry for the purpose of professional development, be it in pre-service teacher education at the university, in-service teacher education at both school and university levels, or adult education within the context of a graduate program.

In the stories told in this section, three common themes emerge that center around the concepts of space, mentoring, and relational knowing. Mary Beattie writes about the need for teacher education programs to create a **collaborative space** for prospective teachers. Mhairi Maeers and Lorri Robison view the concept as a **time space** which allows teachers to come to terms with their beliefs about subject matter and to make sense of new programs. Helen Christiansen and Janet Devitt suggest that teachers in universities and schools need to create a **pedagogical space** in one another's classrooms where collaborative partners from each of those institutions can get to know each other (and themselves) better through different forms of shared planning and teaching of classes. Next, Sandra Blenkinsop and Penelope Bailey suggest that each was able to deepen her understanding of teaching and teacher education through the creation of a **curricular space** as they engaged in a two-year collaborative inquiry into the integration of elementary language arts and science methods courses at the university. Finally, Karne Kozolanka and Bert Horwood return implicitly to the notion of **collaborative space** in their description and analysis of Karne's initiation into "academic life and work."

Mentoring is a second underlying theme. In her work as a teacher educator, Beattie mentors her students as she enables them to engage in collaborative experiences with each other, with her, and with their earlier selves as they make sense of learning to teach. Maeers, in her role as university researcher, mentors Robison, a classroom teacher, in the implementation of a new mathematics curriculum. Each learns from the other as they work together, at first with the children in Robison's classroom and later with education students and teachers within the context of a summer institute at the university. Christiansen, a university professor, and Devitt, a seconded teacher, mentor each other as Devitt helps Christiansen study her own teaching and Christiansen, in turn, initiates Devitt into life in a faculty of education. Blenkinsop and Bailey were also involved in mutual mentoring as they engaged in self-reflective inquiry. Kozolanka, as a graduate student and later as a beginning academic, and Horwood, as an academic advisor and later as a more experienced professor, write about "andragogic accompaniment" as a mentorlike relationship which "emphasizes the collaborative nature of the exchanges between the two parties."

Finally, all these chapters share a view of learning that is relational where, as Kozolanka and Horwood suggest, "humans are seen to develop expertise by acting in the world in communities of practice" or, as Beattie points out, "teaching and learning to teach are about working with persons rather than with transmission of subject matter."

◇ Chapter Nine

Collaboration in the Construction of Professional Knowledge: Finding Answers in Our Own Reality

Mary Beattie

All experience is an arch wherethru'
Gleams that untravelle'd world, whose margin fades
Forever and forever when I move.

—Alfred, Lord Tennyson, Ulysses

This chapter is about a university setting where pre-service teacher candidates engage in collaborative experiences that encourage and enable them to make sense of becoming teachers within the context of their whole lives. The context for the construction of a professional knowledge of teaching in a relational setting is established within two sequential foundations courses during a year-long pre-service teacher education program. Students in this program are prospective secondary school teachers who identify two subjects

they wish to teach at the secondary level. All have advanced degrees in one of these subjects and a number of university courses
in the other. Most of these students have had one or more careers
since graduating from university, many have graduate degrees and
professional qualifications in the arts, law, business and social work,
and they all bring richness and wide range of experience to the
teacher education setting. All students are required to take two
foundations courses as part of the teacher education program. In
the first semester all students take the mandatory course, "Teaching: Schools, Students and Systems." In the second semester, they
take the second course, "Developing a Personal Philosophy," which
they have chosen from a number of available options. The assumption that teaching and learning to teach is about working with
persons rather than about the transmission of subject matter, and
that good teaching involves the creation of settings and experiences
where students are encouraged to question, inquire, analyze and
construct their own meanings is at the heart of these courses and
this chapter.

Students who choose the optional second semester course,
"Developing a Personal Philosophy," are grouped together for the
mandatory course in the first semester. They remain as a cohesive
group throughout the year and I teach this group in both these
courses. The framework provided by these two foundations courses
provides a setting within which the persons involved can enter into
collegial relationships with one another, where we can come to
know one another over time, and can learn to trust and to support
one another as we collaborate in one another's learning. The setting can provide the structures, support, and conditions for inquiry
and can facilitate development of a professional knowledge of teaching, authentic to each individual and the teacher he or she can
become. Through a range of classroom experiences (cooperative
presentations and reading groups; reflective writing and feedback;
group seminars; sharing of resources and discussions) pre-service
teachers are encouraged to actively engage in the reconstruction of
what they know and in the creation of a professional knowledge
which involves growing understandings of the students they teach,
schools, systems and the self as teacher. The year-long arrangement provides us diverse and numerous opportunities to connect
theories and practices of teaching and learning. We collaborate to
think critically about the issues surrounding the purposes and
functions of education in a democratic society, look at the organization of schools and classrooms, and the process of reconstructing
the self as a professional teacher.

Many researchers in the field of teacher education and teacher development call for teacher education programs within which teachers' epistemological, cultural, and historical content and frameworks are recognized and acknowledged in the professional learning setting. Connelly and Clandinin (1988) and Elbaz (1983) have demonstrated the personal character of teachers' knowledge of practice. Butt and Raymond (1987), Goodson (1988), and Knowles and Cole (1993) show the role of biography and life histories in teachers' work. Connelly and Clandinin (1990) offer a conceptualization of professional development which is both personal and professional. The connections between the teacher's personal narrative and professional practice have been well documented elsewhere (see Beattie 1995; Clandinin and Connelly 1987; Clandinin, Davies, Hogan, and Kennard 1993; Knowles and Holt-Reynolds 1991). These researchers point out that when we learn to teach, we bring our life histories to the learning situation and enact our beliefs, values, and understandings in our behavior and practices. We draw on our previous experiences in learning and teaching to make sense and meaning of our new and predicted future situations; the ways we have been shaped by these experiences shapes the ways we enter into and begin to shape our new learning and teaching experiences. This continual involvement in the process of inquiry—choosing among possible alternatives in order to grow professionally, of expanding and reshaping one's knowing within the context of one's whole person—builds the capacity for reflection and action and is a process of self-empowerment, emancipation, and professional development.

It is this view of teaching and learning that informs this chapter and on which the understandings documented here are based. The purpose of the chapter, therefore, is to advance the ways we understand the connections between knowledge created through past experience and the creation of new professional knowledge. Through presentation of two portraits of students, I show how this kind of teaching—and the reflective writing and feedback which is an integral part of it—provides a way in which a teacher and students can collaborate in meaning-making that is grounded in the individual's experienced knowledge and enables individuals to construct a professional knowledge related to the past they have experienced and the future they envision. In this way, the process of teacher education can be one of personal and professional development that has a high degree of autonomy, self-determination, and personal freedom associated with it.

Creating a Setting for Collaboration and Collaborative Meaning Making

The prospective teachers in the program described here take their coursework at the university between September and April. This is interspersed with four two-week blocks of practice teaching in secondary schools where they are required to spend at least one practice- teaching session in each of their teachable subjects. Many students enter the teacher education program expecting to teach as they were taught and have expectations that the process of becoming a teacher will be one of acquiring strategies, skills, and techniques to teach the subject disciplines they have chosen. Many have experienced learning in their own lives as an individualistic, competitive, objective activity and have been successful in school and academic settings because they are highly motivated, high-achieving learners. The process of adapting what they know from their experiences as learners to their current roles as teachers, requires that students reconstruct this knowledge within the new professional context. The process involves gaining an appreciation for the diverse learning styles and interests of the students they teach; coming to an understanding of perspectives on teaching and learning other than their own; and becoming familiar with policies, practices and necessary understandings required to teach in a multicultural, multilingual, urban environment where the fabric of everyday life for a classroom teacher is concerned with the creation of conditions of both equity and excellence for all students.

Throughout the year, the readings provided, classroom discussions, presentations, and response to students' writing seek to encourage participants to make connections with issues in education and understandings from the perspective of their own experiences and their own realities; to hear the views of others, and integrate the new with what is known. Students are encouraged to identify and describe the critical incidents of their experiences as learners; to tell stories of teachers who have been significant to them, learning situations which nurtured or impeded their learning; and to explore the meanings of their reflections within the context of becoming a teacher. Through storytelling and joint reflection on experience, students explore ways they and others make meaning and learn to see the connections between knowledge they already have and development of their classroom practices and professional knowledge. With ongoing feedback from colleagues on their ideas and understandings, many individuals make further connections and use their writing to explore patterns they perceive in their practices over time, and to document dilemmas, contradictions, and challenges they experience in making the transition from being a student to being a teacher. The written feedback from the teacher on selected writings focuses on extension of this thinking and provision of further questions, resources, and support. Through these various forms of oral and written collaboration, many students come to see that the transition from student to professional teacher requires new understandings of the other in the teaching-learning relationship; new understandings of the connections between what teachers do and what happens for the students they teach; and new understandings regarding ways to encourage inquiry and analysis amongst their own students.

The university classroom setting where students collaborate in this way with each other and with the teacher is one that provides the learner with a high degree of respect, and in which trust, valuing, and reciprocity can be felt within the relationships and in the learning community. Sharing ideas, understandings, dilemmas and the questions which are compelling to them at any given time takes place in small group settings, in whole class discussions, and in the privacy of written journals. Students decide what and how much they will share. They make decisions regarding the extent to which they will expose their vulnerabilities and weaknesses to others, and have control over the level of risk and challenge which they will take. Thus, it is hoped that prospective teachers, who will create classroom situations where inquiry and collaboration are emphasized, are able to experience these kinds of learning situations for themselves. It is hoped that through creation of a setting where inquiry into teaching is ongoing, acts of teaching and learning are continually explored and critiqued for what they teach about teaching, practice and theory are linked in ways that inform both, students will be enabled to make links between this and settings they create for their own students. This kind of setting and this kind of teaching is centrally concerned with enabling prospective teachers to become more perceptive about: people and how they learn; teaching practices that enable and encourage them to learn; and distinguishing between those school and system structures that enable and disable learners. It is also centrally concerned with the extension of perceptions and transformed understandings into practice, and into developing competencies, practices and habits of mind which teachers can use to bring about change in themselves, others, and the settings in which they work.

Relational Learning: A Teacher and Her Students Meet Through Writing

As a teacher, I understand my role as creating a setting for teacher education where each person's present life is brought into a significant relationship with the past so connections can be explored and used to construct a professional knowledge of teaching that is authentic to the self. I believe I am responsible for providing educative experiences for all students I teach, providing appropriate readings, activities, and discussions that provide information on diverse ways of thinking about schooling, teaching and learning, challenge and extend commonly held views, and provide frameworks, support and challenges for students to conduct their own inquiries and create their own meanings. Students' reflective writing and the feedback I give are a significant part of establishing a relational setting, whose purpose is to enable students to document details of their professional journeys and explore their meanings. Throughout the year students keep a professional journal. At regular intervals they select pieces to which they would like a response and feedback.

The writing students do is of particular significance to articulation of experienced knowledge and to construction of a professional knowledge. Through the documentation of details of practice and their own learning about themselves as teachers, students become increasingly more aware of the complexities of teaching within its wider context, and work with the epistemological, historical and experiential content and frameworks of the knowledge they hold. Reflective writing and feedback provides students with opportunities to examine the ways they have constructed their world views, confront the notion that their vision of the world is not universally shared, work out solutions to problems of practice, rethink what they have thought about, and do so with a teacher in a way that is both private and collaborative. Students receive detailed written responses to the writings they submit including: suggestions for resources, teaching strategies; other possible interpretations of events; new questions, challenges and avenues for exploration; and a caring teacher's response to patterns, recurring themes, and evolving meanings she hears in the writings over time. In this way, students have a documented trail of their own thinking and thought processes, a teacher's responses to their thinking, and the opportunity to use the text they have created to become more articulate about their own knowing and learning. Their text enables them to probe the complexities of their own developing professional knowledge and use what they know to create new knowledge.

Students share selected writings with their colleagues on a regular basis and provide each other with feedback. This enables them to have their own knowledge validated and authenticated, contribute to each one another's understandings, provide alternate views and perspectives and, over time, expand the horizons of their own knowing. Many students come to see reflective writing as a valuable framework for continuous, self-directed inquiry into teaching and learning—a practice which they can continue into their teaching careers.

The structure provided by the ongoing writing and feedback the students and I engage in over the course of a year, gives me a framework within which I can be in a relationship with each individual student. I can meet each one at the point of his or her own questioning and meaning making and I can collaborate with each person in adapting and extending what is known to make new knowledge. Within this context, I can engage in a private conversation with each student where, through joint reflection, new meanings are made—each person is both teacher and learner. Through their writings, students show me their patterns of thinking and meaning making, the ways in which they are making connections between prior experience and current inquiry, and the ways in which they are making sense of the process of becoming a teacher. In short, they teach me how I can best teach them and how I can provide the kinds of responses, support, feedback and challenges which will enable them to further their inquiries. This provides a setting within which I can work with students on a one-to-one basis and respond to their current anxieties and questions. In the early part of the year these questions predominantly focus on the acquisition of teaching strategies, planning lessons, evaluating students' work, and classroom management. Later on in the year, when many students have learned how to deal with these issues, more complex questions come to the fore in the writing. Then I can participate in the intimate process of collaborating with the individual in an inquiry into what it means specifically for this individual to become a teacher.

Through constructive feedback I can encourage students to enter into conversations with their earlier selves and study their past experiences in teaching and learning for what these experiences have taught them. Values, beliefs, assumptions, expectations, and what is taken for granted are questioned and challenged. Through these conversations, students build the observational, reflective, communicative and performative capacities necessary for a career of reflective and inquiring practice. Through making connections between past and current writing I can sometimes lead students to make their own connections between past and present, see the contradictions between held theory and current practice as it is described, and enter into a dialogue with the self regarding the process of negotiating between the teachers they are and the teachers they want to be. The feedback given to each individual is focused on helping that particular person identify and articulate his or her own knowledge, knowledge structures, and learning processes, and enabling each prospective teacher to identify the epistemological, historical, cultural, and experiential wealth being brought to the learning situation. This kind of collaboration through writing involves extending each individual's inquiry into the connections between past, present, and future experiences and knowledge, and moving towards recasting the self into a new unity where personal and professional are one.

Collaborating in the Construction of a Professional Knowledge of Teaching: Portraits of two Students— Barbara and Patrick

To illustrate teaching and learning lived out in a setting where reflective writing and feedback are an integral part of the process of collaborative meaning making, I present two portraits of students I constructed from the writing done during the pre-service year (students have granted their permission). These portraits are presented to show how two individuals used their experienced knowledge to construct professional knowledge that was authentic to the person involved. Each individual came to connect prior experience with the experience of becoming a teacher and with the process of coming to understand the role of teacher in new ways.

Portrait of Barbara

Seeking and finding answers in my own reality. . . .

When Barbara came to the faculty of education she had already taught piano to private students for several years. She had a master's degree in English and had chosen English and music as her teachable subjects. In response to a suggestion Barbara wrote about a significant teaching experience she had as a piano teacher when she and her student had almost given up and declared failure. She described how her student could not understand what she was trying to teach her. The obstacles seemed unsurmountable. Both teacher and student were frustrated and discouraged. Having tried every method she could think of to solve the problem Barbara went back in her memory to recall the conditions in which she had connected to this music as a learner. She tried to remember the details of the connection. She went on to describe her joy at being able to turn a near failure in teaching into a success by creating parallel conditions for her student and enabling the student to connect with the music in her own way as Barbara had done when she was a learner, rather than in the teacher's way.

As the pre-service year progressed Barbara encountered difficulties teaching English in high school classroom situations. She began to question her decision to teach English to secondary school students. She found the process of becoming a classroom teacher much more difficult than she had expected and found that suggested strategies and random ideas offered by kindly colleagues and teachers didn't help at all. Barbara described her frustration at finding the techniques and strategies offered by others inadequate and unsatisfying to her sense of herself as a teacher. She recognized that other's suggestions were, in fact, distractions which prevented her from working out her own solutions; they added to her frustration and to the recognition that she was "constantly seeking answers in someone's reality." Barbara came to see that helpful others were impeding her own inquiry into what it meant for her to be an English teacher, and were preventing her from getting at the real issue of connecting her personal self to her professional situation. Through writing about all this, getting feedback on her writing, and the teaching of one of her associate teachers, Barbara came to recognize the value and significance of her own knowledge and the processes by which she had created it. She came to understand how to use this knowledge to solve the dilemmas and difficulties of teaching English in a high school and came to new understandings of herself as a teacher.

Recognizing the need to begin with her own reality, Barbara came to understand the necessity of understanding the reality of the other in order to teach and make connections between curriculum content and the lives of students. She came to see teaching English to high school students as more than the transmission of curriculum content. Successful teaching in her terms required her to create experiences for students where they could see how she was connected to the content of the curriculum and begin to make their own connections and meanings. Barbara came to see her role as a teacher of English from a new perspective. She changed her perceptions of students' attitudes towards learning English and gained new confidence and trust in herself as a learner and inquirer. At the end of the pre-service year Barbara was able to articulate her own learning in this way:

> My story here is the story of becoming a teacher of poetry, a story of finding my own poet-teacher.
>
> It begins with me hating to share my literary self, my pleasure in poetry and words, my delight in finding resonance in the sound of others as voices in their writing and my knowing the world through my own articulation of it.
>
> It ends through the generosity of my associate teacher (in the fourth round of practice teaching), who showed me that I could teach literature beginning from my own poetic soul. Lessons could grow around my feelings about how literature works, instead of being contrived according to some detested formulas. It is a story of how a rambunctious bunch of adolescents do not hate poetry and, from what they wrote to me afterwards, did not hate studying it this time.
>
> In looking for a little something like Pooh Bear, I have found that a little something becomes a big hunger when I seek my answers in someone else's reality.
>
> I have come to see that understanding begins and ends with my own storehouse of experience and learning and knowing. All else, useful and seductively decorative though these bits of colored string and feathers might be, becomes but a hindrance when it is time for me to find my own meaning.

The process of recalling and analyzing her dilemma with the music student led Barbara to continue to explore the connection between learning and teaching throughout the pre-service year, and make connections between her personal knowledge and her growing professional knowledge. By the end of the year, she was able to see how she had made connections between her past and present and used them to solve problems of professional practice and construct her professional knowledge of teaching. By this time also, she no longer regarded herself as unsuitable to be an English teacher. In remembering the role of literature in nourishing her own mind, heart, and soul, she was able to succeed in her practice by creating a classroom setting that grew out of her feelings about how literature works. Students were invited to make their connections to literature as she herself had done.

Portrait of Patrick

Patrick left his job as a television instructor in an Inuit community in northern Labrador to come to the faculty of education where he was a prospective high school teacher of environmental science and math. He had worked for a year in Labrador where one of the major aspects of his job was to teach the Native television crew some of the skills necessary to improve their cultural programming. In the course of his work with the Native people Patrick came to see that those he had come to teach had very valuable lessons to teach him. Some of his best teachers had been children. During this time he documented details of many of his experiences as an accepted member of the Inuit community. These writings provided a rich resource for him in his teacher education program and in enabling him to come to an understanding of the teacher he could be.

Through the writing he did during his pre-service year Patrick explored his understandings about teaching and learning, made connections between his previously unarticulated knowledge and his developing professional knowledge, and used what he knew to design his own professional education. In the writing he was encouraged to draw on the journal he had kept while in Labrador and juxtapose excerpts from past writing with what he was writing about developing professional knowledge of teaching. With encouragement Patrick allowed the writings from the two different periods in his life to enter into a dialogue with each other, and to highlight connections between his existing knowledge and the professional knowledge of teaching he desired. By engaging in a conversation with earlier self and using his reflections on his earlier learning, Patrick was able to shape and direct his inquiry in the pre-service teacher education setting. He provided himself a framework within which he came to recognize and value different ways of knowing; reconsider his role as a teacher; begin to consider relational learning and the establishment of a learning community; and reconceptualize teaching within social, institutional, economic and moral contexts wider than he had first imagined. Through the use of intertextual meaning-making Patrick came to reconceptualize his role as a teacher and see wider possibilities, responsibilities and opportunities available to him through bringing about change in his life, lives of students, and structures of communities and systems.

Patrick described details of how he came to a new understanding of his role as teacher and moved beyond thinking of teaching as the transmission of knowledge, skills, and strategies to the creation of a learning environment where learners with different needs and abilities are enabled to learn. He explained how his exploration of significant learning experiences helped him identify the way in which he came to appreciate others in a learning community, understand the other's perspective, accept multiple realities, and shift the focus from the self in a relationship to reciprocity between persons in relation. In this excerpt from his teaching journal he writes about his role as a member of a community. In his analysis he hints gently at a possible connection between this role and his new role as a teacher in the classroom community:

> (March 1993) When I was ice fishing in Labrador, (I was one of the few "whites" travelling with the Inuit) we all had an ice hole and we were fishing within eyesight of each other. People would patiently stand by their jigging hole all day long and pull in Arctic Char at the rate of about five an hour. Once, while I was pulling up my catch, the fish slipped off the hook just as it was emerging from the water. I immediately jumped onto my stomach and struggled with the big fish that was thrashing all around the ice hole and threatening to swim back in. After a brief battle, I finally grabbed it and threw it high in the air, far away from the hole. People all around watched my antics and laughed out loud. Momentarily, my response was to feel insulted and mocked, but then I looked at the hilarity of my own situation and laughed along with them. At that moment, and in their own way, the Inuit showed that they accepted me as part of their community. The Inuit love to laugh and it is one of the reasons they manage to survive when others fail; they have learned to make light of difficult situations. I realized that, had the Inuit not laughed at me, they would have been showing an indifference and quiet politeness for the stranger.

> Through examining this episode, I realize that my brief need to protect my honor stemmed from a vain and foolish pride to

project an outer shell of calm, controlled artificiality. I see that the moment we stop thinking about ourselves first, we start understanding the other and only through the caring and understanding of others, can we come to understand ourselves.

The shift from thinking of teaching as performance, where the focus is on the teacher-self, to the conceptualization of teaching as the creation of conditions where others make meaning within the context of their own realities, is a major reconceptualization of what it means to be a teacher. Later on in the year, Patrick used his new found understandings to make sense of the frustrations he was feeling with regard to certain aspects of his teacher education program and to question and analyze the expectations about teacher education which he had brought with him. In his writing, he described his growing appreciation and understanding of the kind of teaching he was experiencing in the two foundations courses. He could see that what he was experiencing in that situation sought to model the collaborative, relational, learning environment that encouraged him to connect with his experiences, study them, and value himself as a knower and maker of meanings. In his writing Patrick had explained the significance of letting go of the tendency and desire to constantly focus on the self and on one's own performance within a relationship with others. He came to understand this anew, within the context of the two courses and within the context of his own education as a teacher. He came to appreciate that the teacher education environment he was experiencing called for a shift in power relations between teacher and learner, encouraged him to trust and believe in himself as a learner, valued his reality and required his participation in the learning process. He described his learning in this way:

(March 1993) I was a real wreck at the beginning of my year at the faculty of education. I thought that teacher education consisted of learning certain rules and tricks on how to teach and handle a class. I was wrong! In truth, I needed to improve myself; I needed to learn how to become a better human being.

Being an effective teacher means being true to yourself and bringing out the best in other people. . . . it means showing people how to believe in themselves and that they are capable of incredible things. . . . and in making your students know that you believe in them.

As the year progressed Patrick extended his understandings of the other in the teaching-learning relationship into a deeper understanding of the quality of reciprocity in the teacher-student relationship. He described the way in which he came to value students as teachers, different kinds of knowledge, and different ways of knowing. He wrote about how he came to value the establishment of a learning community within which reciprocal relationships with students could be initiated and developed and students would have knowledge they brought to the situation validated. Extending this into his future practice, he imagined and described his future classroom where students would be provided with meaningful, purposeful learning experiences which would enable and empower them to play increasingly more responsible and contributory roles within their communities, inside and outside school. In such an environment, the students and teacher continually learn from each other and are transformed through their interactions. Selected excerpts from his writings show how he used his experience as a meaning-making framework for his professional development and used writing as a way of accessing his understandings and creating new meanings:

(March 1993) I didn't know how to fish before I went to Labrador. My father was never a sporting type of man. He watched a lot of TV and my idea of the natural world came from our Sunday ritual of "The Wonderful World of Disney" and from our tortuous two-week car-camping marathons across the United States. My best teachers were least expected. They were all figures of respect and admiration to me. Some of my best teachers were children.

(July 8, 1991) I never had much luck fishing with the rod until today. It was an absolutely fabulous Labrador morning! The water was so still and beautiful that it was possible to see the fish swimming to your lure. The Native children, who often fished alongside me, frequently volunteered information on how to improve my fishing technique: "Pull the rod like this," or "You're reeling it in too fast," or "Cast it over your head, it'll go farther." This particular morning there were at least eight of us perched on our rocks jutting out on a sea whose tide was falling. We would call to each other when a school of fish were swimming our way. The schools were ten to forty strong, sometimes small ones, sometimes average ones, and other times varied sizes with a few large leaders who actually led the troupe! We fished for a good two hours in this fashion watching school after school of fish swim by. One amusing boy who fished right next to me, sang a little song calling out for "iqaluit." He did not know the English word for trout or char. I joked about how we rated the schools of fish by being grade three (small fish), grade eight (medium fish) or grade eleven fish. The variable-sized schools were rated in terms of "There's a principal, a few teachers and some students." The young boy said that he was fishing for the "graduating student" and we both knew how important this fish must have been. We often moved from rock to rock where opportunity was best. At one point, perched on a rock barely six feet wide, there were four of us: myself, another adult, and two boys casting our lines one over the other, competing for the same fish.

(March 1993) I have seen Inuit children, from five- to eight-years-old, catch and cut up fish with the same skill as their parents. In many Native societies, children achieve independence very early in their lives and are expected to play a contributory role in their families. They therefore develop a stronger sense of their value and responsibility to the community. In our society, children play with plastic tools or "easy bake" ovens and, by encouraging this sort of play, we are telling them by inference that they are a diminutive of us, and that their true value to society will not be recognized until ten to thirteen years down the road. Is it any wonder that teenagers rebel against parents and teachers—the very people who have raised them to be incompetent?

By contrasting the Native mind-set with my own, it becomes evident to me how the educational system is often fighting against the natural tendencies of human beings. We have a lot to learn from our youth.

The patronizing approach of the school system must stop. Like parents, teachers are raising children to be incompetent. We tell them what they should know and assign them homework which is just a diminutive of the real world and has no true purpose other than providing a mark and, therefore, a promotion into the next grade. Students have grown to feel that they can contribute nothing of real value to the world because for the last thirteen years of their lives they have done nothing but obey, memorize, and conform to a system that has institutionalized their worth to society.

(July 1991) Looking at the accumulated files of previous trainers who had worked before me (all white Southerners), I couldn't help but think that I was just another Southerner, coming up with good intentions and my own vision of how they should be making good films. The irony of having the Inuit do television programming. I once thought that the Inuit had a hope of developing an aboriginal documentary style, but this seemed as absurd as expecting a white southerner to develop a unique Native drum dance. What we are doing to the Inuit now is essentially what we've done to ourselves long ago: allowed a certain mind-set to dictate the fabric of a people. While we acknowledge that each individual has the same right to education as everyone else, we seem to think that this right is congruent with a universal and standardized educational system. What we fail to see is that there are different people, different modes of thinking, and different values that must be addressed. What needs to be done is a change in thinking mode, in short—reforming the educational system.

This will never happen as long as our modern world views continue to emphasize western scientific knowledge as the means to technological power, order and control. We need a paradigm shift which changes the frame of reference within which the fundamental thinking in major disciplines such as economics, social studies and science is done.

(March 1993) I am troubled by a school system where standardized educational testing is being advocated by a public who demands academic parity across the world. I see it as an effort to socialize and empower our already overempowered institutions (while disempowering those they claim to help most). These people forget that students are human beings. Let us not manufacture competitive, aggressive machines out of these young people. Let us allow them to think for themselves instead of perpetuating this ridiculous edict that they must always measure up to each other instead of themselves. We are no longer catering to students' needs but to the parents' or to society's best intentions of how things should be. It is dehumanizing and disempowering our students—the community leaders of tomorrow.

Patrick's growing understanding of the structures of his own learning and knowledge and the extention of his understanding into his professional development led him into increasingly complex conceptualizations of the role of the teacher. With positive and constructive feedback, he gained confidence in his own knowing and began to trust his own judgement. Gradually he began to question and challenge the structures and frameworks of classrooms and schooling as he saw them, and to understand and articulate his need to actively change them. His writing here shows a strong belief in his own knowing and an understanding of the moral conflict he feels regarding how schools are and how they might be if they were to provide good learning conditions for all learners. The writing shows this prospective teacher in the act of developing the reflective capacities and understandings necessary to bring about changes in the school system. He shows how he has transformed his own understandings and a conception of himself as a teacher who has both the need and the capacities to bring about change and transformation in the lives of students, schools, and communities.

Collaborative Experiences in Pre-service Teacher Education Settings

The landscape of teacher education needs places and spaces where prospective teachers can reflect on their lived experiences and recover the significant aspects of what they know as they relate to becoming a teacher. The description of the setting provided by the two foundations courses given here is an attempt to show one way in which this can be done. Through inquiry, reflection, practice, and feedback from a number of colleagues and teachers, prospective teachers are provided with support and alternate perspectives as they construct a professional knowledge of teaching. Within the context of these two university courses students can bring past and present experiences together, make meaningful connections between theory and practice, and take an active part in the construction of their own professional knowledge. Within this setting students can receive continuous feedback on their meaning-making and avail themselves of the experienced knowledge of both their colleagues and the teacher in a setting which is collaborative, collegial and supportive (as opposed to individual, competitive and isolated), in spite of organizational structures, obstacles, and requirements. The portraits of the two student teachers provide insights into the processes of becoming a teacher and into the ways these two prospective teachers brought their personal knowledge to the process of construction of professional knowledge. The portraits provide understandings of what is involved in the transition from being a student to being a teacher who understands the complexities of teaching within a personal, professional, social, institutional, and moral context. Together they highlight the different paths prospective teachers take on the journey toward acquisition of professional knowledge and different kinds of knowledge, skills, and understandings they bring to the teacher education situation.

Creating professional knowledge requires ongoing opportunities for bringing the past—with its patterns, frameworks for understanding, systems of beliefs and values—into a significant relationship with the present and for the providing of constructive support and feedback on the process of this inquiry. Our teacher education programs could be enriched by: the provision of experiences and opportunities where teachers and learners reflect together on issues of significance to the learner; the provision of a variety of responses and feedback to learners; and development of new ways of living, learning, and relating to others in learning communities. Learning to teach needs to be understood within a relational context and within the context of working with people. Thus, the development of professional knowledge is focused on the continual development of knowledge, skills, and capabilities to better meet the needs of the people being taught and of the situation being lived. In Barbara's words, learning to teach must begin in students' own realities and extend outwards to an understanding of the realities of others. This eschews the kind of packaged learning Patrick rejects for students and for himself and espouses the concept of a school curriculum co-created by the persons involved. Programs that do not take account of prospective teachers' prior experience and held knowledge cannot provide them with the kinds of experiences necessary to enable them to teach their own students in a relational way, learn how to co-create curriculum with students, or enable students to find answers in their own realities.

Our teacher education programs will be enriched when we create space for prospective teachers to collaborate with each other and with their teachers as they question, challenge commonly held ideas, learn to see and understand the realities and perspectives of others, and are supported in their individual inquiries. Prospective

teachers need to see and experience the process of reflective teaching and inquiry into their own teaching in their lives as students
of teaching, so that they can learn to teach this way with their own
students. To teach them otherwise is to disenfranchise and
disempower them, providing them only with distractions which keep
them from addressing real issues, and frustrate and delay their
professional development. With rich collaborative experiences and
relationships as an integral part of their make up, teacher education programs can be the arching frameworks through which the
past horizon is re-viewed and the future "untraveled world" is created by prospective teachers. Such programs can provide the permanent structures and habits of mind for a career of reflective
practice and ongoing inquiry.

✧ Chapter Ten

Making Sense of Mathematics Within Collaborative Communities

Mhairi "Vi" Maeers and Lorri Robison

This chapter describes the experience of a classroom teacher and a university professor as we worked collaboratively on two action research projects. The first project involved mathematics program implementation in a Grade Four cross-cultural class; the second involved the two authors and others in a mathematics summer course teaching experience at the university.

A very powerful professional development tool, the purpose of action research is to examine a problem situation and determine a disciplined path towards solution. Action research often results in increased understanding and changed practice, enabling teachers to become more conscious of their actions and decisions, and ultimately more responsible to their students and to their school. Lorri could have conducted her own action research in her school classroom without any help from Vi. However, as we both worked together to make sense of a pilot program, we enjoyed a synergy which would not have been present had either of us been working alone. As we had not previously worked with the new mathematics program, we approached the task of understanding its require- ments as learners. We had to understand the mathematics that was to be taught and at the same time keep in mind the children we were teaching. Through our interdependency, nurtured in the unfolding understanding of the new program and of the children, we became collaborative partners in learning.

Pervasive in the collaborative inquiry literature is the model outlined in Oakes, Hare, and Sirotnik (1986) and Tikunoff and Ward (1983). Our initial study allowed the teacher, who is the consumer of the research to "be involved in the process of inquiry when the outcomes of the research are intended to inform . . . her own practice" (Tikunoff and Ward 1983, 455). Other important fea- tures of collaborative research, identified by Skau (1987), are to share increased personal understandings, assume transactional roles, and be free and able to relate to others in new ways. Further- more, collaborative research necessitates the development of rela- tionships and collaborative decision making about roles. Lieberman and Miller (1990) emphasize the importance of a trusting, open relationship of collegiality. Whether the research is conducted be- tween two or more teachers within a school, is school-wide, or between a university and a school, a trusting collegial relationship which is open to change, promotes productive inquiry. Initially, collaborative action research may be like the beginning of a friend- ship as partners get to know one another. Our collaborative action research arose from a need identified by the teacher which met the need of the university researcher. Early in our relationship we believed ourselves to be in agreement with respect to our mutually negotiated goals, and consequently not working under what Maloy (1985) calls the "multiple realities" (p. 342) of different perspectives and motivations.

Much of the initial collaborative action research occurred between us at the verbal level as we examined and attempted to understand the program implementation material, or, as we de- briefed students' actions in relation to our instruction using this material. Much of this interaction occurred in the midst of children working or during recess times. There was thus little time for us to keep formal records of our collaboration. Formal data collection in the form of taped interviews, for instance, occurred whenever time could be found in our busy schedules. Ongoing findings from the action research which we discussed together and reflected upon, informed us as to how we organized the implementation material into a workable plan for classroom instruction. Through our collaborative interaction within this community of two we developed an understanding of the mathematics program requirements and the way in which each of us approached the task of operationalizing these requirements into practical activities for Lorri's Grade Four classroom.

Formal research involved investigating and documenting our feelings, uncertainties, connections, and critical moments as we worked together to implement the pilot program. Data from field and meeting notes, transcriptions of audio recordings, and journal records were all examined and analyzed.

The Classroom Collaborative Learning Community

The major theme arising from the recorded data of our collaborative research was that of community of learners. The two of us participated in a shared experience, worked toward a shared, negotiated goal, and as such participated in a "shared endeavor" (Rogoff 1994, 209). This theme also relates to Lorri's sense of living with her children in her classroom as they participated in shared experiences. This theme was evident in each of the contexts we shared—the action research classroom study, and the intensive summer school course at the university. The latter focused on new strategies in teaching mathematics. Here we collaborated for the purpose of educating other teachers.

The concept of a community of learners suggests that more than one person is focused on the tasks of learning. Lorri previously felt alone in her planning for and teaching of mathematics. She felt equally alone in her personal learning of both the content and pedagogical knowledge of mathematics. She had no one to share ideas with, or to work with in order to make sense of the mathematics curriculum. Working together offered us opportunities to share our ideas. It enabled Lorri to realize that her fears and anxieties with regard to mathematics were not uncommon. Within our community of two learners we developed an open trusting relationship of collegiality (c.f., Lieberman and Miller 1990). In the following excerpt, Lorri discusses her involvement in the community of learners:

> I realized that I was not alone in my feelings and anxieties about the learning and teaching of mathematics. I talked to Vi about my fears, and later, in July 1994, in a summer class

experience, I further shared some of my past fears and anxieties about both the learning and teaching of mathematics. I
realized from talking to Vi that many pre-service teachers
have these same fears, and I realized from the summer class
students that many long time practicing teachers have these
fears also. I sensed that somehow all of us were part of a
larger community of learners, striving to overcome the mathematical fears of the past. What I had experienced over the
school year with Vi were a series of mathematical experiences, or encounters, where either I tried something new in
the classroom, or Vi did and I watched, or together we talked
through some of the suggestions in the pilot program. By the
time the summer class came along, I no longer felt the same
fear or anxiety. I felt now that I could encourage others, and
help them to feel part of a community of people trying to
overcome negative mathematical experiences from the past.
(interview transcript, July 1994)

Interacting with Vi during the school year, interacting with
her class, and interacting with the summer school students all
reinforced Lorri's understanding of a collaborative learning community. Vi's participation in this community was initially one of
encourager, facilitator, and questioner, as she believed that Lorri
needed to talk through some of her earlier mathematical experiences. The sense of trust and collegiality that developed between
us enabled us to work together as learners in order to understand
the new program. As Vi said:

I realized from the start that Lorri was nervous and almost
hesitant to embark on this pilot program, as she had many
untold fears and anxieties about her mathematical experience. I knew the best way I could help her was to let her talk
through some of her fears. I endeavored to establish a bond of
trust between us, where each could speak freely about her
concerns. Lorry was very open to relating to me all her past
mathematical experiences and I was able to share with her
many of my own, as well as tell her about the experiences of
others. Lorri began to realize that she was not alone. This
seemed to give her strength to continue. She began to feel
confident in her teaching of mathematics and was able to try
out some of the ideas in the pilot program. We began to work
together in the classroom with the children. A sense of community is developing between us—we are sharing our ideas,

developing trust, and negotiating what we are going to do. It feels good to work with someone in the field on a topic of interest to both of us. (interview transcript, October 1993)

As the year progressed, it became evident that Lorri was much less anxious about her mathematics teaching and was beginning to take risks with classroom groupings and mathematics activities. Our small community of two learners helped her validate what she was doing and gave her confidence to continue. It was becoming increasingly apparent that Lorri's initial fears and anxieties about mathematics were quickly being replaced by her fears and anxieties about implementing the new pilot program. She felt there would have been more chance of success in effecting change in her teaching of mathematics without the restrictions imposed by the new program. She stated in an interview that "it was the program and not the mathematics that was the barrier to change" (interview transcript, October 1993).

We both agreed that our **collaborative** interpretation of the requirements and our consequent **collaborative** operationalizing of these requirements, followed by our **collaborative** debriefing and reflection on this operationalization added depth and focus to our understanding of the features of the pilot program and its connection to the new mathematics curriculum in the province of Saskatchewan. As we interacted in relation to the topic under investigation (e.g., how to plan and implement instruction on place value, for instance) we found that our separate shared understandings enabled each of us to think differently and more deeply about the topic. For example, Vi would suggest an activity that had previously worked for her, only to discover that it would not work for this group of children. Or as we were planning, Lorri, who knew the children better, would have to change an activity that Vi suggested in order to meet the needs of her students. This would, in turn, encourage Vi to create collaborative environments for her own pre-service mathematics students at the university. It would further encourage her to guide her students in the creation of structures to allow others, such as teaching partners, cooperating teachers in field placements, or parents to collaborate in the planning of mathematics activities. The two of us worked together as learners engaged in a collaborative conversation whose focus was that of making sense of mathematical requirements. We learned from each other, but more importantly, we learned together within an environment of trust—one where taking risks was validated.

The Summer Course Collaborative Learning Community

Both of us participated in an exciting professional development opportunity in the summer of 1994. Vi initiated a summer course, suitable for undergraduate and graduate education students, on new strategies and approaches to teaching mathematics. To assist us with this class, the late Professor Richard Skemp from the University of Warwickshire, England, acted as resource person. Professor Skemp was recognized internationally for his theory of intelligent learning in mathematics (Skemp 1989). The summer course was intended to explore Skemp's theory through discussion, lecture, and making and doing of Skemp's structured activities (Skemp 1993a, 1993b). We worked with groups of students during the making and doing of the activities, while Professor Skemp focused on the lecture aspects of the course.

The summer course teaching experience found us in two separate, albeit connected, collaborative communities. Over forty undergraduate students and three graduate students participated in the summer class which met in the mornings. The graduate students worked as group facilitators. This meant they had to meet with Professor Skemp every afternoon in order to construct, talk through, and practice the following day's structured activities. Although Lorri was an unofficial student in this class she assumed the same role as the graduate students in that she facilitated a working group in the morning and participated in the meeting with Professor Skemp in the afternoon. In addition to this the two of us reflected upon the entire class experience from the perspective of our research interest. We focused on making sense of the structured activities in relation to the new provincial mathematics curriculum. From the very first day of the class it was clear that all of these students shared a common focus. This was demonstrated initially by their attempts to make sense of Skemp's theory and its application and further demonstrated by their enthusiasm in sharing their mathematical experiences.

Lorri's Experience in the Summer Class

During the summer class teaching experience Lorri realized that everyone was there because of a desire to learn about new ways to teach mathematics. She further realized that her earlier anxieties about teaching mathematics were shared by almost all of the summer class participants. During the morning sessions Lorri was able to share her recent, more positive experiences with the new program.

Through listening to Professor Skemp's lectures, participating in discussion following the lectures, and preparing the structured activities, Lorri understood how the mathematical concepts were organized into a conceptual network. She was able to link those concepts to the curriculum, and to her previous and present teaching of mathematics. Everything seemed to "click together" as she began to conceptualize complete networks of mathematics concepts. In the group she facilitated she was enthusiastic as she helped others make similar connections. Her new sense of community was enhanced as she found herself confidently sharing many of the ideas the two of us had worked through together the previous year. In her group, Lorri created a caring environment which enabled her students to discuss their fears and anxieties about teaching mathematics, and to share their own plans for implementing some of the new ideas in their future teaching.

Lorri had many occasions within the summer school community to talk with the other students. It was somewhat disconcerting for her to learn that some of these teachers "were still using the text book." She "saw herself as one of these teachers."

> People were saying that of me. Only a few months ago I was using the textbook almost exclusively...I don't have to defend my dependence on the textbook. It doesn't matter any more that I was dependent on it. I know I'm not going to be any more. (interview transcript, July 13, 1994)

Lorri had come to the decision that the textbook would not be the authority of knowledge when she taught mathematics. It would no longer direct what she would teach. She felt fortunate to have had a "before and after experience" of textbook dependency. It seemed to her that many of the teachers in the summer course were just began to have an "after" experience. She observed that for many of the summer school students, it was difficult to "let go of the traditional way of thinking, doing and being" and "how easy it is to do that" (interview transcript, July 13, 1994). Lorri had experienced first hand what it felt like to let go of the secure boundaries of her past mathematical teaching experience. She encouraged her summer class group to do the same.

Lorri's Experience in the Afternoon Group

The two of us reflected upon some of the summer course discussions we had with Professor Skemp and the graduate students. Lorri was impressed by the confidence that the graduate students (all successful practicing classroom teachers) had in their nontraditional approaches to teaching mathematics. She realized that "they (had) been teaching mathematics in a nontraditional way for a long time" and so "they had a firm philosophy as to why" they did so (interview transcript, July 13, 1994). Lorri had come to an understanding of that philosophy and had begun to put it into use in her own classroom. Lorri also realized that, for the most part, she and the graduate students thought about and taught mathematics quite differently from most of the other students in the class. The summer course offered an occasion for Lorri to articulate her newly worked through philosophy of teaching mathematics. It also provided an occasion for her to come to terms with her past mathematical experiences. She was able to help and encourage other teachers to share their experiences and embrace new knowledge. The summer course may have been the most pivotal event in the development of her new philosophy. As Lorri participated in the community of learners with Professor Skemp, Vi, and the graduate students, she found strength and excitement. Or as Lorri put it:

> As this group prepared and practiced for the next day they supported and encouraged each other. I felt welcome and very much a part of the group, and very much a contributor within the group. (interview transcript, July 13, 1994)

The afternoon community was collaborative in that all participants shared a common focus and purpose: each encouraged and supported the others; each worked at developing a bond of trust; and each had different strengths and different ideas which became the common shared understandings of the group. The collaborative community established by the course facilitators enabled Lorri to increase her understanding of teaching mathematics. In the following excerpt, she describes her feelings:

> I was impressed with these women. I knew them and I thought they were, and had always been, creative teachers who kept current with new developments in teaching. . . . I had not previously considered that many had had similar past experiences as me in both the learning and teaching of mathematics.

I could easily relate to their stories . . . The level of confidence and commitment to this new approach was solidified and unquestionable within this group. The experience which I had in this afternoon group gave me the opportunity to participate in a shared community in a way that supported my own philosophy of teaching and living with my children . . . We got to know each other in a relaxed way and were able to share things that otherwise would not have come to light. Nobody had worked through these activities before, so we were all learners together. (field notes, July 1994)

Vi's Experience

The afternoon group was for Vi a powerful community of learners. Group members had to interpret our directions, practice the activities in preparation for teaching them to the undergraduate students, and gather together materials necessary for the following day's classes. All needed one another in order to understand what to do. Within this afternoon collaborative community, Vi was able to share her past experiences and current thinking as a learner and teacher of mathematics. She found herself participating in a community of learners, the nature of which was indeed a "participation in a shared endeavor" that involved "working towards a shared, negotiated goal" (Rogoff 1994, 209). In this community no one person had all the knowledge about what to do, and no one person tried to prescribe what others should do. All were aware and committed to the task at hand. Professor Skemp had given them an outline of what he wanted to do but it was up to the facilitators to make personal sense of that outline and to become familiar with all of the activities, many of which were new to them. Being part of a collaborative community as they assumed the behavior of mathematicians (Fellows 1991) was an exciting experience for Vi. She resolved to develop this manner of working in her pre-service elementary methods classes at the university.

It was apparent to Vi as she observed the students during class time in the mornings and when she read the course evaluations later, that all of the students had experienced success in the course. For the most part, it seemed that their learning had been enhanced by participation in energizing collaborative learning communities. Once again Vi saw that the power and support of such a community can have a significant impact on the mathematical learning and the mathematical experiences of participants.

When Vi observed Lorri interacting with her group of five students during the morning classes she realized the importance of the time the two of them had spent together during the previous year. As she said:

> The first year of our time together was a developmental phase, during which we learned to depend on one another for inspiration, for constructive criticism in planning for and implementing our ideas in practice. . . . We learned that neither of us had sufficient knowledge to operationalize the pilot program effectively. Through our support of one another and our evolving ability to make sense of that program collaboratively, we were more confident and more articulate in sharing with the summer class communities our sense of curriculum and the way it was being addressed by Skemp's structured activities. (field notes, July 1994)

When the Class Was Over

Throughout the summer Lorri continued to work on an interactive mathematics program for the following school year. She had seen how strengthening for her a community of mathematical learners could be. She wanted to create such groups in her own class. She began to transfer the most favorable conditions for her learning into pedagogical decisions which would affect her learners. Both her mathematical content knowledge and her pedagogical knowledge had been changed as a result of her participation in collaborative communities.

Vi's experience reinforced for her the powerful effect that a collaborative community can have in enabling learners to make sense of a topic, and in encouraging them to take risks as they learned.

Reflecting on Our Experience

This chapter has focused on some features of our collaboration as we worked together, initially in Lorri's classroom to make sense of a pilot program in mathematics and later to prepare for and teach a summer course in elementary mathematics methods. At the end of our collaborative teaching each of us reflected on our experience:

Lorri: Learning mathematics changed from learning from an external authority—a series of formulae, routines and skills—to learning mathematics in a more interactive sense of personally constructing mathematical knowledge within a community of people who were also striving to learn. I have come to understand that my students and I are creators of mathematical ideas, and that mathematical knowledge can be nurtured through interactive communities of learners. With this evolving belief system of learning mathematics came a change in my teaching style. Where previously I had almost exclusively used a textbook and had children work straight from it, I now have children working as a whole class or as a group, using manipulatives, and generally being much more actively involved in their mathematical learning. I have begun to plan mathematics by considering what I am teaching in other subject areas and I am also planning thematically with mathematics becoming part of the theme. My participation in a collaborative community with Vi, and with the summer students, has helped me realize the power of community in learning mathematics. (self-report, July 1994)

Vi: I have found the entire collaborative process with Lorri exciting and professionally rewarding. It was exciting to see Lorri approach the teaching of mathematics in a more interactive way, but it was even more exciting to realize the power of the two of us working together to make this happen. Working with Lorri in the two situations where a sense of community developed, made me realize the need to establish pedagogically sound supportive collaborative communities to bring about change. I had previously considered that this was important, but over the past year, through my participation in both communities as a learner, I felt the strength of the supportive collaborative community to enable me to learn. I have also realized that such a community takes time to develop. It is much more than a workshop presentation or an in-service visit. Changing one's approach to teaching mathematics cannot happen in a few days. It requires a significant change in beliefs about mathematics, the nature of mathematical knowledge, and about how children learn mathematics. Such change needs to be developed over time within a supportive collaborative community. (self-report, July 1994)

Looking Ahead

We did not begin our collaborative research experience by observing each other teach or by observing children learn. Instead we spent the first few weeks exploring our personal understandings of the nature of mathematics and the ways children learn mathematics. We took time to reflect on the program and ways in which its requirements related to our evolving beliefs about mathematics. Through our collaborative endeavors during the first year of our study our deliberations were related to our problem situation—the implementation of the new mathematics curriculum. Consequently we were both able to participate more confidently in the summer course as we shared what we had learned about mathematics and mathematics teaching and learning.

In both communities the participants determined the knowledge appropriate to our ongoing making sense of a situation. Members of a collaborative community need to determine the path they lay down (Varela 1987) as an adequate solution to a problem situation. There may not be an ideal path or there may be more than one acceptable path, but whichever path they choose, they need to justify the adequacy or viability of that path as a solution to the problem. In our earlier collaboration the problem situation in Lorri's classroom was an external prescribed situation which we needed to understand: the new mathematics curriculum had to be implemented. As we did so, we laid down a viable pathway that addressed the requirements of the programs; the children who interacted with our pathway, in turn, laid down viable pathways of demonstrated mathematical understanding. In our collaborative community we did not ask ourselves if we were right, or if we had chosen the best activity. Rather, we considered whether or not an activity would create a space for Lorri's students to become engaged with the material and interact appropriately with the topic.

Often teachers are called upon to implement new curricula. Usually some in-service is provided. As a result of our experience we wonder, Is present in-service practice sufficient to create a space for teachers to make sense of requirements of curriculum implementation, and to come to terms with their beliefs about learning and organizing content for instruction? After all, we had met and worked together collaboratively for an entire school year.

In both communities, specific situations which had been externally prescribed were reformulated into solvable problem situations. Participants in both learning communities worked collaboratively as they decided upon viable pathways to solution.

The nature of the collaboration in each community enabled participants to engage in conversation such that an adequate solution
was found. Furthermore, collaboration had a powerful effect on our
learning about each other in relation to the topic. We did not simply take the pilot material and implement it in the classroom.
Rather, we took time to understand what that material was asking
us to do, and then collaboratively worked out a plan of implementation—our viable pathway. This took time but in the end it was
worth it. We reached a greater understanding of mathematics and
of each other in relation to mathematics. Most of all, working
collaboratively enhanced our confidence in ourselves as learners
and teachers.

✧ Chapter Eleven

Collaborative Conversations at the University: Creating a Pedagogical Space

Helen Christiansen and Janet Devitt

> *Collaboration is always fraught with difficulties and*
> *complete equality is probably impossible to achieve in*
> *any partnership [G]iving each partner equal power in*
> *the research process ... require[s] us not only to*
> *recognise the differences in the ways we construct our*
> *worlds (and our castles) but to recognise the need to*
> *respect, and learn from, each other—in terms of Bruner's*
> *metaphor, to inhabit each other's castles.*
>
> *(Somekh 1994, 9)*

In any collaborative undertaking between researchers whose teaching occurs mainly in school settings and researchers whose teaching is carried out mainly in universities, there are issues that need to be addressed so they can indeed learn from one another. This chapter shares the experience of its two authors who came from

different "castles" (cf., Bruner 1986), but who conducted their research in Somekh's "castle of the academy" (p. 1). Jan is a French
immersion teacher who is presently on secondment in a faculty of
education on the Canadian prairies and Helen is a professor in
that faculty. We had originally met in Jan's Grade Two classroom
when Helen was a faculty advisor for a student teacher assigned to
Jan. When Jan began working at the university we undertook to
collaborate in the planning and teaching of different sections of the
same course each of us taught—a French language adaptation of a
generic teaching methods course required of all students in the
faculty of education.

Our decision to collaborate arose from a shared interest in
improving teacher education. Moreover, there were concrete advan-
tages to working together as closely as possible. First of all, it enabled us to share the workload while benefitting from each other's
perspectives and insights. Secondly, we needed each other. When we
began working together Jan needed someone to initiate her into life
at the university. Helen was looking for someone who was interested
in conducting research within a collaborative framework. Finally,
believing that a good teacher educator needs above all to be a good
teacher, we wanted to set time aside for sharing reflections and
observations of our own and each other's teaching. Working together
on a research project which involved a collaborative self study of our
teaching at the university appealed to both of us.

Jan's arrival on campus coincided with the publication of what
became known as the "Smith Report," a document whose principal
focus was an appraisal of university teaching in Canada. In that
report, teaching is said to be "seriously undervalued at Canadian
universities" (Smith 1991, 63). Like many other institutions of higher
learning across the country, our university had taken up the challenge of improving the quality of teaching while striving to maintain a balance between teaching and research. It made sense,
therefore, to integrate the two by making our teaching a center of
inquiry. We found out very quickly, however, that before we could
collaborate as teachers we had to learn to collaborate as individuals. In other words, we had to develop a collaborative relationship.

In this chapter we describe the development of that relationship. We agree with other educators who argue that in collaborative endeavors the relationship between research partners is of
prime importance (e.g., Clandinin, Davies, Hogan, and Kennard
1993; Cole and Knowles 1993; Hollingsworth 1992; and many contributors to this book). In our case, each individual brought into
the relationship the baggage from the institution she represented

and with which she identified. That baggage had to be unpacked so each could understand the other's context, or, as Somekh (1994) puts it, we had to learn to "inhabit each other's castles" (p. 9).

We use the castle metaphor as a conceptual framework for this chapter which begins with sharing extracts from early and more recent conversations. Next, we explore the ambivalence of Jan's situation as a seconded teacher and the effect this had on our research. We go on to examine ways in which we collaborated in the "middle ground" (cf., Clandinin, Davies, Hogan, and Kennard 1993) of our own teaching. We conclude with a gathering of threads and an examination of possibilities for future collaborative endeavors in the school "castle."

For much of our first year together we met formally in Jan's office once a week. These sessions, which were recorded and later transcribed, lasted about an hour. During the first six months of our inquiry each kept a weekly journal to which the other responded. The first journal entry was autobiographical. The rest were reflective pieces that became part of our ongoing conversation. On several occasions we observed each other teaching, keeping field notes we later shared. There were countless other collegial exchanges during the two terms. Sometimes one or both of us kept field notes of these.

At the end of that first year we began to examine our data, moving into another phase of our project. Since that time we have been engaged in a process of "restorying" (c.f., Connelly and Clandinin 1990)—talking and writing about our experience. Our collaboration took on added meaning for us as we look backed over the transcripts of our taped conversations and journal entries. From time to time we followed up on themes that emerged and either became stronger or faded into the background to make way for new themes. We learned to accept this as part of a narrative process—as we analyzed old stories we became involved in creating a new shared story. Much of the data presented here comes from what we now consider to be three key conversations about our evolving collaborative relationship: a conversation we had early in Jan's secondment; another at the beginning of her third year which revisited our earlier conversations; and a recent conversation as we revised an earlier version of this chapter. These conversations were significant for us because each was an occasion for new understandings in our thinking about collaboration. Each conversation demonstrated to us the power of "restorying" (cf., Connelly and Clandinin 1990) as we found new meanings in the data—meanings that changed both the process and the product of our collaborative inquiry.

Lowering and Raising the Portcullis

Although we had originally met in Jan's school classroom we began our formal collaboration in the castle of the university where Jan was the outsider. It is highly likely, however, that as Somekh suggests, the school "castle" from which Jan had come had "just as many turrets, secret passages and grassy courtyards, (and was) as well defended by moat and portcullis . . . as the castle of the academy" (Somekh 1994, 1). In medieval times an iron grating (portcullis) which hung over the gateway of a castle was lowered between grooves to prevent the passage of any possible invaders. In contemporary schools and universities it could be argued that a metaphoric portcullis is lowered and raised to control the entry of possible invading ideas which threaten not lives, but the traditions and cultures of those institutions. Unlike the knights of old we cannot be easily identified by the colors of our banners. Nonetheless, in our exchanges with one another, university teachers and school teachers often proudly display the "colors" of our "castles" using verbal "banners" such as "theory" (i.e., ivory tower) and "practice" (i.e., the real world).

In our early conversations it was clear that each was proud of who she was and of the castle she defended. It would take time for us to learn to appreciate each other's perspective. We probably made a good beginning during our first recorded conversation by stating our positions as honestly (some might say bluntly!) as we could:

> You're in a very funny position, Jan, because you're not a professor, and you'll never be accepted as a professor . . . I must say I have a problem with that. I don't mean to be cold, but you know, I spent five years doing a Ph.D. To come here I had to go through a whole day of interviews. I've got to publish or I'm not going to get tenure. There are so many rules and conditions for me and for anybody who is a professor here, that a phone call from a department head doesn't make you a professor. It's not that I don't appreciate you as a person. It's just that I don't think of you as a professor. (October 2, 1992)

Two years later, as we attempted to make sense of that early conversation we looked back at what Helen had said that day. The honesty with one another, a key element in our collaboration, has continued.

Jan: That first year, when we were meeting on a regular basis, exchanging journals and so on, you made it clear to me on numerous, numerous occasions that there was a difference in our levels. I didn't take it personally because I didn't feel you were annoyed with me as a person [but rather that] you were annoyed at the way this whole thing [secondment] came about. I just came sailing in here and had a nice little office without going through the . . .

Helen: Sweat equity (i.e., the university hiring process).

Jan: Exactly. And that wasn't breaking down the barriers. That was putting up barriers. I didn't take it personally because I didn't have any illusions about who I was, and where I fit in here. I like the fact that I was brought in here to teach. I don't have all of the other things that you have to deal with. I feel like I can concentrate on the teaching part and not have to worry about anything else. (August 22, 1994)

Jan, on the other hand, made it very clear early in our relationship where she stood with regard to theory, expressing what many believe is a practical view of the role of theory in teacher education:

I'm not academically inclined and theories more or less leave me cold. I'm interested in theory and I like to know what it is, but only because I want to see how it applies practically in the classroom. (October 2, 1992)

When Jan reflected upon what she had said that day she saw her reluctance to discuss theory in a different light—linked more to her lack of theoretical background than to a lack of interest in theory per se.

Part of the reason I felt so uncomfortable always getting into the talk about theory/practice was because I knew I didn't have the theoretical background. I didn't want to shortchange the students because I didn't have the educational background to provide what they needed. (August 22, 1994)

When Jan started teaching at the university, she was quite determined to get the students to "start making the connections between what they were doing in class and what was happening in the school classroom," even though she remembers being "worried about [her] lack of theoretical background and being afraid someone was going to ask [her] a question [she] couldn't answer." Helen, on the other hand, had noticed right from the start that the students were eager to hear what Jan, with her more recent school experience, had to say.

> **Helen:** I've always felt that I really know my content, but when we started teaching together, and people found out where you were from, they just ignored me and listened to you.
>
> **Jan:** Do you really think so?
>
> **Helen:** Sure, I do. If you're going to be a teacher, you're in a tough job market and "everybody knows you don't learn anything in university". So who better to listen to than a teacher? Whatever I know is considered to be more or less irrelevant anyway. Who am I, after all? Just some "theoretician." (August 22, 1994)

When we looked back at these conversations we saw at the end of nearly three years each had moved toward the other's earlier positions. While we are both still in the "castle of the academy" (Somekh 1994, 1), we are beginning to move freely (at least in a figurative sense) between our two castles. Each has come to understand and to trust the other.

The Ambivalence of Secondment

Our collaborative self-study of teaching began in the first year of Jan's secondment at the university. We gradually developed a relationship of trust as we planned, taught our courses, and reflected on both the collaborative process and what we were learning about ourselves as teachers and teacher educators. That first year, Jan, who was used to "knowing her parameters and working within them," often found her situation at the university to be rather ambivalent. As a seconded teacher she was on loan from her school board. This meant she did not have official status as a faculty member although her teaching and supervisory responsibilities were similar to those of her new colleagues. In the school system Jan had been considered a senior colleague. At the university she felt like an outsider "on the edge, sort of looking in." Jan could not help but think there was a "lot going on between the lines"—a lot she was unaware of because she was not a faculty member. She wished her role was "more clearly defined" as most of the time she had "no idea what, if anything" was expected of her.

Whereas Helen was happy to have found a colleague with whom she could plan her classes and conduct research, she too found the ambivalence of secondment difficult at times particularly with regard to her obligation to publish. Sometimes, she felt she was being unfair to Jan for, after all, the latter was not under the same obligation. Under such conditions was it possible to engage in collaborative inquiry? What, if anything, was Jan getting out of this?

From time to time, the ambivalence of Jan's role affected the way in which we worked together. Early on, for instance, we wondered about how our students perceived us as teachers and teacher educators. It will be recalled that Helen believed Jan had more credibility with the students because she was "fresh" from the school classroom. Jan did not share this point of view. As a matter of fact, during the whole of her first year on campus Jan continued to struggle with her perception of the role of university professor. As she told Helen one day:

> It's funny that you were under the impression that people listened to what I had to say because I was a recent classroom teacher. I felt just the opposite. I didn't think anybody wanted to hear about what happened in my little classroom. That first year, I purposely didn't talk too much about my own classroom and share much with the students. I remember, though, that towards the end of the year, in elementary language arts, I brought in some slides that I had of the writers' workshop in my classroom. That turned out to be the class in which they had the most questions. I realized, then, that they did want to hear about my classroom experience. It took me the whole first year to realize that the students wanted to hear about what I had done. I had thought that because I was just a classroom teacher, and not a "real prof," I would be less credible in their eyes. (August 22, 1994)

Although our university, like many others, has had teachers in seconded positions for quite some time there is no policy describing how these people are to be integrated into the life of the faculty. Often this places individuals in awkward situations, such as the one recently when a special faculty meeting was called at the request of a subject area chairperson. As the purpose of the meeting was to reexamine an earlier decision on a controversial matter, considered by some to be at the heart of our teacher education program, the room was packed with people on both sides of the issue. This included a number of seconded teachers. As it turned out, however, only faculty members could vote. Yet, among the disenfranchised were instructors who would have to live with the consequences of the faculty decision.

Some might consider it ironic that a few of those instructors, such as Jan herself, had already been with the faculty longer than some faculty members. What does this type of situation mean in terms of the unfolding story of a faculty of education? What is the contribution to that story of a seconded teacher who works there "temporarily" for many years? What is the role of a seconded teacher at the university? Is it "just" to teach? If so, what does that mean? We do not have any answers to these questions. Nevertheless, as time goes on and we work more and more closely together it is with the knowledge that one of these years Jan will leave. On the one hand, this would be an exciting turn of events because of the potential for moving our inquiry into teaching into Jan's school classroom. On the other hand, it will bring new challenges for Jan because as the years go by it is highly likely that she has become identified with the faculty of education. Indeed, one day this past year, after a presentation on evaluation by a former school colleague invited for the occasion, Jan's students commented on the value of having someone in from the school system—someone who knows what is going on. At that point, it became clear to Jan that students do not necessarily consider her a school-based practitioner. The ambivalence of secondment continues.

The "Middle Ground" as a "Collaborative Space"

In an earlier chapter, Margaret Olson describes the "middle ground" (cf., Clandinin, Davies, Hogan, and Kennard 1993) as a "collaborative space . . . [that] develops in relationships built with others over time." As we collaborated in teaching our classes we developed trust on both a professional and a personal level. This did not happen overnight. As a matter of fact, it might not have happened at all had we not decided to collaborate as teachers, where "everybody's on a level playing field" as Jan said recently (August 22, 1994). Teaching together and talking about our teaching allowed us to encounter one another in a nonhierarchical space, a "middle ground," where we could "construct meaning through collaborative conversation" (Olson, this volume).

When we were planning and teaching our classes neither of us had time to be concerned with who was the professor and who the seconded teacher. In the complexity of the teaching situation it really didn't matter. As a matter of fact, in the university classroom, Jan was probably more credible than Helen in the eyes of the students. We believed each was making a contribution to the other's professional development. We often observed one another teaching, discussed our observations and reflected upon them. Whatever the focus of the conversations, there was opportunity for personal growth for both as can be seen from the following excerpts, typical of our honesty with one another and the ways we have come to discuss our teaching:

> **Jan:** Have you ever considered that your level of thinking and understanding is so much higher than that of the students?
>
> **Helen:** Yes.
>
> **Jan:** The feeling that I have when I see you talking to a group is that at this level [indicates with her hand] it's clear, and it's obvious, and it can be followed. But at another level, it's not. It would be hard to come down.
>
> **Helen:** It is. And yet, part of me has a problem with all of this. I find it hard to accept that people get to third year university, and have never been given the opportunity to think about some of these things which are fundamental. Is that the teacher's lament? You know, the old "didn't anybody teach these students anything before I got them?"
>
> **Jan:** Yes, it is.
>
> **Helen:** And that's a contradiction. I'm always saying that you do what you can with what you get. Yet I'm not doing it in my teaching. (October 9, 1992)

On occasion we conducted formal observations of one another, taking data on whatever it was we were working on as part of our ongoing professional development as classroom practitioners. When it was Helen's turn to observe, Jan was surprised to find she was a little apprehensive about having Helen observe her teaching.

> **Jan:** I was a little bit nervous when you were observing during the seminar last Friday. And I found it kind of strange,

because in the last few years in immersion I've had people in and out of my room all of the time and it has never really bothered me. But now I find myself in a new situation. I knew you were doing what I asked you to do [i.e., take notes on student participation in the discussion], but at the same time I just felt there was somebody at the back of the room keeping an eye on me. I found myself saying to myself, I wonder if everyone around me knows how incompetent I am? So that was the case I guess. I was afraid of exposing my incompetence.

Helen: I'm always afraid of exposing my incompetence. But that's funny anyway, because I WAS judging you. I was sitting at the back of the room saying, Wow, is her French ever good! Is Jan ever together! Damn! Why isn't my French that good? Why can't I be that together?

Jan: I never in a million years would have dreamed that you would be having these positive thoughts.

Helen: I don't know how positive they actually were. I do know that I was doing a number on myself. (October 16, 1992)

As we looked back on our early conversations about Jan's teaching we wondered if Jan had been nervous because the teaching and observing had taken place in a university classroom. Would Jan have felt as uncomfortable if Helen had observed her teaching in her own school classroom? On the other hand, would Helen have found herself in an awkward situation if she had been the one teaching in a school classroom? We concluded that each of us probably feels more comfortable in her own castle, i.e., the classroom of her own institution.

Threads and Possibilities

In an earlier chapter Helen Stewart reminds us that in a collaborative undertaking trust emerges as a central constructive factor. We certainly found this to be true in our case. Like Stewart, and Clandinin (1993) we have seen that our research relationship was "founded within conversations"—oral and written. One such conversation took place at the end of the first phase of our ongoing collaborative adventure. For some time we had been working on preparation of a document based on our transcriptions and journal writing of that first year. When we finished each wrote a personal letter to the other which we exchanged. Neither had yet seen what the other had written. As we read them we were profoundly touched by the mutual mentorship and caring relationship that had emerged. The following excerpts testify to this, and to the success of our collaborative work in the middle ground of shared pedagogical space:

Helen to Jan: When I asked you if you wanted to be involved in a collaborative research project which had teaching as the focus of our inquiry, I imagined us in long philosophical discussions about the meaning of teaching. What did we actually talk about? Stuff that all teachers talk about, I imagine— classroom and student-related matters. We did something very worthwhile in asking our students to videotape themselves working in school classrooms. The sessions in which we worked with them in small groups were wonderful. I felt like a "real" teacher!

As both of us know, I had a rough fall term. I am still licking my wounds. What would I have done without you? My weekly updates on how I was faring really cut into our "philosophy time." Thank you for listening.

I am excited about what our collaboration has led to. Most of all I am happy to have found through this experience a colleague and a friend.

Jan to Helen: My personal growth in relation to this project has been enormous. You did more than ease me into my new situation. You exposed me to an exciting world of research, reading, and reflection. I feel like I've taken a graduate class without having paid any fees. I've always considered myself a reflective teacher but now I realize I was reflecting in a vacuum; there was no connection to meaningful context. Our collaboration motivated me to begin an exploration of narrative inquiry as a form of research.

As a teacher, I have always valued collaborative work. On the rare occasions when I was able to enter into a collaborative venture with a colleague, I have benefitted greatly, both on a professional and a personal level. This experience was no exception. It has reaffirmed my belief in the need to organize a teacher's timetable in order to accommodate collaborative efforts. The benefits would resonate throughout the system— from top to bottom.

Bridget Somekh (1994) suggests that "to inhabit each other's castles" means that "change for each individual in the partnership arises from understanding that in collaboration both contributing and learning become a single process" (p. 6). Each of us has changed as a result of this experience—Jan has become more aware of herself as a theoretician; Helen, has become more skilled as a practitioner. In our collaborative partnership each has contributed to, and learned from, the other. We have begun to imagine other possibilities in the castle of the school, as this excerpt from a recent conversation illustrates:

> **Helen:** Think back to when you were teaching. Suppose that I, or some other professor arrived at your school for a year on secondment. How would you feel about that?
>
> **Jan:** That would probably be wonderful.
>
> **Helen:** Why?
>
> **Jan:** You would have a colleague who was probably more up to date on all the recent research—who'd been reading far more than any of the teachers. I would suspect that a person who chose to go back to the classroom would be going back to try new things out. That would probably be the main reason for going back. It's nice to sit and read about all the new ways of doing things, but maybe you want to go back and try them out and see how they would work. I think that would be quite exciting. I would also suspect that the person would want to engage his or her colleagues in discussion, so that there would be some chance to learn from each other, and that would probably be beneficial to the staff as a whole.
>
> **Helen:** How do you think the staff members would feel if they had one teacher who was more equal than all of the others?
>
> **Jan:** But that person wouldn't be considered more equal because when you get into the classroom everybody's on the same playing field. In fact, the teachers would probably feel that they had an advantage because they were in the classroom the year before, whereas the professor probably wouldn't have been in a classroom for a few years. They would probably watch and see how this person managed, coming from the ivory tower down to the classroom. (August 22, 1994)

Toward the Improvement of Teacher Education

In this chapter we examined collaboration from the perspective of an ongoing relationship as partners in pre-service teacher education. Our experience points to both possibilities and pitfalls for school-based and university-based educators. On the one hand, collaborative undertakings that give partners opportunities to come together as teachers in either school or university classrooms open up new possibilities for the improvement of teacher education. Secondment would seem to be an ideal vehicle for such endeavors. Experienced teachers have been seconded to faculties of education. Occasionally, faculty of education professors have taught in school classrooms. Perhaps more formal arrangements need to be made where professors are routinely seconded to schools to conduct research—but also to teach and to become part of the life of the school. On the other hand, the parameters of secondment need to be more clearly established so individuals do not find themselves in situations of ambivalence. Furthermore, there may need to be a time limit for secondment. After all, it should not become what amounts to a permanent or semipermanent transfer. Finally, through collaborative partnerships we can learn to inhabit one another's castles and, in so doing, provide mutual support. Honesty in our relationships should enable us to move forward in authentic collaborative experiences. Such authentic collaboration among practitioners in the two castles would lead to creation of new knowledge about teaching and, in turn, to improvement of teacher education.

✧ Chapter Twelve

Creating Reciprocal Relationships in Language Arts and Science: A Collaborative Exploration of Subject Area Integration

Sandra Blenkinsop and Penelope Bailey

For a university classroom, the noise was astonishing. Students huddled around tables laden with beakers, scales, water, task cards, role cards, books, documents and pencils. They poured water, weighed, measured, argued, questioned, observed, predicted, gave advice, read aloud, wrote, crossed out, spied on other groups, fudged results, and searched through articles, papers, and handouts. The students planned and conducted tests on competing brands of products. They role-played scientists working for competing companies, for consumer groups, or for environmental groups. They prepared and presented reports for company directors and for subscribers to newspapers and environmental newsletters.

These middle years, teacher education students were participating in a workshop designed to provide a hands-on experience with the integration of language arts and science. This workshop was the outcome of a two-year collaborative inquiry into the integration of language arts and science methods courses in a teacher education program. Over the course of the collaboration, as we struggled to model integration for our students, our own understandings about the concept of integration evolved and deepened.

We embarked upon our collaborative inquiry shortly after a meeting at the beginning of the academic year in which instructors of methods classes for middle years education students discussed course outlines, assignments, and student work load. At the time, Sandra was teaching a language arts methods course and Penny was teaching a science methods course to a common group of students. Even though we were strangers at the time, the few words we shared at that first meeting ignited a spark and our collaborative journey had begun. We initially sought to integrate course assignments to help reach a program objective—reducing student workload. As our collaboration continued, however, we sought more fundamental integration of our subject areas. We explored the philosophical links between our courses and discovered ways in which the content of one subject area could be addressed in conjunction with the other.

We were motivated by strong personal interests in each other's subject areas and by our mutual belief in the educative value of the integration of subject areas. We were especially interested in the concept of integration because the textbooks and local curriculum guides we were using in our courses (Carin 1993; Irvin 1990; Saskatchewan Education 1993; Thompkins and McGee 1993) advocated this practice. Additionally, we wanted to "borrow" motivation from each other's subject area. We recognized, however, that most of our students lacked prior experience with integration, and curriculum guides and textbooks could not be expected to provide adequate background knowledge to support our students' use of integrated experiences in their school practicum placements. Our students needed to have integrated subject area learning experiences to achieve a real understanding of what is meant by integration. The struggle to provide our students with that understanding provided the impetus to our collaborative planning and teaching over the course of our study.

Methods

The design and process of our collaborative inquiry was informed by several research perspectives. Because we intended to engage in a self-reflective inquiry aimed at deepening understandings of our own teaching practice, we used action research (Carr and Kemmis 1986; Elliott 1991; Kemmis and McTaggart 1988) as the methodological framework for our study. Within this framework, we explored the evolution of our personal practical knowledge (Clandinin 1986; Connelly and Clandinin 1988; Connelly and Clandinin 1990). Reflective letters written to each other along with agendas and meeting transcripts constituted a written account that chronicled and contextualized our inquiry. Informed by our experience, and inspired by the work of Aoki (1991, 1993), we noted the ways in which the ongoing dialectic we had created between our subject areas transformed our understanding of integration. To describe our common thoughts and experiences in this chapter, we have used the pronoun "we." To present our individual thoughts, we have constructed narratives that capture the essence of lengthy, free-ranging discussions. In these we have used the pronoun "I."

Beginning Steps

In the weeks preceding our first attempt to integrate our science and language arts methods courses we had many things to learn about each other's courses. In the early days of our ongoing dialogue each of us described the general perspectives in which our courses were grounded:

> **Sandra:** In my language arts course, I approach the teaching of reading and writing from a holistic perspective in which literacy is understood as a socially constructed practice. I emphasize the importance of experience. I believe that teachers should give children a multitude of authentic opportunities to read and write in which reading and writing are used to explore and respond to real topics as opposed to opportunities in which reading and writing are done for the sole purpose of learning to read and write.
>
> **Penny:** My ideal of science teaching is to facilitate children's active engagement in inquiry activities. This approach to science

instruction is experiential. Learners' engagement is authentic in that they are employing scientific processes such as observing and measuring to address their own questions relating to a particular topic. I want to help my students to feel confident enough in their knowledge of science and pedagogy to attempt this type of science teaching in their own classrooms.

In the course of our dialogue we realized how eminently compatible a holistic view of language arts was with an inquiry view of science. Both of these views are characterized by their emphasis on the importance of experience and their insistence that the experience be authentic and meaningful.

As our collaboration progressed, we revealed our individual understandings about what form integration of our methods courses might take:

Sandra: I see integration of language arts and inquiry science as the incorporation of reading and writing into science activities. Science could provide the content focus and reading and writing could serve as tools for recording and reporting. As far as our methods classes are concerned, some of the content and activities from the science methods course can be dealt with in the language arts course and vice versa.

Penny: The hands-on, science inquiry activities in which the students participate could provide the context for meaningful reading and writing. I like the idea of using the science activity package from my class as the starting point for students' planning of related reading and writing experiences. I would like to experiment with using reading and writing to help students to investigate their science questions more fully and to ask new questions as part of a cycle of inquiry.

As we learned more about the key concepts, processes, and activities at the heart of each other's courses our teaching began to change. Each of us presented the concept of integration in our separate classes. We did this by referring to content, processes, and activities that were being presented in each other's classes. Additionally, Sandra asked students to prepare reading and writing extensions for the science activity packages required in Penny's course, and she gave them the option of preparing an integrated science-language arts unit plan instead of a literature-based unit plan.

At the end of the semester we observed that the reading and writing activities the students had developed as extensions to their science activities were merely afterthoughts that didn't promote further inquiry. We also observed that none of the students had taken advantage of the option to develop an integrated science-language arts unit. Overall, we wondered how much our students had really learned about planning for integration. We felt, however, that we had gained new understandings about what it meant to integrate subject areas in a teacher education program.

> **Sandra:** I now see a problem with our attempt to model integration for our students. I realize that what we presented was an example of the integration of methods course content in a teacher education program. What our students needed to see was the integration of reading, writing and science as it would appear in a middle years classroom.
>
> **Penny:** The concept of integration in teacher education is a lot more complex than I had originally thought. To our students we were still dealing with integration at the level of abstract knowledge. In effect we conveyed the message "Do what we say," rather than "Do what we do." We didn't actually get together and show them how it would work.

In planning and teaching our first integrative component we had presented an example of integration of the content and requirements of university courses. In retrospect, we realized that an example of integration of science and language arts activities suitable for a middle years classroom would be more likely to provide the type of background experience our students needed in order to plan and teach in an integrated fashion in their practicum placements. At this point the focus of our inquiry shifted to the development of hands-on experiences.

The Integrative Workshop

Inspired by the professional satisfaction we felt working together and our ongoing questions about integration, we embarked upon the next phase of our collaboration. We made time as instructors to meet and plan an integrative component for the middle years courses we would teach the following year. We agreed that the appropriate relationship between science, reading, and writing would be for science to provide the primary content focus, and reading and writing would be relegated to an instrumental, secondary role. Our shared belief in the value of experiential learning prompted us to choose a workshop format as the vehicle through which we would involve students in integrative experiences. We engaged in lengthy discussions about the topic focus of the workshop, types of science activities to include, and forms of print appropriate to those activities. We decided to focus on the topic "Consumer Product Testing" found in the middle years science curriculum guide (Saskatchewan Education 1993). This unit suggests that students perform scientific tests to compare different brands of the same type of product. For the purpose of our workshop we decided to use disposable diapers as the product to be tested.

In keeping with the spirit of inquiry science, we decided to provide appropriate science equipment and suggest that students devise and carry out tests on two brands of disposable diapers after which they would compare the results. We reasoned that through these activities the students would naturally engage in authentic science processes such as hypothesizing, experimenting, measuring, and observing. We decided that the only requirement related to language arts would be: whatever they wrote should be appropriate for their communicative purpose, and it should enhance the inquiry and decision making process. To support the students in recalling and constructing various forms of print typically used to record and report scientific information we decided to place samples of writing—lists, charts, graphs and diagrams—at each work station.

At the last minute the element of role-playing was added to the workshop. The roles were intended to provide purposes for writing other than having reporting and recording as ends in themselves. The roles were also intended to provide a meaningful social context within which science and language arts activities would take place. The roles required that the students act as teams of scientists working for and reporting to different employers such as diaper companies, consumer product testing organizations, and environmental groups.

Throughout the planning of the workshop we wrestled with the issue of time. Both of us found it very difficult to find room for the workshop in our already overloaded course outlines. We also found it difficult to resolve other time related questions such as:

Whose class time should be used for the workshop? How long should each of us speak? How long should students spend on science activities and on literacy activities? We realized that the time apportioned to each subject area reflected its relative emphasis in the workshop. Because science was the major focus of the workshop we agreed to present the workshop in the science lab period. Science activities would occupy a greater share of the time.

Once the workshop was planned, we field-tested it with inservice teachers. Feedback from participants convinced us that our integrative workshop would indeed provide the type of practical experience we intended to offer our students. It also demonstrated the need to supply additional print materials such as the original diaper packaging, magazine articles, advertisements, and books so that students could see different types of writing conventionally used for specific purposes and audiences. In addition, participant feedback prompted us to develop individual frames for the workshop which we would present separately in our own class periods to introduce and close the workshop. The preceding parts of these frames would feature Sandra showing examples of specific types of reading and writing that could be incorporated prior to, during, or following science activities, and Penny exploring different types of inquiry teaching ranging along a continuum from less to more teacher-centered. The closing parts of these frames would include discussion of science and language arts activities the students would have participated in during the workshop.

When we finally presented the workshop to our middle years students we were delighted with their response. The vignette used to introduce this chapter is a snapshot of what we observed as the students went about their inquiries. We could see that the written records of their inquiries and the reports they shared led to discussions and arguments in which scientific processes and findings were compared and questioned:

Penny: The workshop accomplished what we had intended. The reading and writing that the students did clearly fed into the inquiry science cycle. Discussion based on the students' written work provided motivation that could lead to further experimentation, replication or reading.

We could see that writing had played a key role in determining the course of the post inquiry activities. Written records provided a permanent document that could be used as a reference for comparison of results. This, in turn, stimulated discussion from which new avenues of interest and inquiry emerged. We could see that the use of writing in the workshop had the power to transform post inquiry discussions from vaguely recalled memories of findings to written records that could be referred to, revisited, and challenged. It was clear that the integration of science and writing activities in the workshop had strong potential to prompt students to further science inquiry and further reading and writing.

When we planned the workshop, little did we know the power role-playing would exert in shaping students' behavior. We were surprised by the strength of motivation the roles engendered. We were absolutely astonished at the unethical practices they unleashed:

Penny: I was alarmed when I saw that some students were deliberately "fudging" data in order to present a more convincing case for the product they were representing to their audience . I was also alarmed when I observed others engaged in a form of industrial espionage in which they "borrowed" experimental procedures and results from peers role-playing scientists from rival companies. I felt that the role-playing element had overshadowed the integrity of the inquiry science process. Accuracy of measurement, the imperative of replicability, and honesty in reporting results had, in some instances, been set aside.

As we reflected upon the influence role-playing had on the workshop activities we realized that by situating science activities within simulated contexts we unleashed the same types of motivations and temptations that influence those who play similar roles in the real world. At first we were disappointed at the behavior of some of the students. As the workshop progressed we began to see that the different types of unacceptable behavior had potential to spark further science and literacy activity. Disclosure of unscientific procedures could be used to prompt extensive reading and writing as students explored current ethical issues in science. Revelation of unscientific and unethical practices had potential to raise questions about bias, accuracy, and honesty in consumer advertising. The interest and outrage generated could easily be transformed into a unit of study that would necessitate extensive engagement in critical reading. At this point, we had a much richer, deeper understanding of integration. We could see powerful forces had been generated by adding social purpose to the science-language arts integration. We could see that by adding a new layer of integration we had intensified the impetus for further inquiry, and we had opened many new avenues of interest.

As we reflected upon the ways in which students engaged in reading and writing during the workshop we observed other unanticipated activities. From the outset of the inquiry we had taken for granted that the students would automatically know how to do the recording and reporting required in the workshop. Our observations, however, showed this was not entirely true:

> **Sandra:** As I watched the students during the workshop, it was apparent that not only were the students engaged in science inquiries, they were also engaged in inquiries about written language. Their use of references such as the consumer magazines and the sample charts and graphs showed that they were, in fact, inquiring into which types of writing were appropriate to convey their particular findings to the particular audience they would be reporting to.

As the students wrote to record and report on their inquiries they constructed forms of written language heretofore unknown to them, and developed new variations of previously known forms. The realization that students had been engaged in learning to write as well as in learning to do science made us reconsider the relationship between science and language arts in the workshop. In exploring the relationship between language arts and science we recalled that early in our collaboration we had agreed science would be the major focus of the workshop and reading and writing would play a secondary, instrumental role. This agreement had been based on the unexamined assumption that because university students are highly literate they would automatically be able to do the type of writing required in the workshop. We now realized by integrating science and language we had asked the students to engage in unfamiliar activities and roles, and hence in new forms of writing. This, in turn, meant that writing became a substantive focus of learning as well as playing an instrumental role.

New Understandings

Overall, our lived experience of integration was much richer than we had originally anticipated. We had started out seeing the integrative relationship between science and language arts as an unequal one: science provided the motivation and substance; reading and writing provided instruments through which students recorded results and reported on their inquires. In the end we could see that our integrative workshop had created a more equal relationship between science and language arts than we had envisioned. We now recognized that science and language arts each played both substantive and instrumental roles.

We have found our collaborative inquiry into integration both fascinating and enlightening. It allowed us to take a currently popular idea in the professional literature and explore it from the perspective of a lived experience. Over the course of our collaboration we created a dialectic between our abstract knowledge about integration and our unfolding experience with it. As our attention flowed back and forth from one subject area to the other we created a curricular space. Within this common space we constructed authentic science and language arts activities that became integrated through the evolution of natural, functional relationships. Through this collaborative experience our early understandings about integration transformed our external experience which, in turn, reshaped what integration meant to us. We had started out with understandings about integration that were bounded by our reading and were essentially academic and abstract. After our collaborative journey into integration we had an elaborated vision of integration-in-action and of the supportive, reciprocal relationship that enhanced learning and motivation in both science and language arts.

✧ Chapter Thirteen

Mentoring as Collaboration: Shaping an Academic Life

Karne Kozolanka and Bert Horwood

Introduction

Traditional views of the mentor-mentee relationship have their roots in the dialectic described in the Odyssey where the role is defined by Mentor, the friend of Odysseus who is entrusted with the care of Telemachus, Odysseus' son. Mentor provides the guidance one associates with wise counsel to the young and inexperienced. This quasi-parental relationship may be described as pedagogical—one where an adult's agenda includes the task of initiating a young person into adulthood. But in current times there is another mentorlike relationship, an andragogic one between adults where the task is to teach people who already have adult status. It becomes relevant to wonder whether a notion rooted in classical antiquity for the education of children is applicable to processes in use today for educating adults.

Yonge (1985) uses the term "accompaniment" to describe the relationship between teacher and pupil, mentor and protegé. The term appeals because it emphasizes the collaborative nature of the exchanges between the parties. Yonge also distinguishes between the forms of pedagogic and andragogic accompaniment in terms of differences between children and adults with respect to position in the community, obligations, social context, responsibility and authority.

> When the pedagogic and the andragogic are viewed as two modes of human accompaniment, the critical differences between them become clear. The pedagogic involves an adult accompanying a child so the latter may eventually become an adult. The andragogic involves an adult accompanying another adult to a more refined, enriched adulthood. Thus, there is a difference in the participants and in the aims. Both agogic events involve a relationship of authority, but Pedagogic authority rests on a different base and is of a different character than Andragogic authority. (Yonge 1985, 166)

This chapter will describe and interpret aspects of the mentoring process between one of us as graduate student, and the other as academic advisor. Our recorded conversations provide the texts from which we construe Yonge's notion of accompaniment as collaborative action—what it means for an established and a beginning academic to have a mentor-protegé relationship. For a beginning academic in graduate school, regular collaboration and reflection with a professor was an important part of acculturation. And now, continuing the apprenticeship in a first year of university teaching, the former student and former advisor collaborate in new ways to interpret and report on the recorded conversations between them. In addition, this research also allows us to reconsider Yonge's distinction between pedagogic and andragogic accompaniment.

Context

The conferences between us were tape recorded during Karne's first year in graduate school. Later, the tapes were transcribed and studied with a view to finding out how the conferences worked to initiate Karne into academic life and work. The conference records were treated as texts for hermeneutic experimentation by both parties. Two conversations were selected as exemplary because: (a) they deal with common issues that graduate students struggle with and (b) because they reveal how Karne's status matures from an early collaborative conversation to a later one. These two conversations serve us in the same way that one or two pottery shards serve an archeologist. The selected shards represent a much larger body of data used to interpret a culture.

Van Manen describes hermeneutic experimentation as the study of essences, "the systematic attempt to uncover and describe the structures, the internal meaning structures, of lived experience" (1990, 10). For example, when Bert responded to questions and statements he was letting Karne know what it was like to live the life of an academic collaborating with a graduate student. The essence of such a relationship is hidden in the discourse. How then to discover the essence? Van Manen is helpful when he suggests: "The textual approach one takes in the phenomenological study should largely be decided in terms of the nature of the phenomenon being addressed, and the investigative method that appears appropriate to it" (p. 173). The weekly conversations between us were characterized by storytelling. Accordingly, this account of what it means to live the life of a beginning academic learning the ropes from an old hand employs a process of reconstructing stories in an attempt to unearth the essences buried there.

This process of collaboration and acculturation can be understood as well through the situated learning research of Lave and Wenger (1991) and their socially distributed view of learning and development. Lave and Wenger describe how adult newcomers are legitimate peripheral participants who engage simultaneously in a number of roles in a community of practice. Lave and Wenger's research is helpful because it sheds some light on the interactive nature of role development. Their research enables us to infer, from our text analysis, aspects of Karne's development as a legitimate peripheral participant in this community of practice. Lave and Wenger also help us to view Bert as one who has certain tools rather than straight answers to questions within this community of practice. We use Lave and Wenger to help understand the benefits gained from these conversations.

Two Conversations

The first conversation appears to deal with Karne's attempt to make sense out of different orientations to curriculum but, as we will show, it has other important content. The second conversation is stimulated by Karne's puzzlement about the nature of research questions and how they are formulated. Each account opens with a summary of the conversation with key words or phrases emphasized in italics.

The Conversation About Curriculum Orientation

In this conversation Bert is responding to Karne's query about making sense of the many theoretical, conceptual, and philosophical perspectives that abound in the field of curriculum studies. In particular, Karne mentions a paper Bert handed out the previous semester in which the writer described three orientations to curriculum: atomism, pragmatism, and holism (Miller 1988). Bert makes the point that there are many *isms that one can get bogged down in* when attempting to understand these different viewpoints.

Bert begins his response by describing the approaches of two botanists who classify species of poison ivy differently. One classifies poison ivy in fourteen species while the other uses only one species category with numerous variations. The former author is described by Bert as a *splitter*, one who breaks things down, the latter is described as a *lumper*, one who pulls things together. Bert uses this story to show that each botanist has his own *intellectual value system* in classification. His point is, while either method may be useful in recognizing poison ivy, it is easy to get bogged down in the *isms* of botany. The same holds true for the "isms" associated with orientations to curriculum.

Bert uses this analogy as a stepping off point to explain the relationship of *atomism* and *holism* in education. He explains that the forces of atomistic and mechanistic thinking permeate curricular thinking, and how we are all *embedded and grounded in an atomistic world view*, raised to believe that to understand something it had to be broken down to simpler and more fundamental elements. But there is more to understanding phenomena than through *classical positivism* which he says is *running its course*, having done what it can do. Bert is saying here that major changes are underway in how one understands the mysteries of professional practice. He is suggesting that the dominant discourse in education is completing its preeminence. Bert makes a pun and calls the contrary position not negativism but constructivism, a synthetical process that differs from the analytical processes used by positivists. Bert describes atomism as a *destructive research method*, destructive in the sense that one breaks the thing down or reduces something into its parts in order to understand it. This runs counter to the other view that says an organism is more than the sum of its processes. Bert uses the example of a newly killed frog in the physiology lab that still has a number of its components functioning—*brain works, heart beating, blood flowing, muscles twitching, et cetera.* Yet, the frog is dead. Bert says it's *the integrity of the whole that makes the frog a frog.* This integrity of the whole is described by Bert in the term *elan vitale* or vital force—the synergistic notion that the whole is greater than the sum of the parts.

Bert explains part of the difficulty in making a shift from positivism to constructivism by describing how we *don't totally abandon analysis because of our scientific and technical training.* He illustrates this with a description of his own research in which he observes how people integrate curriculum. For example, still engrained is the perspective he has held in the past—a teacher's expertise or disciplines approach. The other approach, which he values more now, has nothing to do with the subject matter but has more to do with *what it means to be human living in the world.* Bert seems to be saying here that both views provide a legitimate base for curricular thinking. Both are now part of his background and come with him to his research. The former is grounded in an analytic tradition and the latter in a more synthetic or synergistic one.

Bert continues by citing Waldorf Education and the Experiential Education movement which put their *images of humanity* as the main factor in forming a view of curriculum thinking. Bert is outlining what he means by *holism,* equating it almost with a kind of enlightened humanism. This differs from the next example in which he describes a totally different view, one that he equates with Plato's Republic which sets out *a recipe, a curriculum for meeting the needs of the ideal state.* Finally, he likens this to Huxley's *Brave New World* with its predetermined instrumental societal roles and compares both with Dewey's vision of *pragmatism* and the scientific method. Bert returns to Karne's original question and finishes his explanation by saying that the shift in moving from an atomistic view to a holistic one involves *more than simply shuffling the cards.* Bert is saying there is a quality which is lost when one breaks something up or simply rearranges things in order to see them in a different light. This quality has something to do with wholeness.

In stepping back from the discussion to examine the conversation between Karne and Bert, we see that the importance of this interaction is not so much in its content but in the nature of the interaction that is characteristic of others throughout the transcripts. While some attention is paid to the content of the interaction, in this case a discussion of curricular orientations, more attention is paid to moving toward an understanding of substance and essence rather than form. For example, form in the presence of educational *isms* is flagged as a potential quagmire to become *bogged down in*. The emphasis in this conversation seems to be movement toward an understanding of essence—what the vital forces are. These vital forces are grounded in the shifting politic of orientations to curriculum and education research which Bert emphasizes with anecdote, analogy and example.

Bert is calling Karne to a view of academe and teaching that says there are moral considerations when one chooses to embrace a particular technique, in this instance an orientation to curriculum. This conversation is about the development of one's intellectual values and is connected to the notion of wholeness—phenomena such as discussions of curriculum, may have transcendent or spiritual dimensions as well as temporal ones.

The pattern seems to be one of simple query based on puzzlement on the part of Karne, a response from Bert that involves analogy or metaphor, and an explanation of issues followed by references to literature and work within the awareness of both. Bert's responses are framed in terms of his own work and research into a high school integrated curriculum. He refers to the relative appropriateness of one approach over another in his research. Bert makes it clear that we eventually need to be certain where we stand with respect to "isms," as it is quite easy to be in a number of different camps. This is an important consideration in academe, for the discourse is complex and establishing one's credibility and position is connected to being situated within a certain epistemological stance that needs to be explicit. This serves another purpose too: it pulls Karne closer to witnessing Bert's reconstruction of his own curriculum practice. In doing so, Karne is learning the ropes of ethnomethodological research. In this instance understanding a macro view is important for his development as a potential academic. This broader view also relates to other more specific issues experienced by Karne. It is to one of these that we now turn.

The Conversation About Research Questions

This conversation begins with Karne expressing his puzzlement over the nature of research questions and how they are formulated. This is a common exercise for graduate students in the beginning stages of writing research proposals. Karne would like to clear up his confusion over the possibilities generated in a recent research class. Karne and his classmates have attempted to formulate a research question which would provide some focus for a course evaluation. *There's questions and there's questions,* he speculates. He had thought questions were best when simple but this experience with his classmates has resulted in conflicting views. For example, his classmates would like to frame a question in which there is a comparison; Karne would prefer a more descriptive direction.

Bert responds by identifying three issues he perceives in Karne's statement. The first issue is what questions are for. *They have a fair amount to do with what it is you're trying to get at,* he says. Bert ties research questions to that of need—the importance of matching questions with purpose. The second issue is the degree of simplicity. He takes Karne's example of a question and describes it *as so simple and broad and so inclusive* that it would be hard to decide what to look for. Instead, Bert makes up a question which demonstrates a specific and simple focus. He then states a third issue, that *one needs to get away from your own answer,* which is something harder to accomplish where questions are loaded. For example, he suggests a research question *should invite the positions of other people who might not share yours.* Bert launches into a short digression on how one can include methodological hints in the formulation of a question while warning of spelling out the methods too specifically. He suggests one may choose to word questions in a more naturalistic manner—the way he tends to—which, he says may be *unsatisfactorily naturalistic.* Bert depicts himself as firmly in the naturalistic camp in which a researcher observes and describes a phenomena. He gives an example of a question which may be too simple and broad and renders it more useful by making it more specific as well as simple. Bert characterizes this as an example of: *research not meant to be psychometric, not to be measured in inches or pounds.* He illustrates what he means by telling a short anecdote about the authors of *Illuminative Evaluation* (Hamilton, MacDonald, King, Jenkins and Parlett 1977)—a research mode based in a socioanthropological tradition. Bert uses the story to describe the shift from a methodology valuing numeracy to one valuing literacy. He calls this shift a naturalistic one: *". . . in other words, you treat the phenomena as though you were a naturalist who chanced by an anthill, very much in the tradition of the 19th century English naturalist."* For Bert, naturalistic inquiry is about describing what he sees and feels about a particular happening.

Karne responds to this anecdote by giving his impressions of a report of Bert's recent research. It described the first meeting of students in an innovative program where students participated in a number of holistic projects such as cultural journalism and research for a federal crown corporation. Commitment to the program was important and the contracting process of the first meeting, as described by Bert in his research, is identified by Karne as an example of the kind of description Bert was referring to.

Bert acknowledges Karne's understanding of his description and continues because he simply wants to *describe events that appear to be critical in the life of a program.* Bert seems to be most comfortable with *just trying to illuminate the whole process and writing up a question to which that would be an answer.* In other words, for him, observing and describing the phenomena precedes the question. This appears to contradict what is generally considered to be rigorous research planning, but Bert has *difficulty fitting into a model of research design that says you must always have a question or must always have a statement of the problem, [when] there isn't a problem,* he says, *there's only a phenomenon.* Bert's method is really quite personal; he says he likes to turn the problem statement around to ask himself, *What is it that I would like to find out?* At this point, he reframes the question to read: *What is that I would like to know that is not yet known?* He hints that there is some relevance here to Karne's original question and illustrates what he means by explaining how one might take the work of someone like Donald Schön (1984) *to see how well it fits* with a particular school experience. When it does not, then he says that either Schön is wrong or *not applicable to what these people are doing.* Bert seems to be saying that even though the framing of questions and problems has some importance in inquiry, research should also include some kind of *crux.* He elaborates with an anecdote about snow fleas out on the ice of a lake far away from their shelter and food sources—*these creatures are being found where they cannot possibly live!* Bert is saying that ordinary happenings or convergence of experience with what one knows is no cause for study, but when one finds inconsistency, contradictions, or a kind of tension then one has a crux which needs explanation.

Karne responds by outlining a similar occurrence at the end of the research class he had been describing earlier. He says that the end of this class was different from the others before it: *everyone hung out, something was different.* He identifies a *crux* or *critical* moment which begs some explanation or illumination.

Bert is interested and recognizes this as a puzzle which may have some value as the introduction to a piece of work. He doesn't use the words "problem" or "research question" but he makes it clear that sometimes *an observation like that makes the best possible introduction to a piece of work*. He illustrates by summarizing a lengthy narrative which formed such a beginning in a successful thesis. Bert returns to Karne's original research question again in an indirect but clear manner. He is advising Karne to avoid becoming entangled in questions and problem statements but rather to search out inconsistencies and contradictions one finds in critical moments or crux statements of lived experience.

This conversation is similar to the curriculum orientation conversation in that Bert has avoided giving Karne straight answers to what may appear to be straight questions. Bert answers with a series of interlocking stories. In other words, his stories build on each other, each painting a partial, metaphoric picture of some issue relevant to discovering one's passion for a particular research direction. Bert is encouraging Karne to explore areas that hold interest for him in academe; a research proposal without some kind of passion for the inquiry often proves hard to sustain. Bert is again addressing issues of essence—for the essence of working on problem statements and research questions is one of finding out what it is that needs to be explained or understood.

This conversation represents a change in the role that Karne is playing. We see that he is not only the presenter of puzzles as in the first conversation about curriculum orientations, but is now acting as a checker of meaning. Here Karne himself tells stories, one of them using an analogy to illustrate the point he has taken. Bert responds to Karne's interpretation with the observation that conundrums such as the one in Karne's story contribute to finding a research project. This is in fact what happens with the next step in Karne's development of a research proposal: he manages to place his own illustration of a problem statement in the context of his own personal schooling experiences.

Collaboration in a Community of Practice

What do these two interpretive readings reveal about mentoring and what it is like to learn the ropes of academic life from an old hand? While both readings give some idea of the details of minute by minute mentoring dialogue (which is valuable detail in itself) one must step back further to tease out the broader patterns of discourse, keeping in mind the lived experience that underscores such patterns. Certain accounts of situated activity within the realm of cultural psychology (Bruner 1990; Cole 1990) help to place these interpretive readings in such a broader perspective.

The situated learning research of Lave and Wenger (1991) is helpful in developing a broader understanding of this relationship. Lave and Wenger articulate a view of learning that is relational rather than analytical in nature—where humans are seen to develop expertise by acting in the world in communities of practice. Knowledgability, according to Lave and Wenger, lies within such communities of practice. In other words, knowledgability is situated activity which exists within a community solving practical problems in the world. According to Lave and Wenger, knowledgability exists in the minds of individuals as portable narratives, not schemata directly transferable to other situations. In other words, we all have our stories, and learning and development are the consequences of sociocultural influences. This social practice view of learning has relevance in examining the conversations of a newcomer and an older hand. These conversations map onto the social roles described by Lave and Wenger as legitimate peripheral participation. This peripheral view is a relational perspective which describes the movement of a newcomer through indeterminate stages which exist in certain forms of co-participation. The concept of legitimate peripheral participation describes the mode of engagement of a learner in the practice of developing expertise. The roles described by Lave and Wenger are linked together by the common thread of learning as fundamentally a process of collaborative production that takes place in participation frameworks— not necessarily in the minds of individuals.

While the concept of legitimate peripheral participation might suggest that participants are somewhat disconnected from full participation, this is by no means the case, for learning as a legitimate peripheral participant is essentially collaborative and "mediated by the differences of perspective among the co-participants" (Lave and Wenger 1991, 15). A popular conception of what constitutes collaborative action is based on the assumption that those who collaborate contribute, if not equally, in an equitable manner. Lave and Wenger help us to reframe what it means to act collaboratively—it does not necessarily mean that one needs to contribute equally or in ways one might ordinarily associate with collaboration. For example, collaboration may mean very unequal contributions by participants. It is this unequal contribution that characterizes participation by different players in a community of practice. Not everyone has the same position or influence but all enact roles important in the reproduction and transformation of their community.

There are similarities between the social roles described by Lave and Wenger and those enacted by Karne and Bert. At face value, the initial conversations show minimal involvement by Karne who confines himself to asking a question or two from time to time, although in the second conversation Karne does contribute an analogy of his own to test the new insight he has gained. A peripheral view of participation confirms Yonge's (1985) conception of accompaniment described earlier, which can be understood in the issues of position, obligation, social context and authority. For example, the nature of responsibility, power, and interaction with peers and older hands can also be understood as essentially collaborative whereas a newcomer or *status subordinate* (Lave and Wenger 1991) must be ready and willing to jettison baggage brought from other situations. For example, a beginning teacher might be encouraged to observe and listen to a number of veteran teachers as part of an internship. In similar fashion, as a status subordinate, Karne begins the process of becoming privy to the storied pieces that compose the narratives of experience which underpin the development of practical knowledge and expertise.

The conversations, while rendered less opaque by these interpretations, also represent a starting point for further investigation by Karne within the educational community with his peers—other graduate students. Bert places a burden on Karne by a degree of indirection and ambiguity in the stories. In addition, there is no advice, instructions, or formulas. Rather, he tells stories, draws analogies and leaves Karne to respond, or ponder, or otherwise work things out. Karne is impelled to venture into the community of practice in order to make meaning of what he is able to glean from their meetings. As the patterns of the meetings unfold, Karne is left to what Lave and Wenger (1991) call "benign community neglect" (p. 93), to find his own way. In other words, Karne is pushed to further collaborative action beyond what he experiences in his meetings with Bert. For as Lave and Wenger point out, a theory of situated learning goes beyond an individualistic or centered view:

> To take a centered view of master-apprentice relations leads to an understanding that mastery resides not in the master but in the organization of the community of practice of which the

master is part: The master as the locus of authority (in several cases) is, after all, as much a product of the conventional, centered theory of learning as is the individual learner. Similarity, a decentered view of the master as pedagogue moves the focus of analysis away from teaching and onto the intricate structuring of a community's learning resources. (1991, 94)

This socially distributed understanding of thought and development owes much to Vygotsky's work according to Stairs (1994), particularly his concepts of "practical activity" and "the zone of proximal development" where the zone can be understood as the qualitative difference in performance between individual and collaborative activity. Stairs concludes: "Human development therefore occurs embedded in and in negotiation with a person's cultural medium in all its dimensions" (1994, 23). Lave and Wenger's (1991) notion of legitimate peripheral participation then, is "a way of acting in the world which takes place under widely varying conditions" (p. 24). It is through these varying conditions that one learns how to act in the world, how to live one's life. This notion of learning has less to do with the acquisition of knowledge than learning how to be. Learning how to be in the world, then, happens as a consequence of collaborative action within a community of practice—of which the master and accompaniment are part. Yonge's (1985) thoughts on accompaniment are also helpful in coming to an understanding that learning and development are situated in communities of practice which contain conversations such as the ones reported here.

It remains then, to speculate on the nature of accompaniment as collaboration—whether it is uniquely andragogic. Can a child and an adult truly collaborate? Perhaps, but the authority relationship referred to earlier by Yonge (1985) is qualitatively different in the pedagogic relationship where it is seen to be authoritarian. This differs from the andragogic which is perceived to be less authoritarian and more authoritative. However, our conversations interpreted in light of Lave and Wenger suggest that asymmetrical collaboration leads to powerful learning. There is no reason to think that an adult and a child could not enjoy a dialogic collaboration much as we did. Thus, the lines between andragogy and pedagogy drawn by Yonge are blurred by this study. Future research into storied conversations between adults and children will shed further light on this question.

While the intuitive and unself-conscious stories and anecdotes told to one another can be mapped onto the research of Lave and

Wenger (1991), there is room for expansion of their ideas. The first example is a natural (unself-conscious) attention to detail. This is not the fussy concern of the novice or status subordinate, but an easy checking of the little things that make the difference between merely competent and expert performance, whether in a university office, a kitchen or a building site. The second is the expert's habit of picturing consequences and sequential patterns in the mind before ever proceeding to action. Again, this is an easy, natural unforced process. For example, in preparing to teach Bert has this ability to identify and correct the flaws in a teaching plan days before he ever sees the class. But, as a novice artist he lacks this ability (for example) when laying out a water color palette and planning a painting. He tries, but the store of remembered relevant experience is deficient. Here he is at best a status subordinate.

Our secondary collaboration in writing this chapter had a comfortable quality which is best described in ancient Chinese thought by the term *Wei wu wei*. *Wei* means act or action. *Wu* means empty, void. The concept, thus, is to act without acting; a spontaneous, natural action whose artfulness lies in its very lack of artfulness—something like an improvised dance. The principle of *wei wu wei* looms large in Lave and Wenger, as well. Flow experience (Csikszentmihalyi 1975) is a closely related idea, although not yet invested with spiritual implications, and Lave and Wenger refer to flow. This can be illustrated by two excerpts from some of our ongoing correspondence as we collaborated on this chapter:

> Part of this is leading from behind . . . a kind of coyote-like dance which reveals essence, not as cause and effect but as spontaneous co-arising. This spontaneous co-arising for example, can be found in the laughter that isn't written out in the transcripts but exists there all the same. I think that this goes deeper, but the laughter is very much symptomatic of it. (Horwood, personal communication, November 1993)
>
> It's like discovering something new—for me it is understanding and for you perhaps the joy one feels as you accompany a person doing so. (Kozolanka, personal communication, November 1993)

There were many times in our conversations when we would come to similar conclusions or would arrive at a meeting with parallel thoughts. The conversations and the relationship reflected something that is beyond our descriptions here.

Finally, it may be important to ask what value there is in exploring the process of collaborative action. The conversations can be re-viewed as thought experiments which transmit lore, of both the topic and the process of accompanied discourse; they are a form of indirect analogy, almost a meta-metaphor. Not only is there content in the stories, the storying itself is a way of looking at the world. These conversations provide a kind of template for puzzling out academe. Karne begins to experiment with the pattern. Using it, he was able to reframe and change his perspective without re-doing the experience. At the same time, Bert was able to recon-struct and recombine his stories of experience to initiate a newcomer. Finally, some stories—such as how an interesting observation can be the beginning of a thesis—explore areas where the instructor is ignorant in some critical way yet applies expertise in the form of intuition pattern recognition, trying to get a better understanding of the situation presented. All, of course, are anchored by the no-tion of accompaniment or an expanded view of what constitutes collaborative action.

This work has shown that Mentor, as an ideal, exists in a contemporary context between adults. Accompaniment, in this case, takes the form of collaborative action in which anecdote, analogy, and checking ideas in sustained regular conversations works to extend an adult's capabilities in a new sphere of endeavor. The profound attention to values brings a recognizable spiritual compo-nent into the collaboration, thus making it a whole.

Part Four

◇

Collaborative Partnerships and Projects

Part Four tells the stories of lived collaborative experiences situated in classrooms, schools, and universities. Each chapter describes and analyzes the development of collaborative partnerships, projects, and research from the individual to the institutional level.

These chapters show there is no one way to begin a collaborative project. Each beginning is influenced by the situation in which it occurs. Susan Drake and Jan Basaraba have tentative beginnings based on commonalties as women and teachers while Caroline Krentz and Beth Warkentin describe a formal institutional partnership arranged by administrators. Debra Schroeder and Kathie Webb find themselves bound to a predetermined focus imposed on them by university guidelines for doctoral research.

The chapters describe how the development of a collaborative project is influenced by its beginnings. Some aspects seem to flow naturally from the coming together of the participants while other aspects are characterized by struggle. Examples of the former are presented by David Friesen as he describes how restructuring the roles of the student teaching practicum shifts the focus to one of learning for all participants through sharing and conversation. Similarly, Jeff Orr found his and the teacher's different roles and needs complemented each other. At the same time, struggle is evident in each project: struggling to achieve equity and share power; exploring beliefs and changing philosophies; establishing ownership through joint decision making; and dealing with the dilemmas of working within the university's guidelines that reflect a quantitative approach to research. In all projects the process, including the aspects of struggle and flow, becomes as important as the outcome.

The analysis used in collaboration varies in each chapter. All reflect on experience and theory but the documentation and analysis take different forms. At the same time, there does appear to be a common pattern in the procedure. Often the authors initiate the process of documentation and analysis then share it with the participants for their response—which leads to joint analysis.

The different chapters refer to various bodies of literature used to inform the authors' understandings of collaboration. Two chapters refer to feminist theory that deals with transformative change and the expression of authentic voice. The literature on metaphoric language is seen as promoting dialogical thinking and innovation of old ideas into new. Change theory states that changing understanding of the self and the relationship to the environment facilitates change in practice.

Although the chapters focus on different aspects of results, they document the power of collaborative projects. Schroeder and Webb express frustration in the barriers to effective collaborative projects by the university requirements for research. Other authors emphasize the learnings possible through collaborative projects: *acknowledged growth, meaning making, insight, validation,* and *creative energy* are all terms used to describe the results of involvement in collaboration.

◇ Chapter Fourteen

School-University Research Partnership: In Search of the Essence

Susan Drake and Jan Basaraba

We are a university researcher and a high school English teacher involved in a long-term collaborative partnership that has undergone several phases. In our own minds we had been successful at the collaborative side of our project; we had developed a strong friendship and felt good about what we had each accomplished through our partnership. With Susan's help, Jan had implemented a new curriculum model that had successfully motivated potentially unmotivated Grade Twelve, English students. With Jan's help, Susan had experienced how the integrated approach to curriculum that she and a group of teachers had developed (Drake, Bebbington, Laksman, Mackie, Maynes, and Wayne 1992) really unfolded in the classroom rather than on paper. Each of us had a deepened understanding of the curriculum model and had used this understanding in other settings.

Confident that we had some understanding of collaborative processes, at a national conference we presented an academic paper that outlined factors contributing to our success (Basaraba and Drake 1993). Shortly after this a researcher from another university interviewed Susan about the project. It came as a shock to both of us to learn that this researcher interpreted our project to have failed on several counts. We had "failed to establish a meaningful relationship" before we began the project and we "had failed to establish the roles and responsibilities of each person at the onset of the project." We discussed this interpretation at length and decided that although we may have failed that particular researcher's schema for successful partnerships, we were definitely successful in our own. This pushed us into a deeper search for our own definition of success and how we had come to realize this. In this chapter we explore the collaborative process by probing below the obvious to discover the essence of an authentic partnership.

Research Framework

We began our study using a practical action research approach (McKernan 1991) based on the work of Elliott (1985). We began here because McKernan (1991) suggested that there is a need for examination of the collaborative process in curriculum-problemsolving through action research. That is, the study was guided by practice rather than theory; the validity of any theory emerging from the study would be its ability to help others. As researchers, we studied our collaborative process, documenting our own behavior and that of the students as they participated in the integrated curriculum project. As we moved on through a series of stages of collaboration, our research methodology continued to take the path of action research.

Data were collected during our ongoing collaboration over two years. Data collection included an ongoing monitoring of the process through dialogue with each other. This ongoing conversation as a method of research was closely aligned with Hollingsworth's "collaborative conversations" (1992) and Van Manen's (1990) "hermeneutic conversations" of lived experience. Written reflections or field notes were shared with each other; these consequently triggered deeper reflections captured in further writing. As in the work of Hunsaker and Johnston (1992), traditional methods of working with the data did not work well, while ongoing writing and dialogue concurrently produced further data and new interpretations. Through "constructing interpretations in the context of conversations" (Hunsaker and Johnston 1992, 368), we narrowed our focus to the patterns that characterized the process we believed facilitated a successful partnership.

Factors for Success

When we reviewed our initial reflections on our partnership (Basaraba and Drake 1993) we found that the factors we had identified as being important to our success were still true. At first glance, two clear factors led to success: our similarities and mutual rewards. Collaboration seemed easier because we both held much in common; we were the same age, had taught for many years and even had some common friends although we had not known each other well before this study. We held similar philosophies on life and teaching which we discovered after long hours of dialoguing together.

Second, there were clear rewards for our partnership. It was an energizing professional development experience. Key to our experience was the learning which occurred for both of us as we struggled to make this program work. For Jan a key reward was the meaningful and personal connection she felt she made with her students. She wrote in her journal:

> One girl shared her experience of (after a previously negative history) coming to know her father because of a trip they had taken together where they were challenged by their need to communicate. Many others experienced challenging stories. Sharing them with the class opened up new lines of communication between students, and between myself and the students. My enthusiasm for this project is growing.

Susan was also pleased by the reception of both the students and Jan. It was rewarding to see ideas she and a group of practicing teachers developed come alive in a real-life setting. Like Jan, she was particularly touched by the stories of students and excited by Jan's enthusiasm. Both of us were willing and able to find personal rewards in the satisfaction of the interests of the other person and this contributed to the success (Clark 1988).

Our experiences also fit with some of the literature outlining characteristics of successful partnerships. Success came from factors such as voluntary participation (Clift, Johnson, Holland, and

Veal 1992), a supportive environment (Fullan and Miles 1992), being culturally sensitive (Hattrup and Bickel 1993), a shared or common language (Crowe, Levine, and Nager 1992), and shared goals. We perceived ourselves to fit more or less into these categories. We had volunteered to do this project and were in a supportive environment. Susan was sensitive to the culture of the school since she had taught there herself not long ago and was still actively involved in another high school setting. This factor contributed to a common language as well. Also, we both valued the teacher-practitioner knowledge base rather than simply a theory base; this was not a contentious issue as in many university-school partnerships (Feldman 1993; Hattrup and Bickel 1993).

However, we felt a lingering disquiet; we had not really captured our experience. Our partnership was not as simplistic as this; these factors did not explain the darker side or the complexities and uncertainties we experienced. And then there was the university researcher who had deemed us to have failed. Were we only fooling ourselves? Were there more layers that we needed to peel away?

Searching for the Essence

As we began to search below the surface, we quickly met with the complexity that had been missing in our first analysis. We had concentrated on why our partnership had been successful. This had seemed more to the point than dwelling on areas where we had experienced conflict. That we had dismissed the dark side in our first analysis was typical of how we had negotiated our process together. Indeed, we had failed to develop a meaningful relationship and to outline expectations of each other as the researcher had pointed out. Instead we had been polite to each other and buried any negative feelings. Challenged from the outside, we dared to sweep away the conventions of polite relationship to define our process more authentically. What we found was a complex network of interwoven dilemmas.

On Equity and Reciprocity

When we embarked on this project it was Susan's agenda to explore the collaborative process; it was also Susan who brought with her a vague notion of "how" collaboration was supposed to evolve.

She knew that when colleagues talked about collaboration they were talking about equity and reciprocity (see Crowe, Levine, and Nager 1992; Tikunoff and Ward 1983). Reciprocity was easy to address. We both had clear rewards. However, equity was not as easy to answer. Equity suggests power in a relationship is equally shared.

Who held the power in our relationship? Was it equally shared? Susan realized that she often felt powerless in this and other teacher-university partnerships. "I would have to be so careful to fit into the agenda of whomever I was working with—not to tread on any toes. You see, these partnerships were all voluntary and if the teacher is not getting rewards there would be no further partnership. I was conscious of not overburdening the teacher—asking too much. Frankly, the research agenda was only my agenda. So why would they write journals, and so on—this was not their goal."

For Jan, issues of power were not relevant. She did not feel she needed to dance around Susan's agenda. Her agenda was to teach her classes successfully and she was able to do this. She was quite clear that if this collaboration did not work for her she would not continue. Although Jan was initially intimidated by Susan's university status, her fear dissipated as our relationship developed into friendship.

"Mutual vulnerability" (Hollingsworth 1992) leveled our playing field. Jan invited Susan into both her classroom and her life and risked negative judgments. Susan felt a need to always be pleasing Jan so she would continue on with the project. She, too, was vulnerable to negative judgments.

After further reflection, we decided the question of power was addressed by our shifting role as expert. Both of us had expertise and authority in different areas. While Susan was the expert on the curriculum model, Jan was the expert in day-to-day implementation and student evaluation. A "complementary relationship" evolved. This term was introduced to us during conversation with Paul Shaw (November 21, 1994); it means partners contribute different things and receive different rewards. We needed each other to fulfill our personal goals. In the final analysis, we were interdependent—stronger together than alone.

Internal Conflict: Driven by Guilt

Conflict seems to be a necessary part of the collaborative process (Drake 1993). Some of our conflict was external and caused by pressures such as time factors in the lives of busy women. Yet much of the conflict was internalized and surfaced as unexpressed guilt. For example, Susan struggled with letting the curriculum implementation unfold as it would. Her journal entries expressed some disappointment when the curriculum did not unfold as she envisioned it should. She sensed that she had to let Jan come to her own meaning; however, it was difficult to do this. She felt guilty for thinking these thoughts and certainly did not intend to express them.

Jan had a history of taking new ideas and applying them to her own teaching, but this time was different. Susan was the expert and so Jan did not feel a sense of ownership as quickly as she might have if she had just adapted the model by herself. "I imported you into class before I knew how to apply this and sat back and let you teach it, so I was slow to take ownership." Jan felt guilty because she was not fully engaged in the project.

Guilt also emerged from other sources. Susan's guilt was driven by the lack of time that she was in the classroom. Caught between her need to be at the university and her perceived need to live up to Jan's expectations, Susan felt she was not being supportive enough. Jan, meanwhile, felt guilt that she had not read all the material Susan had left for her and that she was not being academic enough. She was used to reading, reflecting, and adapting new ideas and had intended to do this. However, her personal life intervened and the breakdown of her marriage and the need to work this through with her two teenage daughters "consumed my extra time."

At first we internalized rather than expressed or negotiated our conflict. We were, quite simply, polite to each other. However, when we came to analyze the data for our academic paper (Basaraba and Drake 1993) we each confessed to being plagued by unexpressed guilt. We believed it was the guilt that spurred us on to give as much as we could to the project in spite of outside pressures. Although this has had positive results, we are now at the stage where we have developed enough of a comfort level with each other and have realistic enough expectations that we can communicate our conflicts to discover what works best for both of us.

After discussion, we decided that the guilt was a part of our larger framework for dealing with others and trying to be all things to all people. We have been socialized to be polite and not express our needs. We are now consciously trying to communicate our needs both in this project and in the larger framework of our lives.

Negotiating the Research

The role as researcher was often problematic for both of us. Problems with the roles of university-school research are pointed out by Clift, Johnson, Holland, and Veal (1992) who reflect on the difficulty, yet inevitability, of the university researcher deciding the study design, data collection, and data analysis. Susan was the trained researcher who had asked Jan to consider this partnership as a part of a research plan. Jan was more than willing, but did not have the skills necessary to fully enter the process at the beginning.

Thus began a delicate process where Susan initiated the research dialogue and Jan responded in kind. Susan was concerned that she not ask too much of Jan who was excessively burdened with the daily demands of school plus an extremely busy personal life. Yet, Jan's voice was essential to the process of doing collaborative research. A solution seemed to be for Susan to guide the research process by modeling the type of written reflections she thought were pertinent to the study. Jan's first responses consisted of an accurate picture of the chronological events of the curriculum implementation. These were accurate field notes that captured the classroom process but did not explore our relationship. As Jan began to respond to Susan's reflections, her attention turned to the analysis of process. In this way, she gradually learned some of the skills of the action researcher.

The writing process also posed problems. Crowe, Levine, and Nager (1992) suggest that creating a narrative that stresses joint voices, rather than a single voice, is an intriguing and difficult problem when people come from different disciplines with different research backgrounds. In this case, the teacher did not have a traditional background as researcher. Susan took the responsibility to write the first draft of this chapter to which Jan gave an insightful and careful response. However, when the chapter was first reviewed, the reviewer did not hear Jan's voice. This led us to a deeper dialogue on collaboration and our respective roles. It also caused Jan to question why her voice was not clearly heard in our first draft. She wondered if this was a metaphor for the role she plays in real life. Like Susan, and many other women, she is in the process of finding her voice and ways in which to express it. This experience, then, was as much personal as professional.

In many ways our journey is not unique and speaks to an evolutionary process of researcher and teacher discovering ways of reflecting, researching, and writing together. It follows much the same sequential pattern Hunsaker and Johnston (1992) did in their path to discovering "the dialogic, multivoiced and evolving character of collaborative work in the content of text as well as in the content of the research project" (p. 365). As we move forward in our partnership we expect we will find new ways of writing and researching that give equal weight to each voice and interpretation.

Finally, we realized that, at this time, the primary job of writing and researching belonged to Susan. This was because it satisfied the reward structure of her system rather than Jan's. The writing process, while enjoyable, did not fit any particular professional need for Jan. She was rewarded by her renewed interest in reading and research and her classroom efforts. Although this did not fit the ideal of equal voice in the research process, it was the way that worked for us. Our attempts at equity were well-intentioned, but led to more conflict and unfulfilled expectations. Finally accepting this reality, Jan said, "Susan, the writing of the final draft is your responsibility." We both were freed from guilt.

On Relationship

The relationship developed naturally. We began over lunch by sharing common interests and pedagogical beliefs necessary to build credibility in curriculum planning (Gehrke 1991). More importantly, we disclosed personal facts about our lives that contributed to the sense of intimacy necessary for collaborative conversations (Hollingsworth 1992). This intimacy was to deepen as we worked together over two years.

Caring for each other was the central principle that guided our collaboration. At first we talked about how trust, commitment, and respect were key to this study. Then we realized that these three attributes could be integrated into one word—caring. It was Jan's caring for her students that opened the path for the initial collaboration. As well, she told Susan she wouldn't have let her continue if she didn't sense that she cared for the students too.

Caring is threaded through the themes previously identified and took us beyond being polite. We have come to agree with Feldman (1993) that we can't work within a definition of collaboration that emphasizes parity and equal responsibility. "It is not possible for university researchers and school researchers to share the same set of goals or to define the same research question unless they change their roles" (p. 343). We have come to accept that our roles will differ and that we can have our own definition of collaboration—one that works for us and shifts according to our needs. In the final analysis, we concur with Heshusius (1994) that building relationships and developing kinship is the most important part of this research process.

Through a Feminist Lens

Recent accounts of collaborative projects among women situate themselves in the feminist camp (Berman, Hultgren, Lee, Rivkin, and Roderick 1991; Hollingsworth 1992; Hunsaker and Johnston 1992; Miller 1990). We, as other women, are seeking new ways of knowing and researching where our voices can be heard in an authentic way. We, too, are open to being changed and empowered by the research process itself—a characteristic of feminist praxis (Lather 1991; Miller 1990). Personal and professional growth has been the most invigorating part of our collaboration. We also recognized that, in our approach to research, relationship and caring emerged as our greatest priorities. Caring as a guiding principle has been associated with feminist theory (Noddings 1984).

We wondered how much of our story and our success was grounded in our being women. From this lens we wondered if the guilt factor in our relationship was more typical of women than of men working together. When Susan showed the draft of this chapter to a young male teacher with whom she is currently collaborating, he offered a clear answer to this question: "If you're wondering if men would carry on the same way about caring and guilt the answer is NO." Although this is only one man's opinion, we suspect he is not atypical. Our concentration on caring and guilt is a part of our socialization. Our challenge now is to maintain the caring aspect while eliminating the unnecessary guilt with open communication with each other.

We have come to understand our partnership as unique and that our way of researching, working together, and even writing belongs to us. We are carving out our own definition—one that works for us and allows us to bridge the two cultures in ways that work in practice. For Jan, "Our shared goals and the experiences of collaboration have led us to a fine friendship. This process of collaboration will continue—reflecting our needs and sparked by this friendship." For Susan, a definition for collaboration became clearer even as she recognized that it will be different for all partnerships:

So how do I determine success? When there is acknowledged growth on both sides. I learn; they learn. We are all pleased with ourselves. Our view of the world and how to operate within it has either changed or been affirmed. We do things differently now even without the presence of the other. And, most important, we are energized by the process.

What Comes Next...?

Now we are at a point of departure. Jan has moved on to collaborate with others in her school. Susan is working collaboratively at another high school with a large variety of personalities. Our relationship is being sustained at another level as we move into sharing our new situations and their accompanying dilemmas. We are wiser for our explorations. We realize the university researcher who sparked these reflections was right. We do need a process by which we can establish the roles and responsibilities of each person involved—and we will be conscious of this in our current and future relationships. However, we agree with LaRocque (1994) that there is no set formula and "a general sense of destination and a willingness to try new routes" will keep the relationship alive (p. 4). More important, we also need a relationship that is meaningful and caring. But we can't necessarily begin this way. These relationships evolve over time and demand care, nurturing, and ultimately being polite to one another. These factors are the essence of success.

✧ Chapter Fifteen

The Meaning of Collaboration: Redefining Pedagogical Relationships in Student Teaching

David Friesen

In this chapter I give an account of several action research projects as attempts to develop collaborative student teaching experiences. As I engaged in these projects with teachers and student teachers, I became aware of our changing discourse and practices. From this experience, I have begun to develop a different discourse of student teaching reflected in several metaphors that capture new understandings of the notion of collaboration. These metaphors have helped me understand and redefine my pedagogical relationships with both teachers and student teachers. This chapter is about learning to live a new story as a teacher educator and expressing it through a different discourse.

The Question of Pedagogical Relationships in Student Teaching

The hierarchical relationship between university-based educators and school-based educators has been perpetuated by the hegemony of one conception of knowledge. Within that view, differentiated roles have been established with the university producing knowledge of teaching, and practitioners applying that knowledge to problems of practice. This technical rational approach (Schön 1983) to teacher education has long been taken for granted until recently challenged by teacher educators claiming that teachers possess a tacit form of knowledge that is constructed and expressed in practice (Connelly and Clandinin 1988).

As an emerging response to the recognition of teacher knowledge, many teacher educators have become involved in collaborative projects with schools in order to understand this alternative form of knowledge and how it plays itself out in practice. These partnerships have altered the conventional roles for all of the participants concerned. The new collaborative approaches are attempting to break down the established hierarchical relationship between university and schools.

I have been involved for many years as a faculty advisor to student teachers in the sixteen-week teaching practicum called "internship." In the fall of the last year of a four-year undergraduate teacher education program, each intern is placed in a school classroom with a cooperating teacher and assigned a faculty advisor from the university. A four-day seminar at the beginning of the experience prepares the cooperating teacher and the intern for internship by focusing on the relationship, the supervisory process, and general role expectations.

The "triad" is the conventional term given to the key players in the internship. However, the implication that the sides of the triangle are equal is somewhat problematic. Gore (1991) claims the triadic relationship has often been characterized by "unequal power, unequal investment, and unequal consequences" (p. 254). Although the cooperating teacher and the intern generally form a close working relationship, I have often felt outside the triangle with little influence as faculty advisor. In terms of power relations, student teachers often "come out at the bottom" (p. 262) afraid to voice their thoughts and feelings because of the authority of the teacher about what is permitted in the classroom.

The recent literature on teacher education suggested to me that inquiry-oriented approaches to teacher education might present the possibility for reshaping the traditional hierarchical roles found in student teaching (Tabachnich and Zeichner 1991). Action research, in particular, seemed to provide a structure to promote collaborative inquiry. This approach appears to stand in sharp contrast to the conventional apprenticeship-oriented approach to the practicum characterized by hierarchical relationships within the triad (Noffke and Brennan 1991). In reporting her experience with action research, Gore (1991) suggests that the primary concern in internship shifts from the performance of the intern to the collaborative involvement and learning of all participants in the internship.

Another problem I had faced as a faculty advisor pertained to the strong socialization of the intern to existing teaching practices and institutional roles. Immersed in the world of practice, the student teacher is faced with the very real pressure of performing competently within prevailing school structures. This pressure privileges technical concerns while marginalizing the need to understand teaching practice in order to bring about meaningful change. Teaching becomes synonymous with knowledge transmission within a prescriptive curriculum. Bullough, Knowles, and Crow (1992) suggest an alternate pathway of learning to teach. Students are considered to be "centers of meaning-making" (p. 190) who go beyond the prescribed roles of the institution. This pathway demands a teaching internship which privileges collaborative inquiry into teaching practice as a model of professional development so that all participants engage in making sense of their practice. It presents a possibility for dealing with negative socializing effects of the internship.

Student Teaching Action Research Projects

As a result of my commitment to collaborative ideals, I explored action research projects as an alternative way to structure field experiences. In one study, I was the faculty advisor for five pairs of cooperating teachers and interns in a sixteen-week internship. During the four day internship seminar, we explored the ideas associated with action research such as collaborative inquiry and reflection on our practice. Each teacher-intern pair identified a puzzling aspect of their practice and devised a plan to study it over the course of the internship. The projects included developing a token economy to motivate middle years pupils; implementing a readers' and writers' workshop approach to the teaching of English;

using experiential learning in social studies; and studying student initiated enrichment projects in a computer applications course.

Each of the projects involved several cycles of planning, action, observation and data collection, and reflection. My primary role as the faculty advisor, was active involvement in the multiple cycles of each project along with the cooperating teacher and intern in order to switch the focus away from student performance toward the teaching practice being investigated by the pair. Specifically, I suggested ways to obtain data on the impact of their attempts at change, and helped them analyze the data. I also conducted weekly meetings with all of the participants from the different projects. These were audio recorded and transcribed afterwards, and a summary of the preceding discussion was presented at the start of each session. In this way, I attempted to stimulate an ongoing conversation about teaching over the course of the internship. This component of the project enabled participants to engage in collaboration beyond the triad by questioning their practice and sharing their projects and classroom experiences with each other. My other role as faculty advisor was participant observer. In this role, I studied the classroom interactions and the transcripts to make sense of the relationships that were developing in the internship.

Revisiting the Experiences: Images of Collaboration

As I engaged in these projects, I noticed a different discourse to guide our practice was being formed. The "game," "conversation," and "struggle" metaphors emerged from my study of the interview transcripts. The three metaphors constitute a new language of collaboration serving to remind me of the kind of relationships that need to be fostered in the triad to enhance learning for all participants.

Metaphor, unlike linear inductive/deductive thought, allows for circular and dialogical thinking to occur. Because of the infinity of meaning it possesses, metaphorical language promotes innovation through the metamorphosis of old ideas into new ones. Whereas scientific rational discourse aims for the same, the univocal, metaphoric language demands interpretation and plurivocality (Weinsheimer 1985). Metaphor "lures thought out of its complacent inertia by challenging it to think more" (Weinsheimer 1991, 182). It contains "the freedom [of language] to form an infinite number of concepts and to penetrate what is meant ever more deeply" (Gadamer 1989, 428). The meaning of an idea is lifted out of its familiarity through metaphor and expanded to mean more than it ever did before. The presentation of these metaphors is a challenge to "think more" about the possibilities for the development of dialogical and democratic pedagogical relationships in the triad.

Collaboration as "Game"

During conversations in one of the action research projects carried out in a middle years classroom, Gerry, the teacher involved, used the metaphor of "game" to describe his experience of internship (Friesen 1994). In his words, the project had created a "level playing field" by inviting him into the game as a participant rather than a spectator. His role changed from that of a coach, the expert cooperating teacher controlling the play from the sidelines, to that of a player engaged in the game of internship along with the other players.

In comparison to the many internships Gerry had been involved in over the years, this one structured by action research resulted in a much less hierarchical relationship between teacher and intern. He claimed that the common focus on a specific teaching approach and its effect on pupils allowed him to establish a relationship with the intern characterized by professional dialogue centered on the project. Gerry viewed Todd as more of a colleague than an intern:

> From my point of view this token economy activity has had an effect on internship. Specifically it has had an impact on our cooperating teacher intern relationship. I believe that it has put us on a more equal level. . . . The other thing it did for me was that it kind of freed me in the sense that since we were on a more equal playing field, I didn't feel that I had to have the answers all the time because were both going into something different, "untried."

Decreasing the traditional hierarchy in the triad during internship meant that the relationship between cooperating teacher and intern became less expert-to-novice oriented.

Action research appeared to highlight the play of the game, the learning process as it is experienced by the participants, not just the performance of the intern. Gerry indicated to me that supervisory conferences, which usually tend to focus on intern performance, began to evolve into conversations about the project and the transformation of the students in the classroom. Gerry's involvement in the project, along with his intern's experiences, became a part of the ongoing discussions about teaching. Todd, the intern, wrote the following in his journal:

> Sharing the successes and failures on an equal level made for easy conference openers and created an informal air or atmosphere which I am more comfortable with and in which I can work better . . . this joint venture has helped our relationship grow much quicker, with a stronger sense of trust than my previous experience. In terms of my personal growth, this semester was like the difference of trying to paddle with the stream's current rather than against it.

As the faculty advisor, I felt more like a participant in this internship than an outside supervisor because of the common focus of the action research project. Each visit to the pair began with a review of their progress, an examination of the data they had collected related to the project, and a plan for the next phase. I experienced internship as a new game that was defining a new role for me as the faculty advisor.

Jardine (1988) suggests, in the words of Ricoeur, "it is in the participation of players in a game that we find the first experience of belonging" (p. 32). The player is defined by the game. This giving oneself over to the game involves a risk "that who we understand ourselves to be might be irrevocably changed, that the familiar ground that we took as our standpoint, our place from which we entered into play, might be one that is unquestionably our own" (p. 33).

The action research game provided a shift in focus from the teaching performance of the intern to the collaborative exploration of the play of teaching. It took us away from our familiar ground of assessing intern performance. This shift in focus had repercussions for my own sense of belonging in the internship. Unlike the participation I had previously experienced as a faculty advisor, this was an enrichment experience in which I learned about middle years classroom practices along with the others involved, because "by our participating in the things in which we are participating, we enrich them; they do not become smaller, but larger" (Gadamer 1988, 64).

The experience of this triad suggests that a collaborative approach such as action research constitutes a new game for internship. Pedagogical relationships within this game are characterized more by dialogue and mutual learning than by the transmission of knowledge from expert to novice. This serves to make them less hierarchical and more democratic in nature. Action research projects promote the collaborative game by privileging inquiry into teaching over the performance of the intern.

The image of collaboration as game reminds us that mutual learning in the internship demands the involvement of all members of the triad in the play of the game; it is less concerned with the performance of individual players. It is a game that requires the commitment of all players in order to achieve the goal of increased understanding of practice for each member of the triad.

Collaboration as "Conversation"

Conversation was an important part of the game of collaboration in this experience. Gadamer (1989) reminds us that conversation is a natural way of being in the world with others. It is "a process of coming to an understanding" (p. 385) through interpretation. Because of the back and forth nature of dialogue, we do not control a conversation but in fact are led by it; it is something we fall into. "We say that we 'conduct' a conversation, but the more genuine a conversation is, the less its conduct lies within the will of either partner. Thus a genuine conversation is never the one that we wanted to conduct" (p. 383).

The point of this, according to Gadamer (1989), is that "conversation has a spirit of its own" (p. 383) and is beyond the control of the participants. The end of a conversation cannot be predicted. When applied to field experiences, this metaphor suggests the possibility of establishing dialogical relationships that resist the control of any one participant and result in mutual learning.

Several ongoing conversations evolved as part of the project. The first began at the four-day internship seminar held in an off-campus residential setting. This was the beginning of a conversation about teaching. The focus of inquiry for the action research projects seemed to, in Gadamer's (1989) words, "come out of a conversation" (p. 383) about teaching. The cooperating teachers and interns were exposed to the new discourse of action research as they explored a mutually engaging project question. Each pair planned to begin their action research project when they returned to the school classroom. After the seminar, teachers, interns and myself as the faculty advisor met once a week over the course of the internship to share experiences and attempt to make sense of them.

This action research project provided a framework in which a conversation could evolve. The topic of conversation drawing us together was the teaching practice under investigation. As such, the focus for the partners in the conversation shifted from the performance of the intern to a specific aspect of teaching practice. Through the cycles of plan, act/observe, reflect, we were drawn further along in the conversation never knowing what the outcome of the specific inquiry would be. The conversation was kept open by questions that seemed to lead to problem posing and the opening up of further questions about practice, rather than finding solutions and final answers.

In one project Alana and her intern, Marian, attempted to explore independent learning by implementing optional independent projects for their students. Marian gave the following example of how she experienced conversation related to the project:

> [The faculty advisor] brought up the question to me after we postconferenced about it . . . he said, "How are you going to motivate all the students to try it?" And so it made me really think and I probably would never have thought of it. I would have just said, "Here it is. If you want to do it, do it. You don't have to. If you want a better mark in this class, you can do it." But it really made me think about how I could motivate all the students in the class. Why should it only be for the better students? It should be for all.

A question posed by me as faculty advisor started a conversation which led to a specific focus for collaborative inquiry.

Marian suggests that the dialogue during the project allowed her to be a contributor to the triad as opposed to a consumer:

> In the triad, with Alana and [the faculty advisor] as experienced teachers, I knew I wasn't alone. We all contributed to this project by conversing about how, what, and why. I also explored teaching as a colleague and not just a learner. To sound off ideas and suggestions with them helped me feel more secure in what I was doing.

Alana suggests that regular dialogue came about from participation in a common project which each participant viewed as beneficial:

> The research we embarked on was to assist the three of us with our work, to help each of us improve what we do. This

sincere attempt by each participant to gain from the experience led us to dialogue regularly about the project throughout the internship.

For me, the image of collaboration as conversation has helped me "redescribe" (Rorty 1989, 39) the role of the faculty advisor in particular. Conversation literally means "to dwell with." The faculty advisor as conversationalist is one who dwells with practitioners in their contexts. It implies a form of interaction that is dialogical and nonhierarchical. It suggests reciprocity rather than expert prescription. To converse implies listening as well as speaking. Far from being an expert in business education or enrichment projects, I had to listen to the talk to understand the questions, the interpretations, and the plans.

In an exploration of the role of experience in the development of teachers' professional knowledge, Russell and Munby (1991) employ the idea of the "reframing of experience" (p. 166). They conceptualize reframing as a response "to puzzles arising within their teaching actions and in the relationship between beliefs and actions" (p. 183). It allows for new meaning to develop and new actions to arise in practice. The central task in the conversationalist role is to help interns and teachers make teaching problematic—enabling them to reframe experience. This role involves a great deal of listening in order to find a compelling question of practice. Initiating a conversation about practice with Alana and Marian involved listening for a question. It was during a classroom visit that the question of independent learning surfaced; from this point in the internship, the conversation became a reframing of experience related to the project.

The image of collaboration as conversation redescribes supervisory practice as a "pedagogic way of being" (Berman, Hultgren, Lee, Rivkin, and Roderick 1991, 25) as opposed to a way of knowing and doing. The faculty advisor and the cooperating teacher cease to be identified solely by what they know or do, but by who they are and how they relate to each other and to interns.

Collaboration as "Struggle"

Richard and Tina's action research project can best be described by me as a "struggle". They both experienced constant frustration in their attempt to implement the readers' and writers' workshop approach. Considerable difficulty was encountered by them, which they specifically attributed to a lack of student responsibility to monitor their own work.

In teacher education, a scientific discourse has evolved that claims to make teaching easier, controlled, and more predictable. The effective teaching approach, which has emerged from this discourse, is an attempt to "depathologize" teaching according to Jardine (1991). It considers teaching to be a "dis-ease" (p. 18) in need of technological treatment. Technical methods tend not to be oriented toward helping teachers understand the characteristic struggles of teaching so that they can be better lived with, but rather are aimed at eradicating them. Along with Richard and Tina, I experienced the struggle to move beyond the quick answers of new methods to participating in collaborative inquiry to understand teaching.

As the internship unfolded, the intern Tina found the exploration of the readers' and writers' workshop approach to be the focal point of her thoughts and activities:

> I think it's definitely a focus and it's something that focuses the intern/co-op relationship, too, because we both care about it a lot and we think along the same lines about it basically. It's the one thing that we've really talked about a lot and shared ideas and how the students are handling it.

Working with someone of a similar philosophy and commitment functioned as an invitation for Tina and Richard to explore teaching together.

A general resistance from students to the readers' and writers' workshop was at the heart of the struggle that Richard and Tina faced. This was manifested in a lack of production in the students' writing. The students voiced considerable disinterest in the process which Tina found difficult to understand:

> They still don't see the benefits and that scares me. I don't like to be a prescriptive kind of teacher, but I'm wondering how do I find a balance, or how do I get them to see that I'm giving them freedom, but they don't want it. Know what I mean? They want to be told what to write, when to write and how to write.

Both Richard and Tina faced a second struggle in taking on the new role of "teacher as facilitator of learning" which was de-

manded by the new approach. For Richard this was a deep struggle
that was not resolved during the internship. At one of the last
meetings, Richard talked about the struggle he experienced during
the internship:

> Here's the question I'm grappling with. How much should I
> diminish my role? I think that I can still play a very positive
> role in guiding students to see things that are important and
> significant and, I think, powerful in the literature that they're
> reading.

Even toward the end of the internship, he was dissatisfied
with his role in the implementation of the program and yet remained committed to the new approach:

> What I've been doing is the lamest kind of thing and I felt so
> awkward and so ineffective and the classes were so dry and
> dead and maybe it's just because I haven't worked it, haven't
> done it properly and I think that's probably it, but now I
> recognize too—and I'm not going to abandon it totally—but
> I'm going to shape it after my own [strengths].

He felt he had failed to be a teacher to the students because
the new approach had alienated him from them. Richard revealed
a strong belief in the central role a teacher plays in the classroom.

In this internship, Tina was invited to participate in the
struggle of knowing what it means to be a teacher. Engaging in the
project exposed her to the same struggle that Richard her cooperating teacher faced. The struggle was intensified because neither
the cooperating teacher nor the intern had the answers concerning
the use of the new approach in the classroom and ways of motivat-
ing the students to write. Unlike many curriculum initiatives, the
readers' and writers' workshop approach does not consist of prescriptive techniques. Richard and Tina experienced it more like
coming to understand a new philosophy and then developing appropriate ways of teaching accordingly.

Other teachers involved in the project also experienced the
struggle that takes place when the internship is oriented towards
making sense of teaching rather than simply implementing teaching strategies. Alana commented after the internship that "as
educators we often have more difficulty with understanding the
pedagogical meaning and significance of difficulty in students'

learning than with reducing difficulty." Technical approaches to improving instruction are aimed at eliminating the struggle rather than understanding it. Alana suggests that for her and her intern:

> The focus for professional development would normally have been on such things as technical skills and management procedures that best ensure a classroom to function. During the past semester and in the current semester, the focus has drifted well beyond the basics to a deeper understanding of what it really means to be a teacher.

Richard and Tina came face to face with the limitations of this kind of technical approach Alana talks about. Initially they were both preoccupied with implementing the readers' and writers' approach to the teaching of English. They were not engaged in examining the claims of this approach. In the process of implementation and development, they became very frustrated that the promises of the new approach were not fulfilled. The various moves they made to overcome the difficulties they encountered led them to problematize this approach and to ask questions about what it means to be a teacher.

Collaboration for Richard and Tina meant an engagement in a mutual struggle to inquire into the use of the readers' and writers' workshop. The hierarchical structure of internship was diminished by the fact that the approach was new territory for both of them. Both in terms of understanding this approach and in terms of classroom practice, Richard and Tina were at the same level of expertise.

The image of collaboration as struggle is a reminder that making sense of teaching is difficult. As a faculty advisor it may be easier to give simple technical answers to complex problems; however, these answers will not deepen understanding of new philosophies of teaching and what it means to be a teacher. Sharing the struggle to make sense of teaching in a learning community helps to create relationships that are less hierarchical and more democratic.

Conclusion

Richard Rorty uses the term "final vocabulary" (1989, 73) to describe the set of words that people use "to justify their actions, their beliefs and their lives" (p. 73). He sees progress as being the replacement of one vocabulary with another through "metaphoric redescription" (p. 28). The old vocabulary is replaced by a new more attractive vocabulary which is a redescription of the way things are thought to be. It is "one more description, one more way of speaking" (p. 57) and not the one "right" way.

The game, conversation, and struggle metaphors presented in this chapter are useful in redefining pedagogical relationships in the field experience component of teacher education. Their use does not guarantee changed practice for, in the words of Rorty (1989), "they are pedagogical aids to the acquisition of such practices" (p. 59). In my own practice, these metaphors are pedagogical aids providing a standpoint from which to examine and change the way I work with teachers and interns. These images of collaboration suggest the possibility of establishing and maintaining dialogical relationships in field experiences that privilege meaning-making rather than promote hierarchical power relations.

✧ Chapter Sixteen

Between Two Worlds:
University Expectations and Collaborative
Research Realities[1]

Debra Schroeder and Kathie Webb

In this chapter we question ways that requirements for doctoral research conflict with the meaning and purpose of collaboration. Drawing on our experiences as doctoral candidates, we describe the ways in which the requirements for doctoral research have conflicted with our negotiation of collaborative narrative research with teachers. We suggest that some of the dilemmas we experienced in trying to do collaborative research were precipitated by differences between the epistemological assumptions of university policies that guide doctoral research and the epistemological assumptions underpinning our research methodology.

The ongoing dilemmas we have experienced as doctoral candidates engaging in collaborative narrative research with teachers arose specifically from: the dominance of an objective view of knowledge in the academy; the university's requirement for the doctoral candidate to have a predetermined focus before being permitted to commence research; the implication that the researcher (doctoral candidate) is "the expert" responsible for the research decisions; and, our different interpretations of ethical guidelines concerning the anonymity and "informed consent" of participants. We are uncomfortable that our institution of higher learning requires only that we make a "substantial contribution to the knowledge of the candidate's field of study" (*University of Alberta Calendar 1995/96*, thesis requirement, 312) and, in doing so, we "avoid or minimize risks to" our participants. (SSHRC Granting Programs 1993, 68.) From our experiences with collaborative research, we suggest that teachers engage in such research because of the possibilities for their own development.

If collaboration is seen as shared commitment, shared responsibility and mutual ownership (the interpretation guiding each of our doctoral studies), then we ask: Can there be collaboration if the focus of the research is predetermined by the researcher? What are the implications concerning knowledge construction when the researcher's voice is the only, or the major, voice heard in the research proposal and report, and if only the researcher interprets the stories told by others in the research? Further, we suggest there is a need to consider the messages to teachers (participating in collaborative research projects with doctoral candidates) about the significance of their contributions when only the researcher has her or his real name on the final report.

Epistemological Conflicts

In (traditional) research procedures that aspire to objectivity and anonymity of "subjects" the questions and issues we have raised would not be considered worthy of attention. However, in collaborative narrative research, a methodology in which the stories of the participants are valued as revealing the way those persons construct and reconstruct their experience and where experience and knowledge are seen as connected, our questions have epistemological significance.

An objective view of knowledge has long legitimized what is counted as knowledge and governed how knowledge is validated and extended through research (Code 1991). We question whether the scientific (objective) view of knowledge and research and the criteria for conducting rigorous scientific studies is an appropriate or adequate basis for the university policies which presently govern both quantitative *and* qualitative research by doctoral candidates. While there is little doubt qualitative research has gained legitimacy at the university, the goodness of fit between the guidelines that presently govern doctoral research and the epistemological base of qualitative methodologies is arguable. If the requirements for doctoral research emerge out of an objective view of knowledge (with assumptions that knowledge is external to the knower and a truth exists that we can ultimately find and verify), and do not reflect a constructivist view of knowledge (that posits knowledge as socially constructed and continually created and recreated allowing multiple interpretations and ultimately dependent on the knowers), graduate students attempting to do collaborative narrative research will be faced with both methodological and ethical conflicts. And if our claims are founded, (assuming university requirements for doctoral research arc drawn from guidelines for research in general) then the issues we have raised concern all researchers.

The pursuit of objectivity in research is based on the assumption that there is a single truth which can be discovered—a truth which will be discovered by the researcher. Collaborative research involves doing research *with* participants. This approach to research recognizes knowledge as socially constructed (Vygotsky 1962) and admits the possibility of multiple truths (Rorty 1991). Similarly, collaborative narrative research works from the observation that humans story and restory their experiences and, hence, that meaning will change over time. Insight into multiple and changing truths within educational contexts is provided by narrative accounts of teachers' work (Coles 1989; Connelly and Clandinin 1985, 1988, 1990; Paley 1979; Witherell and Noddings 1991). Although universities have made room for qualitative research in education, many requirements for doctoral students still reflect the assumptions of the quantitative paradigm. This dichotomy may be a source of conflict for students who choose to conduct their research using a collaborative narrative methodology. Our intent is not to reduce a discussion of university doctoral research requirements to a dichotomous comparison of quantitative and qualitative research principles; nevertheless, we are concerned that the epistemological differences underlying these two paradigms will result in ongoing dilemmas for both graduate students and the teachers they are working with if these inconsistencies are not addressed. A researcher trying to maintain an objective stance will have difficulty establishing a collaborative research relationship.

Conflict of a Predetermined Focus

Doctoral candidates attempting to negotiate collaborative research with teachers experience the double bind of having enough focus to satisfy their committees that they should pass the doctoral candidacy examination, and insufficient enough focus to allow participants to help construct the research questions. Prior formulation of the research question by the researcher can affect the participants' ownership of the research and the extent to which they can trust that collaboration will occur.

Debra initially envisioned her doctoral research to be both a collaborative conversation about her research topic, "Curriculum as a Middle Space," and a jointly constructed space for the professional development of the four teachers with whom she worked and herself. Her first dilemma arose as she wrote her research proposal. Although she attempted to write in a way that would satisfy the university's requirement that the doctoral candidate have a predetermined research focus, she also tried to construct her proposal in a way that would allow the research agenda to evolve. She wanted her proposal to be perceived as an invitation for others not only to enter into and personalize her questions but also to ask questions of their own. Debra also wanted the participants to be involved in constructing the research process and in determining the meaning this research would have. This was difficult because the requirements of her university and department for doctoral research emerged from a fixed view of research which allowed for little flexibility. Indeed flexibility in a research proposal was perceived negatively and little space was allowed for the research model to change once research had begun. The assumption that we can know ahead of time what needs to be known and that this will not change significantly once the research commences is implied in the requirements.

Kathie's interest in doctoral research emerged from her long experience as a classroom teacher. She wanted to do research on a teacher's personal practical knowledge (Clandinin 1986; Connelly and Clandinin 1988; Elbaz 1983) which would reveal how a teacher's caring informed her practice and her knowing. She avoided some personal dilemma concerning a predetermined focus by commencing research in the teacher's classroom following acceptance of her three-page proposal for ethical review and constructed her more detailed thirty-page proposal four months later, following much discussion with the participating teacher and after their research relationship had time to develop. She was, however, daunted by the university's expectation that the candidacy examination would determine if she had a clear understanding of her research topic and that she knew *how* she would do the research. At that time she and the participating teacher were much less clear as to where the research was heading. Although they were negotiating a study that they wanted to be developmental for both and would include both of their meanings of the data, the methodology and their responsibilities in the study were aspects they were working out as they got to know each other better and as they came to understand how the study fit the context of the teacher's classroom.

The Story of the Researcher as Expert

The university requires the doctoral candidate to author the research proposal and the research report. At the candidacy examination and the thesis defense it is the candidate who must respond to questions and defend the findings. There is an implication in this process that the researcher has sole responsibility for the research question, the methodology, the findings and the interpretation of the findings. This assumption is in conflict with the reality of collaborative narrative research that involves a joint construction and reconstruction of knowledge.

Even as she wrote her proposal and prepared for the candidacy exam, Debra questioned whether she could call her research collaborative. As the doctoral student, she was the one who had to prepare the proposal before she was officially allowed to proceed to candidacy and ethical review—before she was approved to involve any of the other participants in this "collaborative project." Although she wanted to do research with other teachers as partners rather than as subjects, simply imagining the teachers she might work with when the candidacy process was completed left her in the position of the expert who could decide both what was needed to be known and how this would be accomplished. It also left those as yet unnamed others in a position where they had to join a process already in progress. Her feeling that this experience of "entering into the middle of everything . . . life going on . . . like a foreign film," using the words of one of the teachers, would make it more difficult for all members of the group to own this research as full partners was confirmed by the comments of one participant at the second meeting of the group: "I'm still not clear enough. I think I will have to read your proposal over a lot of times to get a sense of the direction we're going." Her attempt to create room for all the participants' voices was not initially understood. (In another chapter in this book Kathie describes with Janet Blond, her partici-pant/co-researcher, how they too experienced the meta-narrative of the researcher-as-expert as problematic.)

Our discomfort with the way the university positioned us as the expert resonates with Janet Miller's experience as described in Hollingsworth and Miller (1994). Miller says that while the hierar-chical structures of the institution commonly indicate she should posit herself as the expert, particularly in relation to her work with her students and K-12 teachers, these expectations have often col-lided with her own and others' internalizations based on race, age, gender or class. She struggles with how the university positions her, how she sees herself, and how others perceive her.

Another perspective of the researcher-as-expert emerged when the teachers in our projects revealed that they also had this expec-tation. Kathie tells of an incident early in her study with Janet where communication was impeded by this belief. In a math class Janet was concerned that Kathie was telling her students too much and that the students were not solving the problems for them-selves. However, Janet didn't say anything at the time. Months later she explained: "I thought Kathie was the expert because she was the one doing the Ph.D." Initially the teachers in Debra's study saw her as the one who was supposed to know and to explain exactly what she expected them to do. They perceived her open agenda as a hidden agenda which they had to guess, and they saw the research proposal and dissertation as hers even after they had claimed the conversational storytelling process for themselves. Simi-larly, Miller (in Hollingsworth and Miller 1994) describes how she struggles with the expectation of herself, shared often by her stu-dents, by classroom teachers and by fellow teacher-researchers, to be the expert "the one who will provide all the answers or will at least point the way (p. 122)." She explains, "That expectation of course, comes with the traditional academic and hierarchical posi-tioning of professor as creator and conveyer of knowledge." Miller also tells how she has had to deal with teachers' anger when she didn't "know" how to go about constructing a critically oriented teacher-researcher collaborative—when she admitted she did not know how to be the expert. These experiences have led us, as teachers, researchers and doctoral candidates, to recognize and understand that issues of power, control and authority are central to the academy's sacred story of the researcher as the expert. With Connelly and Clandinin (1994), we draw attention to the limited possibilities for teacher development inherent in the hierarchical relationships between universities and schools and the way these are perpetuated by the story/expectation/myth of the researcher-as-expert. In their most recent book (Clandinin and Connelly 1995), these researchers further explicate the negative consequences of this sacred story for teachers' professional development.

Ethics Review Issues

We have several concerns with present ethical guidelines established by the university as they relate to collaborative narrative research with teachers, including interpretations of informed consent, the requirement for anonymity of participants, and the expectation that doctoral research will constitute no significant risk to these persons. The university's (and often the school system's) requirement for anonymity in research involving human participants is designed to protect the privacy of individuals who take part in academic research and ensure they, or their ideas, are not personally identified. However, this requirement also serves to prevent participants from getting credit for their contribution to the research. Schulz (1994) draws attention to the contradiction between the attention university researchers pay to acknowledging the ideas of their colleagues' work (verbal and in print) and the readiness with which they hide the identity of the persons in their studies. As two teachers doing research *with* other teachers, there seems to us something hypocritical and very unfair in the university's requirement that only our names are listed on the final reports of our research projects. The implication is that the work is entirely of our own doing and that collaboration with the teachers, so essential to our findings and the significance of our work, is denied.

The notion of informed consent expressed in the ethical guidelines for research that each of us was issued by our departments is also intended to protect the research participants. However, the university's expectation that participants who sign a research agreement at the commencement of a study are fully informed as to what they have consented to implies that the research project has been fully explicated prior to the commencement of the study. The reality of collaborative narrative research with teachers, however, is that the research tends to change over time. The teacher's role in the research may change during a study to include being a data collector, a data interpreter, and even a co-writer of the research reports. Such roles may not have been anticipated at the time the researcher initially approached the teacher to participate in the study. Since collaborative narrative research is an evolving process, rather than an established procedure which can be planned in advance and rigorously adhered to, the concept of informed consent is a misnomer in need of further discussion. It is not enough that we gain consent prior to commencing research. In collaborative research the consent of participants needs to be renegotiated throughout the project. Another reality is that participants' circumstances and commitment to the project may change throughout the life of a collaborative research project, and they may become more or less involved. It is reasonable to expect that some collaborative projects might be discontinued when the interest of participants wanes or they see that there is little future benefit for them in continuing. What are the ethical issues, however, when the researcher is a doctoral student who has a dissertation to complete? The need to bring the research to an acceptable conclusion may necessitate changes to the collaborative relationship(s).

In the context of our research projects informed consent was redefined. It was not seen as something that could be given a priori, even with the usual provision stipulating a person in the research is free to withdraw at any time without penalty. Rather, it was incorporated as an ongoing part of the research process. For her study Debra constructed a participation agreement which all participants signed after reading her proposal and meeting for the first time. Though they had signed this agreement, the teachers made it clear they wanted to be able to renegotiate at any time. They recognized they might change their views over time and they wanted a flexible approach to data collection and reporting that would honor the way they reconstructed their knowledge. They wanted to be able to change their final story as reported by the researcher. Kathie and Janet also resisted a binding research agreement and acknowledged that change was expected. We see the teachers in our studies as having argued for including reflective practice in our research methodologies.

Our applications for ethical review were based on the principal of informed consent and granted on the provision that each of our studies would pose no significant risks to the participants. Our concern with this ethical guideline is that emphasis is placed on "not doing harm to" the research participants. As teachers doing research with other teachers, we question if "not doing harm to" is a sufficient goal to strive toward in research agendas. If we are going to engage teachers in an ongoing collaborative research process, which requires them to commit significant amounts of time to the joint construction of knowledge, we also need to ask questions about the potential benefits of the research to the teachers who are involved. It does not seem sufficient that we not do harm to the participants or that our research make a significant contribution to knowledge in the field of study.

Linking Feminist Theory and Collaborative Methodology

Through valuing the experience of participants and mutually constructing and reconstructing the research knowledge, our collaborative projects with teachers are designed to lead to transformative change. We, as women teachers doing research with other women teachers, have found the need to make our own interpretations of qualitative research and question the boundaries that constrict our work. In the same manner that Luke and Gore (1992) question the implementation of the theory of critical pedagogy in their classrooms, we feel that the literature on research methodology and the university requirements for doctoral research (informed by the literature) fail to address the realities we face in doing collaborative narrative research with teachers.

Whereas we acknowledge that there are many feminisms and recognize that not all feminists are trying to understand collaboration, we identify some commonalities between our collaborative narrative inquiries with teachers and feminist theory. Feminists share the assumptions held generally by qualitative or interpretive researchers that interpretive human actions, whether found in women's reports of experience or in the cultural products of reports of experience, can be the focus of research (Olesen 1994). For feminists the ultimate test of knowledge is not whether it is true according to an abstract criterion, but whether or not it leads to progressive change (Weiler 1988 cited in Lewis 1993, 4). We, like Hollingsworth and her co-researchers' (1994), claim that our collaborative research is feminist research. We agree with Olesen (1994) that feminist qualitative research assumes intersubjectivity between researcher and participant and the mutual creation of data. Further to this, Lewis (1993) frames experience as a feminist issue and provides a rationale for why the personal has been so problematic for the academy. She states: "It is precisely because of the power of the personal that, traditionally, the academy has encouraged us to believe that knowledge is possible only if we set our looking outside of the context of our lived realities. Contained by the blinders of 'objectivity' our peripheral vision has been limited by those restrictive codes which forbid personal discourse" (Lewis 1993, 5). We draw attention to the restrictive codes which "guide" doctoral research and render problematic the omission of any reference to transformative change, subjectivity, or the personal.

Implications for Changing the University Landscape

One of the most profound changes in the university landscape we are arguing for is the recognition of collaborative narrative research with teachers as developmental for both teacher and researcher. For this to happen, the language and emphasis of the university's requirements for doctoral research need to change. The language of the ethical guidelines for research (*University of Alberta Calendar 1995/96*, 62) is framed in terms of "good scientific enquiry." However, the language of scientific enquiry is not neutral (Keller 1992). Keller critiques "good science" and argues that it distorts how we see the world due to its embeddedness in particular cultural, political, and linguistic frames. Even though the words "human participant" have replaced subject or object in our university's guidelines for research, there is no recognition that research may be a mutual construction and reconstruction of knowledge as is possible in collaborative research. For example, the statement, "Human participation in research includes the direct or indirect involvement of persons who are the focus of a researcher's inquiry" (*University of Alberta Calendar 1995/96*, 62) implies research is "done to" human participants. We argue that such language constrains the possibilities and limits the purpose of educational research, particularly for doctoral candidates attempting to negotiate collaborative research projects with teachers.

University research policies need to change to recognize the flexibility required for effective and meaningful collaborative narrative research that benefits both researcher and participants. The requirements for doctoral candidates to proceed to candidacy emerge from a fixed view of research, which allows little flexibility for the research model to change. One criteria commonly used by doctoral committees to determine whether candidates are ready to undertake research is the preparation of a research agenda. The logical sequential nature of these flow-chart plans assumes that research proceeds in a linear fashion, each step can be predetermined, and it is reasonable to estimate how long each phase will take. Collaborative research, however, is a changing process that involves reflective, cyclical and even regressive steps. Planning for such research needs to be open—not fixed—and university guidelines (and doctoral committees interpreting the guidelines) should be flexible enough to reflect this reality. What is needed is recognition of collaborative research as an active, creative and interpretive process. Negotiation and renegotiation are central to this research process. Both the timing and purpose of candidacy examinations may need to change to reflect these realities.

Time continued to be an issue throughout our research projects as we attempted to create collaborative research milieus while sticking to predetermined schedules. It takes time to develop a relationship, to get to know teachers well enough for them to tell their stories. Collaboration is relational; building relationships is an ongoing process. In the requirements for doctoral research, however, there is no acknowledgement of the significance of the research relationship or the time required to develop this relationship. Zajano and Edelsberg (1993) reveal the development of a trust relationship between researcher and practitioner enhanced their research and changed the nature of their study. They suggest (as do Cole and Knowles 1993; and Connelly and Clandinin 1990) this has profound implications for how we think about research.

We raise for concern the ways a doctoral research agenda may cause abbreviation of the development of the research relationship. The demands of doctoral research require that people make commitments to relationships they would normally make much more slowly. We have found some participants try to shorten the time needed for trust to develop, whereas others volunteer personally revealing information much more slowly. Within this context, it is not surprising that participants withhold potentially important information they do not yet feel safe to disclose, but it leads us to wonder how valid the findings will be. At the first meeting of Debra's group, one of the teachers identified time and relationship as a concern when she said that under normal circumstances she would not say the things she was saying until a trusting relationship had been established but, because their time was limited, she was not going to waste it by engaging in the usual rituals of small talk and safe talk. In doing this, she was putting herself in a vulnerable position. She was also putting Debra (the person the university held ultimately responsible for ensuring the research participants were protected) in the vulnerable position of hoping her trust was not being misplaced. If participants disclose personal information more quickly than they would under circumstances where trust is built in a reciprocal relationship of self-disclosure, we wonder how vulnerable the participants might be, both in the group and in the published findings. The current requirements for doctoral research do not seem to address the kind of vulnerabilities, for participants or researcher, we have experienced in our collaborative studies.

The major requirement of doctoral research is that it make an original contribution to the field. In negotiating collaborative research with teachers, it is not enough that only this expectation be met. We suggest it is unethical to expect teachers to commit themselves to projects that may be of limited professional and personal value. To address this issue, we would alter present requirements for judging the worthiness of a research proposal to include the provision for teachers' comments concerning the potential usefulness of the project to them. If based on Noddings' (1986) notion of fidelity to persons, then collaborative narrative research needs to answer critical questions of how we care for all the persons in the research (Webb, Schulz, Schroeder, and Brody 1994).

Caring for teachers in research could begin by asking: Why would teachers be involved and of what benefit will the research be to them? It might include providing them with time, space, and freedom to engage in research they see as professionally developmental. Ethical behavior, based on an ethic of caring in collaborative narrative research, might mean that teachers are named in the research and that the final research report be presented as multiple stories and interpretations, rather than as one truth where all voices have been melded into one story. There is a need to question how research can be called collaborative if only the researcher's voice is heard in the final research report. From our perspective, this is an ethical issue. Collaboration which benefits teachers may require providing the opportunity for more than one person to author the final research report. It might open up the possibility for more than one person to own the research data and for all participants to use jointly constructed data as approved by the group. However, all of these suggestions create dilemmas for the doctoral student using a collaborative narrative approach working within current ethical guidelines.

Conclusion: The Challenge of a New Story

The power of the researcher to control the research is implied in current requirements for doctoral research. While issues of power, control, and authority are central to negotiating collaborative research, there is little, if any, recognition in our university's regulations that teachers can be full partners in research. We argue for doctoral research guidelines that recognize working collaboratively with others requires flexibility, a willingness to renegotiate the working relationship, and mutually agreeable expectations throughout the life of a collaborative study. Substantive changes to the language and intent of doctoral research requirements are needed in order to recognize that in collaborative studies human participation in research means more than the direct or indirect involvement of persons who are the focus of a researcher's inquiry. Additions to current university ethical guidelines for research might include statements such as: In collaborative research, human participation means person(s) engaging with a researcher in shared inquiry. This shared inquiry may include shared responsibility for determining the research focus, and/or decisions about data, and/or joint interpretations of data, and/or coauthoring the research reports.

Faculties of education could take a proactive step in redefining teacher development through recognition of teachers' contributions in collaborative studies of teachers' work. This recognition could take the form of requiring applications for ethical review of collaborative research projects at department levels to include statements by participating teachers as to potential benefits of the study to their development as teachers. Further, teachers' perceptions of the potential for transformative change as a result of their participation in research (doctoral or otherwise) should be valued and, consequently, requested by all authorities (university faculties of education and school boards) giving permission for research to commence. The ethics review process for doctoral research also needs to ask questions about how consent might be renegotiated throughout collaborative studies. This is both an ethical and a methodological issue.

Traditionally in doctoral research, the ethical review, candidacy examination, and permission to commence research happen in close sequence; however, for doctoral candidates planning to engage in collaborative studies, permission to start research may be needed well before the candidacy examination. University doctoral advisory and examining committees should allow candidates wishing to engage in collaborative studies time to develop constructive relationships with participants/co-researchers and time for these persons to mutually decide the research focus before requiring the doctoral candidate to present a research proposal at a candidacy examination.

The changes we suggest challenge an old and accepted story of educational research in which the university researcher decides and controls research. When we tried to create a new story of research in our doctoral studies by collaborating with teachers to co-construct the research knowledge, we found ourselves challenged by doctoral research requirements. If we, as educators and educational researchers, want to tell a new story of collaborative research, we must be aware of the existence of the old story. Unless we take the time to bring it into our group discussions, it will continue to exert an invisible power and control that will sabotage the collaborative research process. Finally, we are mindful that doctoral candidates are expected to make a substantial contribution to the knowledge of the candidate's field of study. Surely this requirement should include candidates pushing at the boundaries of what we call "research" and what good research is supposed to do.

NOTE

1. This chapter was presented as part of an interactive panel presentation, Collaborative Narrative Inquiry and Teacher Research: Issues Emerging From Three Studies, by K. M. Webb, D. Schroeder, and R. Schultz at The Conference on Qualitative Research in Education, University of Georgia, January 1995.

✧ Chapter Seventeen

The Same but Different:
Classroom-Based Collaborative Research
and the Work of Classrooms

Jeff Orr

I met Marlene through my work with schools as a facilitator of pre-practicum experiences in the fall of 1992. I will never forget the picture that came to my eyes as I peeked through the glass separating her classroom from where I stood in the hall. Marlene saw me standing in the hall and invited me into her classroom with a wave of her hand as she continued circulating around the room. Students were engaged in paired or group reading of a novel in their own spaces. Some sat curled up on the rug in the reading corner busily taking turns reading paragraphs to each other. Others sat at their tables and worked eagerly. Several boys read purposefully as they lay propped up on their elbows like walruses on the carpet. When the class ended, I told Marlene her classroom brought forth my image of community. She stated that it was very

247

important to her that her classroom function as a community. She saw her classroom as a place where a community could be built together as students learn to help each other both socially and academically.

When I began to make preparations to do my doctoral research, my thoughts were continually returning to Marlene's classroom. I asked Marlene if she would share her classroom with me for several months. After several conversations in which we negotiated what we would be doing, we formed a research relationship to try to better understand her classroom as a community. As a doctoral student, I was intrigued by the sociality of Marlene's classroom and wanted to know how her classroom community could help me understand the place of classroom environments in shaping students' social responsibility. Marlene wanted to know how she could make her own classroom more of a community so her students could grow in their sense of social responsibility. I joined her and her students as a researcher, co-teacher, and learner, as part of this classroom community at the beginning of April 1993 and stayed there until late June. The following letter, which I wrote to Marlene, clarifies the parameters of our research and the ethics which framed it.

January 12, 1993

Dear Marlene

I feel the need to engage in a research relationship which honors the knowledge and skill of you as a classroom teacher. It seems to me that there is too much research that wrongs teachers and suggests ways that they could make things better, and not nearly enough that sees teachers as knowing, competent professionals with an important story to tell. Teaching is a difficult job, and is filled with problems, dilemmas and complexities. In our research relationship, I hope to understand the complexities with which you live, and try to convey your understanding, and mine, of your classroom as a place where children work together as a community of learners. I guess I believe that it is in classrooms such as yours that children get the real lessons that our society can teach them about the true meaning of citizenship for living and working together as a community. I hope to capture in words, some of the biographical and classroom context that has shaped and shapes your teaching and practical knowledge. I hope to work with you as a co-researcher, with both of us aiming to help each other learn about the classroom as a community. I plan on writing about the meaning you give to your work as a teacher and not to judge it from an outsider perspective. I intend to guarantee you the right to approve the accuracy of my observations and comments, and for you to reserve the right to withdraw from the study at any time that you wish.

Things I would like to do in your classroom:

1/ Work with children on projects, hear them read, help them with editing and any other appropriate activities. 2/ Do as much of your busy work as I can, such as xeroxing, organizing things, etc., so that you will have the energy to talk to me when we need to discuss things. 3/ Talk with some children about what they are doing in your class to try to understand their meaning of the classroom as a community. 4/ Spend some time with you figuring out how you organize your classroom and talk with you about this so that I can better understand your views on classroom as a community. 5/ Observe and describe your approach to running your classroom as a community. 6/ Become involved in the planning of your focus area for April to June so I can figure out where you are heading and how it all fits with your view of the classroom, and so I can help you collect some materials for this area. 7/ Keep a journal of my time in your classroom and have you read it for accuracy and provide you with the opportunity to note things I might miss, or fail to understand, or to suggest a different direction for me to take. 8/ Hear the stories about your classroom both past and present so that I can help tell your story of teaching through these and other means. At the same time I hope to share with you my story, so that you can better understand where I am coming from and how it relates to you and your story.

I would also like to assure you that I have spent quite a bit of time in other peoples' classrooms and feel that I can make myself both useful and scarce when each is appropriate! What I mean by this is that I will be very sensitive to making your life as stress free as possible. . . . I will go with the flow, and I am perfectly aware that this is a reality of classrooms.

Sincerely,

Jeff

Classroom-Based Collaborative Research

There has been considerable attention paid to collaboration in the education literature (Clandinin, Davies, Hogan, and Kennard 1993;

Cochran-Smith and Lytle 1990; Connelly and Clandinin 1988; Schubert and Ayers 1992), but only a few researchers have heard the voices of teachers *and* children (McKay 1990; Paley 1986). Noddings (1986) calls for an approach to educational research that investigates problems which interest and inform teachers, students, and researchers and is aware of the possibility of wronging the researched. This chapter shows how I attempted to follow Nodding's notion of fidelity by engaging in personal experience research *for* teaching and teacher education, not *on* teaching and teacher education, and by remaining committed to collaboration with a teacher *and* her students. It, therefore, explores the nature of collaborative research between teacher and researcher, researcher and children, and teacher and children in a classroom community. It reconsiders the meaning of research in conjunction with the needs, interests, and concerns of all those who are part of it, and tries to insure that "diverse narratives" (Giroux 1992, 25) are not excluded.

The way our various voices, with their differing intentions and meanings are shared and interpreted, provides an opportunity to explore meanings constructed in a collaborative context, and to consider the promises and challenges that classroom-based collaborative research holds for education. Three themes that have relevance for collaboration in classrooms emerged during this study: (a) the need to recognize differing conceptions of time by the researcher and the researched, (b) the significance of differing intentions that individuals bring to the research question, and (c) a recognition of some of the issues associated with collaborative research with children. Following these themes, I discuss their implications for future collaborative research in and for classrooms.

Collaborative Classroom Research and Differing Views of Time

Recognition of the busyness and immediacy of classroom teaching is a key principle that guided our research in Marlene's classroom. The many demands placed upon the lives of teachers often make it difficult for them to find the time to co-labor with university researchers. This study showed the need to recognize the importance of time for teacher-researcher and university-researcher, and to keep this at the center of the research agenda.

It became evident from the beginning of my research relationship with Marlene that the rhythm of her life as a teacher meant she had little time to herself during the teaching day. Not only was

she busy with teaching, but she was also inundated with responsibilities from other aspects of her work. She had interviews with
all the parents of her students. A film crew videoed her classroom
for an educational television production. Four teachers from other
schools visited and observed in her class. Two writers of a math
textbook she was piloting spent a number of math periods with her.
Several parents of future students observed in her classroom to
find out about her education program, and four parents regularly
volunteered in her classroom. These events were in addition to
regular school routines such as collecting money for the spell-a-
thon, organizing cross-age events for the entire school, being on
regular morning, recess, and noon hour duties, planning for the
school-family barbecue and the parent appreciation tea, organizing
the field trip to the dinosaur exhibit, carrying out a weekly set up
and take down of the gymnastics equipment in the gym, and planning and preparing for day-to-day happenings.

Time was a significant issue for Marlene, as it is for all teachers, because of the immediacy of teaching and the many pressing
and often difficult to fulfill needs her students had. This pressure
to fit the many school demands into her day was a major theme of
her teaching life.

Marlene: I guess my biggest worry right now is the time, and
I guess that is always a worry for teachers. The year always
seems to fly by and you've only got half of what you want to
get done. I am getting worried about conference reports because I know that takes me a very long time to do that. I am
trying to think when am I going to do it. And with our dinosaur commitments for the next three weeks that sort of comes
out of your social time. I can't give up my math time because
of the testing that is coming up and that kind of thing, and
then this pilot, and just trying to sort out when I am going to
do things (personal communication, April 27, 1993)

Marlene was excited about the possibilities of researching her
own classroom but she was concerned that her time remain in her
control. One of the conditions she wanted to place upon her involvement in this collaborative study was that she be free to choose
the time we met to discuss our research. She maintains her professional health by getting out of the school at noon and after school,
so that when she is in the school she can remain focused on the
children and the many demands of teaching. The conversations we

held about her classroom had to fit into her time frame so she would not be pulled away from her focus on her students. I was one of many individuals placing demands upon her time and I knew I could easily become a major burden on her if I was not careful. Nevertheless, she indicated it was normal for her to have many people in her room and she was comfortable with me being there.

To me, time was also important because I was on a tight research schedule. I would only be available for the three months of April, May, and June. I had to get our conversations taped and transcribed so I would not fall behind in providing these for Marlene to read. I was constantly wondering: Do we have enough data? Are we meeting enough to discuss classroom events? Am I getting enough time with the children during and after classroom activities so we can get a broad perspective of classroom life? This meant my view of what should be happening was focused upon my concerns for seeing as much of the classroom as I could, to meet my obligations as a doctoral researcher.

Marlene's time pressures confirmed for me the need to help her with the daily chores of her classroom so she would be free to talk regularly. I made a special effort to do as many of the time-consuming preparatory activities such as marking math each noon hour, planning social studies activities, doing her photocopying, and generally taking on emerging activities and duties when they appeared necessary. This helped Marlene and it gave me empathy for the demands of her teaching role.

Time has very important implications for classroom-based collaboration. Respecting time concerns allows researchers to show their caring for one another as they live and work together. Marlene and I had differing concerns about time, which alerted us to the need to respect each other's goals for the research project and to realize the research project was but a small part of Marlene's work-related obligations. Our collaboration was about working together, not simply researching together. As the outsider in Marlene's classroom I was not unlike a guest in her home. Just as a guest who is around for an extended period of time will pitch in and help out with household chores and show a caring for the general well-being of the events of the house, so, too, should a researcher who is around for extended periods of time. Collaborative research in classrooms must aim for more than theoretical or practical understanding; it must demonstrate a sense of caring for the work of practice through a mutuality of labor and a sensitivity to each other's intentions.

Differing Intentions for Educational Research

Differences in our respective educational intentions became more and more evident as we labored together in the classroom. These differences were manifested in the roles we found ourselves playing in the teaching/research process. The classroom research in which Marlene and I engaged meant that I was interacting with the children on a regular basis in order to help us figure out what sense they were making of her classroom as a community. Although I saw this through my doctoral research lens, Marlene saw it through her teacher research lens:

> **Marlene:** Your role with the kids. I think that is important. Trying to get to know them through working with them at gym, playing ball, that kind of thing, because you get to see different aspects, particularly the social aspect of what is going on. Things that maybe I have missed too. Listening to the kids in the group, and helping them. I think it is important for the role of the child in the classroom. I guess I am always thinking of what is best for the child, and I think if I wouldn't have thought there was going to be a benefit to the children in this then I wouldn't have agreed to do it. It wasn't making it easier for me, but can make it better for the kids in this room. You are extra help for them. A role model, as a male. Because I am a female. Things like that. (personal communication, April 27, 1993)

I performed as a teacher assistant for many tasks and taught some lessons, but my role in the classroom was different than Marlene's. I did not have the power Marlene did and, although I could lighten her teaching pressures by doing some teaching, my position was subordinate. Marlene and I commented about our different roles:

> **Jeff:** When it comes to many teachable moments you would probably transform those situations, whereas on a number of them I don't act. One reason is that I can't do it the same way because I don't have the power in here to do it.
>
> **Marlene:** I think it is neat when I do handle them. You can watch and see exactly what I do and you can say to yourself,

"Would I do it that way?, or would I change it to a different way?" or "Now I see why they do certain things." (personal communication, May 3, 1993)

We talked about the different roles we played in the research process. When I asked Marlene for her opinion about how I might express her actions in the classroom in words, she indicated this was something she saw as my responsibility and not hers:

Jeff: There are all these wonderful things. How do I begin to capture it in print?

Marlene: I'm glad that is your job and not mine. (personal communication, April 14, 1993)

Marlene was interested in researching her classroom, but forays into the literature to contextualize issues in a broader theoretical framework did not really interest her. When I raised my interest in her classroom as a way to understand other classrooms, Marlene commented about the meaning of this research for her classroom:

Jeff: Part of my goal is to see how your classroom speaks to *other* classrooms.

Marlene: I have always said "What is best for working in *my* classroom?" That is why the things that I find really interesting reading . . . are the little anecdotal things that come up when you talk with the kids or conversations that you hear. (personal communication, May 3, 1993)

Although we had different interests in the collaborative relationship, they complemented each other. As we tried to make sense out of Marlene's classroom as a community, Marlene always pushed for more relevance for the children in our talk. When we were discussing the meaning of a classroom activity for a group of children, my desire to understand the children's world was not enough for Marlene. She used our emerging understanding to try to make the learning environment more focused upon developing a sense of community for the children. As time passed, I saw this as much more central to our agenda and came to respect and honor this dimension to our collaboration more fully:

Jeff: The math lesson between Marvin, Linda, and Kristen was almost like a fairy tale. There is a problem and a solution that comes about when Marvin learned his math. You can see by the end of it that he knew how to do that.

Marlene: Maybe that is something that we could talk about with the kids, so that they can see the reason for me wanting them to do this. James and the ones that are having trouble know that is going to help them with their math, but does Edward think it is helping him? It would be interesting to pose the question to Edward and Randy, who are fairly strong, and ask them, if they couldn't do a question, how would they solve that? (personal communication, May 3, 1993)

Marlene saw the children's voices as being central to our research. When I was interviewing the children about their classroom creed (their written statement of principles of classroom beliefs), I was interested in asking them about the purpose of their creed, but Marlene saw these interviews as an opportunity to empower her students to further shape their community:

Marlene: I think it would be neat to ask them what is it that they like about this class. What do they like about this classroom? What kinds of things do they like in the classroom? It would be kind of neat to ask them if there was anything that they could change in this classroom, what would it be? What kinds of things would they do to make this a better classroom, besides having more gym? (personal communication, May 13, 1993)

"Tell and Guess" is an activity in which Marlene gives students ownership for developing their own examples of word families. When I observed some children not beginning their "Tell and Guess" activity with the customary invitational comments, and mentioned this to Marlene, she saw this as another opportunity to have her students consider the activity as a way to help them be more responsible members of their community:

Jeff: Sometimes during "Tell and Guess," people will be good watching and then others won't. I wonder if they just forget.

Marlene: Sometimes they don't need to because the other children are watching. Sometimes they forget too, because I have to sort of prompt them. It would be neat to ask them why it is important to watch, because it is important to watch. (personal communication, April 20, 1993)

Part of the promise of collaboration relates to the possibilities it holds for meeting peoples' differing needs within the same project. As Marlene and I talked with a shared understanding and purpose about the issues of community that concerned us, we came to realize our research agendas were "the same but different." I was interested in seeing how understanding Marlene's classroom community could tell me something about living responsibly in other contexts. Marlene was focused upon using the data from our research to understand her own classroom so she could make it a better place for her students. It is the complex differences which are made possible in "same but different" research that helps make classroom-based collaborative research a potentially educative experience. This "same but different" agenda was also evident in my conversation with the children.

Co-Laboring With Children

Children's comments allowed us to see the way they were making sense of their social context, which greatly influenced our understanding of community. This helped us approach our work with more certainty that we were doing what was best for children. Although many of the children's comments strengthened the convictions Marlene and I held about community, they also added new perspectives that showed how children were experiencing their environment, activities, and classroom routines from their unique place as learners. Their perspectives both confirmed and challenged our notions of community.

Children confirmed the significance of this classroom as a place that created a sense of community for them. For instance, Cheryl's talk reminded us of the powerful message being sent to children through the physical environment of the classroom. She told us, "All over the room it says we are special and I am special. It always says we are special. So everybody knows, there's a whole bunch of signs" (personal communication, May 6, 1993). Terry let us know about the importance of each child's uniqueness as an aspect of this community. "Every person is unique in a way. . . . They all do things their own way. I might do something one way and they might do it a different way" (personal communication, May 6, 1993). The feelings children registered about their classroom environment helped convince Marlene and me of the importance of the hidden curriculum in sending positive messages to children.

By listening with curiosity (Paley 1986), we heard students' perceptions of their classmates' place in their community. After I observed Carl, Marvin, Karne, and Art during a readers' theater practice, Carl told me, "Nobody else picks Marvin and Karne for anything. They are getting better at plays cuz we are helping them." Art supported Carl's comments and told me the reason for the boys' isolation was, "Marvin is new and Karne is sort of new to this class" (personal communication, April 30, 1993). These comments helped us see the children's awareness of their classroom as a place that welcomed others and showed us the need to put more emphasis upon developing this kind of social space in this and other classrooms.

Children's expressions of their points of view also showed they were internalizing both social and pedagogical reasons for community-oriented activities in the classroom. Tanya noted, "Ms. G. tells us why she puts us in groups and with partners, to teach us to work with other people, because when we get a job we will have to work with other people. We can't work by ourselves" (personal communication, May 31, 1993). Terry said, "I have learned to be cooperative with other people and to help them when they want help" (personal communication, May 28, 1993). Kristen internalized the problem-solving focus of the cozy corner:

> We are supposed to be in a circle and we work out problems there like if someone is throwing snowballs. She will remind us not to do things like that because some people throw snowballs and you forget about it. She doesn't say you have to do something. She just asks us what we can do about it. (personal communication, May 6, 1993)

Karne talked about the sense of support provided by others.

> This group has been good because we have a partner and we share books. They help me by sounding it out. They cover the word half of it, and that's all. It is okay when they help me. I learn to be a good reader. (personal communication, May 31, 1993)

Tanya felt good about collaborating with Susan through peer editing.

Instead of doing it just by yourself you have help. When you are doing it by yourself it is not very much fun because you have to lift your dictionary in your hand and then you have to do this and then when you find your word you have to write it. It is easier if you have two people. One can do looking up the words and one can do the writing down. It is just so fun. (personal communication, April 27, 1993)

These children's stories remind us that children are making sense of their classroom community and its purposes in ways adults do not. This shows the value of listening carefully to their voices to better understand what they are experiencing in the classroom. Their stories reveal their feelings about being in community with others and the feelings they come to hold for each other. This confirms this classroom as a place that teaches social and educational responsibility.

Although many of their stories were in support of the way Marlene's classroom community was organized, children also openly showed dissension from the way community was being lived in the classroom by challenging the reason for some classroom routines. This research formed an important forum through which they voiced their desires for changes in their classroom. When classroom activities were frustrating them, they did not hesitate to tell me. Although sharing gym with another class was intended to help students learn to work with a wider community, Mandy questioned this activity in a conversation with me:

Sometimes it is kinda really not fair when Ms. Andrew's class comes with us, because sometimes I just want to be with my class. I don't know why but it is kinda boring when other people always have to come with you. You can't be with your same class for phys. ed. or anything. (personal communication, June 14, 1993)

Kristen's frustration with being expected to work with two partners in math exemplifies her struggle to live in community:

I don't like working with partners that need a lot of help, but just a little bit of help because I get all mixed up. Linda needed help on rounding and Marvin needed help on rounding and I didn't know who to help first because Linda forgot how to round and Marvin didn't know how to round. It is okay except for when I have two people at once. That gets sort of hard. I feel frustrated. (personal communication, May 3, 1993)

Edward also found it frustrating to be asked to work with others. "I didn't like switching books because it slows me down. I am finished and they are still writing the question down" (personal communication, April 30, 1993). Donald talked about his desire to work alone when he had to work with partners:

> Sometimes when we have to work together I just want to work by myself. I kind of have no choice even though the person is slow at math. I didn't really like slow partners but sometimes you just have to wait up. A fact of life. (personal communication, May 20, 1993)

Engaging in research that strives to involve students as collaborative participants by including their voices in the research text had pedagogical significance for classrooms. Listening with curiosity to what children had to say allowed us to hear things that would not normally be heard. Their stories, in turn, helped Marlene understand how her classroom community was, and was not, meeting the children's needs for social responsibility.

Classroom-Based Research and the Work of Classrooms

Marlene wanted to know how her classroom could become more of a community to improve her students' social responsibility. Her comments about our new understanding of the children's perceptions of the classroom creed are indicative of how she made use of the knowledge which I uncovered:

> **Marlene:** I think it is really good bringing in the children, and having them talk about what they think. I am learning from this that I need to spend more time on talking about the creed and revisit it more often, because the kids aren't able to articulate it. From reading the interviews with the students I know that I need to do more of that next year. Some can, but not all of them, so that is telling me that I need to talk more about that. (personal communication, May 13, 1993)

After reading about my interactions with the children, Marlene developed new understandings of her students' perspectives on the classroom, which she then used to transform her practice.

> **Marlene:** How can I help my philosophy be more strong by looking at the voice of the kids? When you are teaching in classrooms by yourself you don't hear that voice as much as I am getting to hear it with you interviewing. Talking about the kinds of things they don't like such as exchanging books. From reading and reflecting upon what I have read in here, I have been looking at how I can change. I really feel that you have to keep learning and keep looking at what you are doing and looking to see what you can do better. (personal communication, May 13, 1993.)

Collaboration with children may be a way to more fully democratize classroom practice, since it can make space for their needs to be heard and, where feasible and appropriate, incorporated into the classroom. It can serve as a form of action research to help teachers see the centrality of their classroom community in shaping education for social life.

Eavesdropping on her own classroom enabled Marlene to make changes which fit with her desire for classroom community, but it also helped her see that her notion of community had to sometimes be more flexible. For instance, when Kristen expressed frustration about being the teacher to two students during math, it revealed to me the struggle to work with others in community. To Marlene, reading my field notes gave her a better sense of Kristen's frustration so she could put this new knowing to work to help Kristen feel less frustrated. "Kristen made the comment that she had a hard time working with three, so I am going to let somebody else have the responsibility of working with three this time" (personal communication, May 13, 1993).

This collaborative research with children has relevance for the work of classrooms and serves as a model of how to provide children with a voice in determining the direction in their own classrooms. When children talked to me as researcher, their intentions were partly to express their satisfaction with their classroom in order to challenge the status quo. Classroom-based collaborative research that hears children's intentions has the potential to shape the future direction of classroom events to make classroom life more positive for children. The issues they surface often have a focus specific to their individual needs and is thus different from what an adult would see in the same situation. Marlene and I became focused upon achieving our own specific agendas related to community, which could have ignored children's voices, if we did not remain curious.

By working with Marlene directly in her classroom, I was able to become attuned to the importance she and her students placed upon classroom perspectives that influenced citizenship education and to reflect upon the meaning of this for other classrooms. For me, this relationship served as a form of research that helped me further my understanding of classrooms as a place where citizenship education is continuously being learned. It showed me that classroom relationships are an important way to contribute to an education for social life.

Implications for Classroom-Based Collaborative Research

Classroom-based collaborative research can serve as an important way to link outside researchers with teachers, in ways that create new and educationally significant perspectives that influence education at multiple levels. Classroom-based collaborative research can be significant for classroom teachers who are able to research their practice by receiving support, comradeship, and educational insights from an outside researcher who shares a research interest and takes time to listen to the children in ways that even the most perceptive of teachers would find difficult to do. This particular collaborative relationship and the new perspectives of children which it uncovered, helped Marlene make her classroom more of a community. Classroom-based collaborative research can be significant for outside researchers and their research audiences by allowing access to teachers' and students' microlevel perspectives while, at the same time, allowing them to consider connections to broader societal issues. Specifically, it allowed me to connect Marlene's professional knowledge to the theoretical literature on citizenship education for social responsibility. Classroom-based collaborative research can be significant for students and allow their voices about classroom issues to be heard in a way that gives them input into the shaping of classroom agendas. The children of Marlene's classroom were able to confirm and challenge the way community was being lived out in their classroom.

Classroom-based collaborative research can be a significant way to hear and respond to the intricacies of the classroom in a way that is more sensitive than even the most discerning teacher.

It allows the outside researcher and the classroom teacher to look more carefully at how children view the classroom intentions of teachers, since the outside researcher can devote more sustained efforts to hearing their voices. It provides an opportunity to become more aware of the differing aspirations children have for their place in classrooms and to represent their perspectives more accurately. Yet this sensitivity will not likely occur if classroom-based collaborative research does not recognize and respond to differing intentions and differing perceptions of time which are at the heart of the teaching-research relationship. Common work can be enhanced if the collaborators sense these temporal needs and differing intentions and account for them through their actions. This is not easy, since the pressures of classroom life and peoples' differing intentions can take participants in opposing directions. Classroom-based collaborative research must have a common purpose to guide the relationship, yet it must also allow participants to develop their different intentions. Classroom-based research must, therefore, weave a fabric of commonality that also has space for difference.

✧ Chapter Eighteen

Are We Partners Yet? From Institutional Agreement to Personal Power

Caroline Krentz and Beth Warkentin

What can a collaborative evaluation tell participants about their five-year partnership? Caroline and Beth present the results of an evaluation of Project Child, a cooperative venture between our faculty of education and a large urban school division. This project was an attempt by two institutions to "cooperate in pre-service teacher education and in-service staff development" (Krentz and Warkentin 1994, 3). Caroline had participated in the establishment and evolution of the five-year project, while Beth had a more immediate perspective focused on what the evaluation revealed about collaboration and partnerships.

What follows is the story of the evolution of the project and how it changed from an institutional, and somewhat formal, agreement to a more personal but professionally empowering experience for the teachers who became the central figures in the project. First, we summarize the background and the context in which the project was conceptualized. Next, we talk about the evaluation process and what we learned from the analysis of the responses to the evaluation. Finally, we ponder the lessons that would inform future collaborative projects between faculty and school staff, and conclude with a view about the legacy of the project.

The Background and the Context

In the initial planning, school division administrators consulted the principal of the selected school but the teachers were not involved. Several faculty members consulted with the Dean of Education prior to developing the final proposal with the administrators from the central office of the school division. The agreement between the two institutions was approved by the elected officials of the school division at one of their formal business meetings.

The site for Project Child was chosen because it was a community school that had a prekindergarten for three- and four-year-olds with empty classrooms to accommodate project activities, and also because of the principal's willingness to participate in the project. In addition, this was an inner-city school with a high aboriginal population. Faculty members hoped that this location would become a laboratory site for pre-service teachers learning early childhood philosophy and methodology. The partners agreed that three major goals would guide the project over its five years. These included: (a) child-centered instruction in the classrooms, (b) involvement of the community and the families, and (c) cooperation between the university and the school division.

As the story unfolded, year-end reports indicated the project had gradually added activities and events that encouraged children to take more responsibility for their learning; community involvement had been enhanced through cross-cultural themes and celebrations; and classrooms had welcomed faculty of education professors and students. The following chart summarizes the project's development over the five years.

The Project's Five Years

1989–1990

The project began in the preschool (prekindergarten) and kindergarten classrooms with a focus on child-centered teaching and developmentally appropriate practice for four- and five-year-olds. Teachers participated in a university course which encouraged increasing cross-cultural understanding in the classrooms and family involvement in the life of the school.

1990–1991

Grade One (six-year-olds) classrooms joined the project. "Kids on Camera"—a family discussion of live video transmissions—became an integral part of the prekindergarten and kindergarten programs.

1991–1992

Grade Two (seven-year-olds) classes were added. The addition of the second grade classes expanded teacher involvement to six. The objectives and focus remained the same as in the initial stages.

1992–1993

All primary teachers (including teachers of eight-year-olds) actively planned and guided the project. University students participated in project classrooms as observers and student teachers. Action research with a faculty member was implemented in one classroom.

1993–1994

Teachers continued to open their classrooms to faculty and students from the university. Community involvement was evident with many visitors participating in the project classes either before, during, or after school.

In the cooperative spirit of Project Child, the evaluation methodology used a responsive and collaborative approach that encouraged interaction and dialogue about its impact. Sirotnik (1988) argues that school-university partnerships are "evolving social experiments by people in the context of their own work, ideologies, and interests" (p. 169) and that these partnerships attempt to foster collaboration in traditionally noncollaborative institutions. The usual canons of research and evaluation in these situations must give way to collaborative inquiry which he describes as "a process of self-study—of generating and acting upon knowledge, in context, by and for the people who use it" (p. 169).

Teachers, faculty members, and administrators jointly decided the purpose of the evaluation was to capture the perspectives of the participants through three processes: (a) teacher questionnaires that included critical incidents describing professional and personal growth; (b) interviews with certain teachers, faculty, administrators, parents, and pre-service teachers; and (c) a review of relevant documents. Beth and Caroline developed the questionnaire and interview in consultation with project participants. Once these instruments were approved, we conducted the evaluation, analyzed the resulting data, and compiled the draft report for review by the participants. Revisions reflected their suggestions and added clarity to the final report that gave voice to their perceptions and experiences.

Results of the Collaborative Evaluation

Conducting a collaborative evaluation was a time-consuming task but the process netted rich rewards. We found we had an abundance of information about the project's impact on the individuals involved, particularly the teachers. The thoughtful responses on the questionnaires and in the interviews indicated professional reflection about respondents' learning and change. As we analyzed the data we recognized a pattern in the responses. Three distinct stages of change seemed to emerge: the beginning, the transition, and the transformation. Each is presented in the following sections.

The Beginning

Initially, this agreement was the top-down type of partnership in which those who were to implement the partnership had little to say about its design. The partnership arrangement had been negotiated by the administration of the school division and by some university faculty. Teachers had no part in the development of the agreement and limited voice during the first year the project was implemented. Rather, they were expected to conform to the terms of the partnership.

As a person who had been involved in educational change in schools, Caroline had some idea of the need for teachers to be involved in the process if fundamental change was to occur. As Fullan (1991) notes, external change agents, in this case the faculty members, "play an important part in initiating change projects" (p. 56), especially at the outset as they work in combination with local leaders. In our situation, the local leaders were senior administrators at the school division level who were very supportive of the partnership with the university. However, the teachers did not seem to fully accept the presence of faculty in the school. As Caroline read teachers' statements about the beginning of the project, she wondered where the project had gone wrong in the early stages. Perhaps a lack of information and limited involvement in making decisions at the outset had frustrated the teachers who suddenly had to adjust to new ways of working.

Community Response

How did the people who were part of the school community feel about Project Child? In the evaluation we heard comments from these participants about their initial frustrations. For example, the Parent Council was informed early in the first year of the project that the school division had decided to enter into a partnership with the faculty. Community members had little opportunity to discuss the implications of the project for their school. One parent remembered her reaction this way:

> I think it was brought in the wrong way. I was on the Parent Council when it was brought in. We were given one meeting, about 10 minutes, saying that this was being brought in. There wasn't enough public relations being done in the community. (interview, December 1993)

Replication of Children's Centre

Some people felt that faculty were trying to recreate the university's preschool, the Children's Centre, which had recently been closed. Strong feelings of resentment about imposing a middle-class preschool into a community school setting were clearly communicated in these comments:

> When it was brought in, it just seemed like they were taking the Centre from the university and dumping it into the neighborhood without any thought of how it would affect our kids and our teachers ... it just seemed like they were trying to take something that worked with university professors' kids and bringing it in with our kids, who are from a totally

different social and economic reality. (interview, December 1993)

Perceptions of Faculty Involvement

To Beth and Caroline, the messages from the participants suggested that imposing the partnership between the faculty and the school division on the community school was, at first, not acceptable. We wondered how the participants viewed the faculty members who volunteered to work at the school as colleagues. One teacher described her initial reactions:

> The first year I felt as though I had no ownership. I felt much like I was at university and there was the faculty telling me what assignments to do. (interview, December 1993)

New Resources and Positive Support

In contrast, others in the school were welcoming the new materials, people, and positive attention the project brought. Classroom support from faculty and large, expensive equipment and manipulative materials from the university convinced teachers there was a positive side to having the faculty of education involved in the school's program. One person noted that the "abundance of good people involved and the support services given" contributed welcome benefits to the school program (interview, December 1993).

Caroline was relieved to find some people saw value for the school at the outset, but she recognized something more than effort was necessary if teachers were to embrace the project's goals. She observed the faculty supported the change process by focusing on the tasks that needed to be done but seemed to have failed to attend to the impact the change was having on the teachers:

> We seemed to be putting out a lot of effort to make the project work—holding workshops, meeting with teachers and the administration, driving a fair distance to the site. Perhaps we were trying too hard to implement the project and were insensitive to the teachers' views. (discussion notes, C. Krentz, December 1994)

Governance

Beth noted that the governance structure was a cumbersome arrangement and top-heavy during the first year. Two groups managed the project: the Project Child Coordinating Team (PCCT) and the Project Management Team (PMT). The first team (PCCT) was dominated by people external to the school: two superintendents and an assistant superintendent (all from the central office of the school division), three representatives from the faculty, and the principal. The second team (PMT) consisted of two teachers, the principal, and one faculty member. The major decision making took place outside the school, while the day-to-day activities affecting the students and the staff occurred within the school. Teachers were clearly in the minority when it came to setting the direction for the project. From the comments gathered in the evaluation, we saw evidence of the need to involve people in the initial stages so that they had some control over their professional decisions. One teacher reflected this view when she observed: "I think my best learning took place in the second and third years" (interview, December 1993).

One administrator sensed there was initial resistance to and concern about the project. She reminded us that problems and questions are normal in any change process:

> I think we need to keep in mind that some things we call "glitches" are really developmental. If you structure something so tightly that there are no glitches, then I think you damage the project itself because, in the end, the people don't have the ownership. (interview, December 1993)

University Students

One of the goals of the project was to encourage more pre-service teacher involvement in the community school. Faculty were aware of the need to offer more experiences to university students in an inner-city school setting. The partnership was to facilitate such placements. When Beth analyzed the records of minutes and the annual reports from the first two years of the project, it was obvious no significant change had occurred in the number of pre-service teachers invited to participate in practicum assignments. As a faculty member, Caroline had intended to address faculty complaints that student teachers were minimally involved n the school. In the analysis of the early year-end reports, Beth noted the recommendations clearly asked that more university students become part of the partnership. Teacher support was certainly needed if students were to be assigned to the project's classrooms.

The notion of interdependence in collaborative partnerships described by Gray (1989) was obvious as we considered the faculty need for student involvement and the teacher need for more information about the project and its goals for the school. Brookhart and Loadman (1992) suggest that problem definition often stems from teacher concerns and joint decision making (between teachers and researchers) is crucial. In this case, joint decision making would ensure that teachers had a voice in determining the direction of the project and that faculty had a legitimate role with their students in the school.

The Transition

As Beth and Caroline reflected on the information the teachers, administrators, and parents shared in the evaluation, they recognized that early concerns began to disappear as teachers became more involved in the project. The agreement that first appeared to be between two institutional partners, gradually took a different shape. At first teachers were uncomfortable having faculty on site because they were seen as instructors rather than colleagues in the change process. Senior administrators continued to symbolize central authority controlling all change and major decisions.

Transitions take time. Initial reactions give way to more experience as people live the new reality. We heard from participants that the initial year of the project was thrust upon the preschool and kindergarten teachers with the assumption they would be able to adjust to a new way of functioning in a partnership with the faculty. However, one person was philosophical about the situation:

> Not all good things have a good start. They just need some time to grow. I think it's just starting to click in for a lot of people and it's starting to fall into place and people [in the community] are starting to realize that it's [Project Child] here. (interview, January 1994)

Governance

The governance structure seemed to reinforce the view that people other than the teachers knew what was the best practice for the first two classrooms involved in the project. Over the first year, teachers and faculty met informally in weekly meetings. The practice continued into the second and third years. Gradually the atmosphere changed. Teachers became more confident about their roles in the project as instructional decision makers. In addition, the school administration recognized the extra burden that the project and its meetings placed on the teachers. To compensate, each teacher was given release time of two half-days per month for planning and meeting. The teachers were encouraged to decide how best to use their release time. As teachers in the next grades became involved in the project, the release time seemed to become a symbol of central office support for the project. The benefit for teachers was obvious from the following comment:

> By being in the team planning meetings I came to understand how children learn best—through hands-on activities rather than only paper and pencil activities. Only through repeatedly hearing this and observing it in other classrooms, did I gain the confidence to put it to the test in my own classroom. (interview, December 1993)

Formative Evaluation

Annual assessments of the project contained information from all participants and informed us of the changes that had taken place or were recommended for the next year. The Project Management Team continued to meet regularly with increased membership over the five years. The teachers were now the majority and plans reflected their growing sense of control over the direction of the project. The joint ownership that Gray (1989) says is a feature of collaborative partnerships began to emerge. The partnership began to take on a new visage. It was no longer the impersonal and institutional image, but rather the familiar and individual faces of those who were involved on a daily basis—the teachers and the faculty who came regularly to the school. Together they began to set the future directions of the project.

One administrator observed that there was a definite change in the view the teachers had held of the project in its first years.

Indeed, teachers' attitudes seemed to become more supportive of the project as they took over the decision making and agenda. An administrator comments on this change:

> I think the biggest highlight is the attitude of the staff toward teaching and toward the program [Project]—it's been an about-face. It took a little longer than we thought it might, and I think it was a real learning [experience] for us in that you don't empower teachers by just telling them that they now have power—there is a growth process involved and teachers have to find that out for themselves. (interview, December 1993)

Attitudes toward teaching became infused with excitement as new approaches and ideas emerged from the planning meetings. One example of a new approach is described by a teacher talking about a cross-cultural fair which "heightened my awareness and understanding of Native [aboriginal] people and their traditions." Family involvement and child-centered education featured in the event as well.

> My personal growth was enhanced by a cross-cultural fair which featured presentations, activities, and programs put on by various people of aboriginal descent . . . . The fair was a cross-grade event in which students chose the event they wished to attend . . . . It also involved many parents and members of the community, creating a feeling of involvement, one-ness, and harmony. (survey, October 1993)

Climate in the School

Gradually there seemed to be a shift in the acceptance of faculty in the school. A mail box for faculty signaled that university people were gradually being included in the life of the school. Faculty members delivered teacher-planned workshops in areas such as math with manipulatives or emergent literacy. Frequently faculty members introduced research findings and articles from professional journals into meeting discussions. New faculty members were invited to join the regular meetings and visitors from other provinces or countries shared their perspectives on areas of mutual interest. An in-school administrator reflected:

I found teachers reading more . . . . some of the materials have been offered by our partners at the University. That is extremely valuable . . . . As teachers learn more and share more, they have more to say . . . . they were more enhanced in their development and have a professional sense of "We do have something important to talk about. We are gaining knowledge and we want to share it." (interview, January 1994)

Parents and other family members had always been welcome in the school. However, most visits usually coincided with interviews at progress report time. As the project progressed, parents became more comfortable through a number of initiatives that teachers and faculty had introduced. The use of live video transmission to a parent/family gathering in the community school meeting room encouraged family members to become more familiar with the classroom programs. A telephone in the kindergarten classroom linked homes with classroom events. One parent commented that "I always feel comfortable" in the school (interview, January 1994). At interview time more than three quarters of the parents or families were represented in the sessions.

Teacher Satisfaction

As the project progressed, the staff felt more comfortable with the changes occurring in the primary grades. Teachers reported spinoffs to the senior grades where teachers began to modify the physical arrangements in their classrooms. Teacher confidence grew as they voiced their views openly about appropriate practice in classrooms. A kindergarten teacher said:

Over the course of the project, people became more vocal and able to verbalize their understanding of the project. I think sometimes, because you are a kindergarten teacher, there are a lot of things you do and don't tell other teachers about. A lot of people might say, "Forget about her, she's just in kindergarten." But what was done in kindergarten was validated [in the school]. It was okay to try things. And you had other people doing those things too. For me, the most exciting part was when you started seeing teachers in the older grades doing some of the same things. (interview, December 1993)

In the staffroom, teachers shared their sense of commitment and good feeling about their work. The sense of camaraderie and togetherness was reflected in comments that described teachers at the school "as a group who come into the staffroom happy—tell jokes, have coffee—it's one big happy family" (interview, December 1993).

Beliefs and Perspectives

School and central office administrators clearly saw the school as a place where university students could "see what child-centeredness is really like" (interview, December 1993). The project, in their minds, also demonstrated to the university community that the school system was open and receptive to participating in teacher education as a full partner. The project's benefit to the children in the school became a common theme among these administrators. This is echoed in statements such as:

> Cognitive skill development and social skill development have occurred through thematic teaching, careful planning, and a wide range of hands-on activities and experiential learning both in the school and out of the building. (interview, December 1993)

Teachers, too, described many benefits to children that were confirmed by parent comments. "Cooperative," "independent," "makes wise choices," "enhanced language development," and "self-directed learners" were some of the descriptors we heard in our dialogue with teachers and parents (interviews, December 1993). One parent felt that "the children have been given the best programs . . . . I just know from my kids' report cards and their enthusiasm for school" (interview, December 1993).

University students who had spent their sixteen-week placement in the school observed that children were valued as creative thinkers and independent learners. Faculty had mixed views about the project. Some sensed change was taking place, but at a very slow pace. Others felt the project would not bring about lasting or deep-rooted change.

The Transformation

Beth and Caroline wondered if there had been real change—the kind that lasts. The nature of the project seemed to change over time from one that was imposed from outside to one the teachers deliberately began to control and own. This was evident in their agenda setting and testimony about their learning. Three staff members reflected on their experience (interviews, December 1993).

> I felt I gained personally as a professional from working with a wide group of people—from having people at the board office more visible, people from the university. You always learn something when you have another person that you're interacting and bouncing ideas around with.

> *I found the project interesting and I learned a lot from it. In fact, it was like a teacher to me. I've been learning a lot of things from other teachers and from practical experiences in the classroom.*

> WHEN I THINK ABOUT WHAT THE PROJECT WAS REALLY ABOUT—AN OPPORTUNITY FOR EVERYONE TO GROW—THEN I SEE THE GROWTH ASPECT AFFECTING EVERYONE IN THIS APPROACH. AND THAT INCLUDES THE UNIVERSITY PERSONNEL WHO WERE INVOLVED BECAUSE THEY HAD AN OPPORTUNITY TO SEE THEORY THROUGH PRACTICE AND TO BE PART OF THE RESOURCES THAT HELPED IT HAPPEN. AND I WOULD EXPECT THAT EACH OF US LEARNED TO fiND HER OWN WAY AND LEARNED MORE ABOUT THE NEED TO FORM THE PARTNERSHIP.

Confidence to Risk

The climate of the project seemed to give confidence to teachers to try new ideas or instructional approaches. A certain comfort level emerged that stimulated dialogue and sharing, especially during planning meetings. We noted that teachers willingly supplied examples of key experiences that indicated how they had made changes. The following comments by two teachers are typical (survey, October 1993):

> I have been able to take all of my beliefs and individualized programs and incorporate them into my program. I am finding the children to be more involved, settled, and willing to work in the centers. They ask me, "When do we do centers?" I have more time to work individually with all the children than I have ever had before. I am going to try "Kids on Camera" and I have a feeling that it will be very beneficial. . . . Project Child gave me the courage and support I needed to try learning

centers. The group members and administration have been wonderful and I feel very lucky to have had the opportunity to be a team member with Project Child.

I discovered that I had enough materials, furniture, space, and energy to do similar activities. I set up twelve centers over a weekend. Students returned the next week and proceeded to work in the centers as though they had always done so.

Students from the university also noted a transformation in the planning sessions. One of the students described the sessions:

When all the teachers got together there was a lot of discussion and openness and explaining. And ideas were thrown out. People would feed off each other and the ideas got better and better. You could just see the plans grow in the meetings. No one had a closed mind. Everybody was accepting. You could try something, come back, and if it didn't work, then you would have all those other minds to help. (interview, January 1994)

Enhanced Collegiality

Both Beth and Caroline noted a high degree of group interaction and respect for colleagues in the teachers' responses. We recognized that the growth in confidence to try new teaching approaches and growth in professional learning were intertwined with increased collegiality. A teacher described one of the project's strengths as the "shared collegial approach which led to more exploration, more inquiry, and a lot more peer support" (interview, December 1993). We heard other voices tell how colleagues in the more senior grades were influenced by the project's initiatives. An example was the change in student evaluation and reporting: "The whole school got involved in student evaluation, which means that the whole school got involved with Project Child" (interview, December 1993).

Improved Communication

The project seemed to encourage dialogue between the staff and the other partners. People told us about conversations in which teachers constructively discussed student needs and willingly shared suggestions:

There's more discussion about students among the staff....
What's happening with the kids, what could be done to help,
what could be done better, how changes could be made. There's
more willingness to share what's happening. (interview, December 1993)

We saw that the school made efforts to communicate more
effectively with parents, families, and the community. "Kids on
Camera," the live video discussions, became an open invitation to
observe children learning in the classrooms:

We get a lot of parents coming in and they are very disappointed if they miss "Kids on Camera." (interview, January
1994)

The openness seemed to encourage community and family
members to visit classrooms and to participate in school outings:

About 10 or 15 parents will come in during the week, just
coming in and out, which is the way it should be.... And
another thing that's really been good is the trips that we go
on. We're getting a lot of parent involvement. For our recent
trip, we had enough parents to help—it was just great. (interview, January 1994)

Teachers made efforts to ensure that parents were informed
about their children's programs:

Perhaps the kinds of professional growth or awareness that
have been brought about is that the teachers are more aware
of the need to explain to parents, to clarify what they are
doing. (interview, December 1993)

Reflections About the Partnership

Beth and Caroline reflected on the responses from the teachers and
other stakeholders in the project. The responses echoed a common
theme of transformation. Slow growth and change grew from a
whisper to a joyous shout at the end of the five years. Initially
there were garbled messages: unclear objectives, unfamiliar terminology, unarticulated philosophy, unsupportive staff members, and
lack of certainty about collaboration and partnerships. "Everything

is finally coming together" was a typical comment by the final year of the project (interview, January 1994).

Participants told us in confident voices that their experiences in the project encouraged them to rethink their practice; to transform their curriculum and methods of instruction; to reflect child-centered, cross-cultural education and developmentally appropriate student evaluation. Furthermore, they had come to value and take ownership of curriculum planning, as well as their professional development. Project Child was the catalyst that enhanced family and community involvement in the school, whereas previously there had been limited participation. University faculty became less directive and more responsive to teacher concerns. In fact, faculty became fellow travelers on the collegial road to understanding what a partnership can mean to each participant. As co-learners, faculty were able to voice their own concerns and needs to have pre-service teachers become involved in the life of the school. More university students were placed in project classrooms to participate in innovative and collaborative teaching experiences in areas such as mathematics and early childhood education.

For us, the project had progressed toward the realization of its initial goals. But perhaps, more than this, the project served, as one teacher put it, "as a teacher" to all who participated. We learned that educational terminology (such as "child-centered learning" or "experiential learning"), introduced by faculty, had created communication barriers that were difficult to overcome until the listener and the speaker clarified the problem. We recognized how important it is to listen to other voices that may use a different discourse. A teacher summed up the constructivist notion of developing a personal understanding of such terms:

> I don't think you can set down a list of things—I think it's something you have to get from within. I think it's only something you develop as you work through some of it. It might not be exactly the same for everyone or in every situation. (interview, December 1993)

Differing "world views," as one person described the situation, may have prevented the dialogue necessary for mutual understanding to emerge at the outset. At first, perspectives about change, how children learn, and how teachers make decisions in their daily practice were disparate. As time and communication opportunities increased, a common language emerged to create mutual understanding among the partners. Indeed, our understanding about partnerships was clarified. Beth observed:

> From what I have heard from the people in the project, I sense that the teachers see themselves as equal partners in the educational enterprise. In fact, they are continuing to be in charge of their planning and the curriculum although the formal project has ended. (discussion notes, December 1994)

For Caroline, there were some unanswered questions about partnerships between a faculty of education and a large school division:

> Perhaps what the evaluation describes for me is the difficulty of influencing change in large established organizations in spite of "good" intentions to support the objectives of formal agreements. How can we work together for change and maintain the integrity of both institutions? (discussion notes, December 1994)

Initially the agreement was formalized at the institutional levels, between the faculty and the school division. But, as Beth and Caroline observed, the subsequent changes occurred mainly at the individual and school levels. This phenomenon is not unexpected when we consider the focus on the school and the teachers in the original objectives. Jones and Maloy (1988) recognized the potential for change in cooperative ventures which serve as vehicles for school improvement:

> When sustained over time through agreements and mutually beneficial projects, cooperative activities between teachers and outside organizations have tremendous potential for educational reform. We have learned that as educators arrive at new understandings about themselves, their colleagues, and their relationships to larger communities, they affect the learning climate for their students and the way other organizations interact with schools. (p. xii)

We were heartened by the perspective of the new but experienced principal who arrived at the school just prior to the school year, following the formal completion of the project. In his view, the teachers in this school live the concept of "team" as they confidently welcome new professionals to the staff. The team approach, fostered by a nucleus of continuing members, has enabled him to observe the camaraderie and support the teachers share with new colleagues. Because these teachers are able to make sound professional decisions without having to first seek approval, he soon realized that confidence, communication, and risk taking were part of the climate. This situation enabled him to make a smooth transition into the life of the school. He noted early on "these teachers made the school work" (interview, October 1994).

Together the team is considering ways to obtain more information that will enhance their understanding of student achievement. Their caring extends to students whose needs are considered paramount in the planning process. According to the principal, "Children's needs are the focus as teachers plan to pick up children where they are in their learning" (interview, October 1994). An emphasis on increasing self-esteem complements the concern for ensuring continuous student progress. As the school year progresses, the school team will consider other issues they identify as essential to effective teaching and learning.

Teachers at this school, who now call themselves "Project Child Teachers," feel a sense of ownership and empowerment that inspires them to continue on their learning journey. They have changed within the supportive environment the project initiated. They are determined to sustain this creative energy as they add new experiences and participants to their project.

Part Five

Looking Back and Looking Ahead

The fifth and last section of the book is different from the others in that it contains a single chapter by the editors. We wanted to take the opportunity to reflect upon our collective experiences of collaboration in all the forms it had taken during the life of the book project—to make sense of our own experience and share a few insights about the nature of collaboration. Our reflection centers around the relationships among collaborative partners.

We begin by describing some of the aspects of the caring relationship that developed in our editorial committee and point out some of the challenges in nurturing such a relationship. Next, we discuss what we labeled "emerging images of collaboration," centering that discussion on the multiple roles of talk in the process of sensemaking. Then we share what we learned from the contributors as we look back at the different chapters. We return to our own collaboration as we examine ways in which we were changed by the collaborative process with the contributors and with each other. Finally, we reflect upon the impact of collaborative communities in bringing about reform in education.

✧ Chapter Nineteen

Making the Connections

Helen Christiansen, Linda Goulet,
Caroline Krentz, and Mhairi Macers

Early in the life of the book project, we realized that collaboration as a phenomenon and as a process was largely undefined and only partially understood by many who participate in "collaborative" endeavors. The book became a means of communicating a better understanding of collaboration to both contributors and readers. As our individual experiences of collaboration were varied, it was possible to present a wide range of collaborative experiences. We were able to reflect upon these as well as on our own work together as editors. A little more than two years later, we recognize that we have come to a deeper understanding of the nature of collaboration. In this final chapter we share our insights. We begin by looking back at the collaborative process as it evolved among the editors.

A Climate of Caring

Our collective experience leads us to the belief that true collaboration occurs within a climate of caring. As a group we cared for each other both in a personal and a professional sense. Early in the book project, it became evident that group members recognized we all had professional and other responsibilities outside of the group. This meant we were not always able to give our entire attention to the collaborative task. Sometimes we were simply not available. Occasionally, too, we needed some time to regenerate. Whatever the reason for a momentary lapse in commitment, the group continued to support and sustain its members.

Caring for each other was best understood by each of us within the context of our collaborative editorial process—the context within which we learned to work together and value each other's friendship and support. That context was rich in situations requiring immediate attention. At those times, decisions needed to be made by all members of our group. Some of these situations were stressful and involved sensitive communication. In collaboration, each individual's work and ideas need to be valued by the others. An idea may be rejected but only after careful consideration and honest, open examination of the perspective from which it is offered. Participants need to be prepared to give and take in a way that respects both self and others. It is within a climate of respect and caring that trust is able to develop; that is, trust and belief in self from the encouragement of others and trust in others as one's work and ideas are received openly and dealt with respectfully.

It became important to listen to one another, to value one another's contributions and to enable each group member to feel a sense of belonging. Within the community we had created, each of us knew she would be more able to take risks, to allow herself to be vulnerable, and thus more open to the "possibility of giving and receiving help" (Benner and Wrubel 1989, 4). Each partner defined her role and level of commitment in negotiation with the group. The group needed to accept and respect each individual's role while at the same time hold individuals responsible to contribute in the manner and to the level agreed upon. If an individual does not fulfill a personal commitment, her actions need to be dealt with openly and honestly so recommitment or renegotiation can occur. Each member has a responsibility to the group, and the group has a responsibility to each member.

Our relational situations gave us freedom to explore the features of collaboration that were emerging as we continued working together. We negotiated shared meanings of collaboration in our many discussions. We learned much about collaboration from what others had submitted, but it was not until these ideas had been explored and practiced within our group that they became meaningful to us in a personal way. We learned that power and decision making need to be shared. Power, however, does not necessarily need to be shared equally, nor do all roles need to be equal. Our experience has taught us a key to successful collaboration is the open negotiation of power sharing and role expectations of each partner as a project evolves. We identify with our colleagues at the Brock Faculty of Education Centre on Collaborative Research who "have effective leadership in many leaders" (Stewart, this volume). In our group, each of us was able to fulfill many roles; leadership came from the most appropriate person in the particular situation.

Emerging Images of Collaboration

As our project approached its successful conclusion, we were able to distinguish and describe some of the prominent features of what we have named "the collaborative landscape." Images of collaboration have emerged. Some are quite clear to us; others are still hazy.

Talk, whether it be written or oral, is at the center of the landscape. It is the mediator between experience and meaning. The talk in collaboration has purpose; it serves to describe and bring meaning to our daily reality. Through talk with self and others, we capture experience for examination. We clarify experience as we share our sensemaking. We listen to and read about the experiences of others and see the commonalities and differences. We become part of others' stories as they become part of ours (McIntyre 1981). Our talk becomes informed talk, informed by the knowledge of self and others, and the knowledge of theory and practice.

Through informed talk, the individual and collective meanings in collaborative experiences come together in relationships. There is judgement in collaboration, both within the relationship and from outside sources. Collaborative partners exercise judgement when they decide which experiences are critical to the project, and which are not. Sometimes events outside the collaborative experience set limits or boundaries to what can be included as part of the collaborative reflection. This is the ethical and political reality of all collaborative undertakings.

There are multiple perspectives in collaboration. Not everyone comes away from a collaborative undertaking with the same understanding. There is always a personal construction of meaning. Through the social aspect of the collaborative relationship, partners sort out the experiences that are the most meaningful to them as individuals. As we reflect on our experiences and those of others from a multitude of perspectives, we arrive at new understandings. We make sense of our actions on a multitude of levels from personal to social. The familiar is portrayed in ways that lead to new understandings (Greene 1973). With awareness and understanding through talk comes the ability to make decisions to change one's self and one's actions in future events. We become empowered to make changes in our own practice.

Our collective experience tells us that not everyone can collaborate. Some people prefer to work alone. True collaboration invites the reconciliation of one's own views with that of a group. Successful collaboration is difficult to mandate. At some point in the process we call collaboration, participation has to become a voluntary undertaking.

Collaboration is challenging. The human element of social interaction is a major part of the collaborative landscape and so conflict is to be expected. Our experience leads us to the belief that if negotiations on the manner in which the group will function are not delineated at the outset, conflicts that arise can become barriers to effective collaboration. Furthermore, ongoing honest negotiation is essential. Without honesty there can be no true collaboration. We agree with Maura O'Neill that "an atmosphere of trust needs to be created in order that one can speak honestly and freely" (1990, 89). The creation of such an atmosphere takes time; the process cannot be short circuited. In other words, in collaborative research the process is as important as the outcome.

The integration of process and outcome is what makes collaborative research so rewarding. We have experiences, talk about them, struggle to understand them and ourselves—all the while immersed in the research as it unfolds. Intuitive knowledge, theory, and experience are all valued. Collaborative research is tentative. Knowing and knowledge go hand-in-hand. Collaboration does not end; it opens up other possibilities. Collaborative research continues the conversation, thereby enabling participants to reach new levels of understanding.

Reflecting on the chapters brings the collaborative landscape of human elements into clearer focus. Each description of collaboration gives voice to personal meaning through stories of lived experience. The personal and individual combine and recombine with the social interactions and relationships within the collaborative endeavors. Layers of interaction spiral through dynamic experiences, changing both the individual and the collaborative group in the relational context. But this landscape has both pleasant vistas and potential dangers. Collaboration seems to need continuous re-creation through negotiation to maintain stability during individual growth and the social construction of knowledge.

Learning With the Contributors

Constructing the manuscript with the contributors gave us many opportunities for collaboration. We were in contact with writers by telephone, electronic mail, and through written comments. Through these social interactions, stories were reviewed, revised, and reconstructed. Contributors' stories spoke of dialogic connections between old (former) knowledge and new insights, of dialectic between lived experience and abstract understandings. Discourse emerged in climates of encouraging support and connectedness.

Strong and clear messages about the importance of nourishing relationships, shared power, caring respect, honest valuing, and responsive fidelity provide the backdrop for continuing collaboration. When these were absent in the collaboration, negotiated meaning and a moral responsibility to hear the other helped participants reexamine their individual roles, assumptions about collaborative work, and their need to go beyond formal agreements. Mutual interests and moral considerations seemed to transcend the tension and, at times, guilt, to empower the contributors to continue their interactions.

Commitment to self, others, and their tasks engendered a caring reciprocity in the continuing collaborations. The resulting respect encouraged openness and risk taking to disclose feelings that projected an image less than the ideal interpersonal relationship. Confidence to share power and to accept diversity in views, assumptions, and goals gave a richness to the experiences described in the stories. Perspectives sometimes varied; the strengths of individual voices changed as situations changed. The collaborative partners did not always agree. We realized diverse views were present as participants strove for harmony within their different goals and intentions.

Central to collaboration was acceptance of personal voice as the essential focus in the developing story. As voices blended in conversation, the productive nature of talk nourished participants' understandings and their attempts to continue their social inquiry. Issues arose in the telling and living of the stories. Time was a major concern. Writers spoke of the need for time to become acquainted with their partners, time to develop common language and understanding, time to reflect on the collaborative process, and time to critique the recent experiences. It was obvious to us that collaboration was not to be entered into lightly; there were heavy commitments to fulfill in joining the process.

Participating in a collaborative endeavor did have its rewards, although not everyone reaped the same benefits. Most contributors spoke of transformations—either at the personal level or, in some cases, for the group. Change was an inevitable part of the interactions among individuals. Collaboration seemed to be the catalyst.

Our Personal Interactions and Change

As editors, we have been changed by the collaborative process with the contributors and with each other. Our collaboration with contributors brought new insights, new perspectives, and new challenges to personal understandings of collaboration and change. Each of the editors had experienced collaborative relationships outside this particular group. Each brought her own history and assumptions about collaborative efforts. These past stories influenced the new story we were creating together.

In reading and responding to the contributors' stories, we were obliged to rethink our earlier beliefs about collaboration. Collaboration does not come with a list of instructions, even from our past. We understood early on that it was important for us to take time to talk, disclose our beliefs, and discuss how this collaboration would unfold. We empowered ourselves to negotiate collaboration in our context.

Our discussions expanded to include the ideas, the constructed knowledge of our colleagues who shared their insights so clearly in the chapters they submitted. Our talking was done on several levels. We talked out, talked through, talked around, talked with one another, and even talked "silently" with people who sent in contributions. All the talk was essential to our collaborative conversation for it enabled us to enter into collaboration with each other and with the contributors. Our beliefs about collaboration included the importance of knowing people and being able to "read between the lines" (discussion notes, January 27, 1995). Talk in collaboration often needs to focus on the relationship before decisions can be made. Decision making in collaboration was accomplished through informed talk rather than through imposing a particular point of view. Voice for us became the means for our collaboration to continue, to shape our relationship, to construct our story. Talking helped us identify the learning that goes along with getting to the outcome. It was "that sense of knowing which is the critical moment" (discussion notes, January 27, 1995).

The notion of a critical moment recalled for each of us the major impetus for our collaboration in preparing a manuscript. We remembered the excitement of the session in Ottawa in which many of the authors and editors participated in a symposium on collaboration. The critical incident jolted us into action, to consider this manuscript as a way to share our stories. We began in our own small way to make connections that would add to the changing educational landscape.

Collaboration encouraged us to explore ways to develop the manuscript. While we were in the process, we saw ourselves living "in" the experience of collaborating with each author and with each other. We learned each of us had to change our individual habits and work together by depending on the strengths of each participant. Change was possible through the respect we developed for each other, through the trust and commitment which emerged, and through the connections to our process in the production of the manuscript. Transformation was possible when we "worked beyond ourselves" as individuals striving together to construct the possibility for new understandings about collaboration and its impact on educational change. We seemed to find the "middle ground," a safe place to take the risk to support each other to achieve a common goal.

The Impact of Collaborative Communities on Educational Reform

The collaborative projects described in this book reflect communities of people working together to bring about change in education Certain features of collaborative relationships arise from the actions of community members. These include the negotiation of the problem situation and thereafter the nurturing of a trusting caring relationship within which sensemaking takes place. We believe these critical features hold true in any kind of collaborative endeavor, whether it is a collaborative research study, a learning community, a university-school partnership, a curriculum planning group, or an editorial committee. Group members need to be prepared to value and reflect upon one another's perspectives. In so doing, individuals strive to understand their own practices and even to change them if necessary.

As a result of our working together in a collaborative editorial community we have come to understand that collaborative projects arise from localized needs, concerns, or situations. Collaborative partners determine the knowledge that is appropriate to help them make sense of their particular collaborative endeavor. Collaborative partners thus determine their collaborative pathway—their unique journey of collaboration. In other words, the members of a collaborative community need to determine the path they are going to lay down (Varela 1987) as an adequate solution to a problem situation. These pathways, as is the case with the ones portrayed in this book, demonstrate many different contexts and situations. No two pathways are identical, yet there are commonalities. What seems to make a pathway successful or viable for the partners who are walking it, is in the justification of the pathway chosen as appropriate and viable in meeting the needs or goals of the partners. An observer may ask, "Does this collaborative pathway create a space for appropriate collaborative activity?" or "How are features of collaboration negotiated in the laying down of the pathway?" In all of the projects described in this book we recognize that each collaborative undertaking constitutes an activity in which features were not predetermined but were worked out in the midst of the action by ongoing negotiation and communication in the laying down of collaborative pathways of possibility.

Helen Stewart's chapter presents four categories of principles that begin to synthesize what we understand about the collaborative process in educational change. One of the foundational principles asserts that in collaboration we accept and study ongoing change within diverse, caring environments. The commitment to constructing new understandings about educational change challenges the broader educational community to value collaboration as a process of renewal.

Within this book are the stories of a variety of collaborative projects. Contributors have moved on to other collaborative undertakings, standing on the experience of the projects described herein, and recursively visiting them. These experiences have been reflected upon, extended, and transformed into new experiences of collaboration. As editors we have learned from the collaborative projects presented here. They affected us in our work together on the book, and also had an impact on other individual research endeavors. We have been changed by our collaborative process.

EPILOGUE

The book has been written. The stories have been told. Contributors have captured their narratives in print for others to read, talk about, and create their own meaning. But, as Connelly and Clandinin (1990) tell us, the narrative continues to unfold even though the "written document appears to stand still" (p. 9).

As editors, we look back upon the lengthy process of collaboration with each writer and each other and acknowledge there are many stories yet to tell. We ask ourselves what we have learned and what meanings we have constructed from our contributions and from those of our colleagues. And, we ponder what the collaborative experience of compiling a written record of so many stories meant to each writer and to the collective. We are all affected by the process.

What we have discussed here are the recorded stories in each contribution, reconstructed from our perspective, that tell us about collaboration and its impact on educational change. In our reflections, we acknowledge the constraints that our personal experiences, culture, and social contexts bear on our interpretations. At the same time, we appreciate how these same contexts free us to see the stories in a new light (Connelly and Clandinin 1990).

The stories of collaboration speak of change and transformation. Some describe how collaboration is possible in a caring, supportive environment, how the collaboration encourages new knowledge about change, and how change occurs through dialogue and interaction. Others challenge us to consider further change in traditional approaches to school-university research endeavors in the meaning of mutuality in collaboration and in providing the necessary support to time-consuming collaborative projects.

Recreating relationships within our ever-changing world offers opportunities for ever-expanding layers of understanding. Readers are invited into the dialogue about the stories captured in the book and about those hidden between the lines—those that yet are to be told. Our dialogue has begun. We invite the educational community to join with us in the continuing inquiry about collaboration in educational change.

REFERENCES

Abbey, S.; Drake, S.; Richards, M.; and Stewart, H. 1992, June. Towards a deeper understanding of the process of initiating a collaborative research centre. Paper presented at the Among Teachers Community/Canadian Association of Teacher Education (AcT/CATE) Preconference, Charlottetown, Prince Edward Island.

Aitken, A. 1993. Critical pedagogy in a Naskapi classroom. McGill University, Montreal, Canada.

Altrichter, H.; Posch, P.; and Somekh, B. 1993. *Teachers investigate their work. An Introduction to the methods of action research*. New York: Routledge.

Aoki, T. T. 1991. Teaching as in-dwelling between two curriculum worlds.

———. 1993. Legitimating lived curriculum: Towards a curricular landscape of multiplicity. *Journal of Curriculum and Supervision, 8*(3), 255–268.

Argyris, C. 1982. *Reasoning, learning and action*. San Francisco: Jossey-Bass.

Auger, F. K., and Odell, S. J. 1992. Three school-university partnerships for teacher development. *Journal of Teacher Education, 43*(4), 262–268.

Barrett, M. 1993. Music education and the natural learning model. *International Journal of Music Education, 20*, 27–34.

293

Barrett, W. 1979. *The illusion of technique: A search for meaning in a technological civilization.* Garden City, NY: Anchor Press.

Basaraba, J., and Drake, S.M. 1993, June. Factors contributing to a successful university/school partnership. Paper presented at the Canadian Society for Studies in Education, Ottawa, ON.

Baumann, R. 1992. Labour-management co-operation in education. *OTF/FEO Interaction, 18*(4), 6–8.

Beattie, M. 1993. The art of teaching: Collaborative story making. In D. J. Clandinin (Ed.), *Searching for connections: Struggling for community* (pp. 108–114). Edmonton, AB: Among Teachers Community, Centre for Research for Teacher Education and Development, University of Alberta.

———. 1995a. *Constructing professional knowledge in teaching: A narrative of change and development.* New York: Teachers College Press.

———. 1995b. The making of a music: The construction and reconstruction of a teacher's personal practical knowledge. *Curriculum Inquiry, 25*(2), 133–150.

Belenky, M. F.; Clinchy, B.; Goldberger, N.; and Tarule, J. 1986. *Women's ways of knowing: The development of self, voice and mind.* New York: Basic Books.

Benner, P., and Wrubel, J. 1989. *The primacy of caring: Stress and coping in health and illness.* Don Mills, ON: Addison-Wesley Publishing.

Berman, L.; Hultgren, F.; Lee, D.; Rivkin, M.; and Roderick, J. 1991. *Toward curriculum for being: Voices of educators.* Albany, NY: State University of New York Press.

Biott, C. 1991. Being a support or advisory teacher: Satisfactions and dissatisfactions. In C. Biott (Ed.), *Semi-detached teachers: Building support and advisory relationships in classrooms.* (pp. xx) London: Falmer Press. p. 346.

Biott, C., and Nias, J. (Eds.). 1992. *Working and learning together for change.* Buckingham, United Kingdom: Open University Press.

Bishop, R. 1992. Te ropu rangahau tikanga rua: The establishment of a bicultural research group under the control of Maori people for the betterment of Maori people. *New Zealand Annual Review of Education, 2*, 205–222.

Boyer, E. 1982. A conversation with Ernest Boyer. *Change, 41*(1), 18–21.

Bresler, L. 1993, Winter. Music in a double-bind: Instruction by non-specialists in elementary schools. *Bulletin of the Council for Research in Music Education, 115*, 1–13.

Brimfield, R. M. B.; Roderick, J. A.; and Yamamoto, K. 1983. Persons as researchers: Observations of the participants, *Curriculum Inquiry, 13*(1), 5–21.

Britzman, D. 1986. Cultural myths in the making of a teacher: Biography and social structure in teacher education. *Harvard Educational Review, 56*(4), 442–454.

———. 1989. Who has the floor? Curriculum teaching and the English student teacher's struggle for voice. *Curriculum Inquiry, 19*(2), 144–162.

———. 1991. *Practice makes practice: A critical study of learning to teach.* Albany, NY: State University of New York Press.

Brock Faculty of Education Centre on Collaborative Research. 1993. [pamphlet]. St. Catharines, ON: Author.

Brookhart, S. M., and Loadman, W. E. 1992. School-university collaboration: Across cultures. *Teaching Education, 4*(2), 53–68.

Brown, L. M. 1991. Telling a girl's life: Self-authorization as a form of resistance. In C. Gilligan; A. G. Rogers; and D. Tolman (Eds.), *Women, girls & psychotherapy: Reframing resistance* (pp. 71–86). Binghamton, NY: Harrington Park Press.

Brown, L. M., Gilligan, C. 1992. *Meeting at the crossroads: Women's psychology and girls' development.* Cambridge, MA: Harvard University Press.

Bruffee, K. A. 1986. Social construction, language, and the authority of knowledge. *College English, 48*(8), 773–790.

Bruner, J. 1986. *Actual minds, possible worlds.* Cambridge, MA: Harvard University Press.

———. 1990. *Acts of meaning.* Cambridge, MA: Harvard University Press.

Bullough, R.; Knowles, G.; and Crow, N. 1992. *Emerging as a teacher.* New York: Routledge.

Butt, R., and Raymond, D. 1987. Arguments for using qualitative approaches in understanding teacher thinking: The case of biography. *Journal of Curriculum Theorizing, 7*(1), 62–93.

Carin, A. A. 1993. *Teaching science through discovery* (7th ed.). Toronto, ON: Merrill.

Carr, W., and Kemmis, S. 1986. *Becoming critical: Education, criticism and action research.* London: Falmer Press.

Carse, J. P. 1986. *Finite and infinite games: A vision of life as play and possibility.* New York: Ballantine.

Carter, K. 1993. The place of story in the study of teaching and teacher education. *Educational Researcher, 22*(1), 5–12.

Castle, J.; Boak, T.; and Drake, S. 1993, April. Collaborative reflection as professional development. Paper presented at the Annual Meeting of the American Educational Research Association, Atlanta, GA.

Castle, J.; Drake, S.; and Boak, T. 1995. Collaborative reflection as professional development. *Review of Higher Education, 18*(3), 242–262.

Castle, J., and Giblin, A. 1992. Reflection for action: A collaborative venture in preservice education. *Teaching Education, 4*(2), 21–34.

Castle, J., and Shuttler, S. 1993, June. Building a teacher development site. Paper presented at the annual meeting of the Canadian Society for the Study of Education, Ottawa, ON.

Christiansen, H.; Krentz, C.; Froc, M.; and Adamack, P. 1993. Creating a collaborative community: Four teachers learning together. In D. J. Clandinin (Ed.), *Searching for connections: Struggling for community* (pp. 27–32). Edmonton, AB: Among Teachers Community, Centre for Research for Teacher Education and Development, University of Alberta.

Clandinin, D. J. 1986. *Classroom practice: Teacher images in action.* Philadelphia: Falmer Press.

———. 1993. On seeing in educational research. A review of *The enlightened eye: Qualitative inquiry and the enhancement of educational practice* by Elliot Eisner. *Curriculum Inquiry, 23*(2), 203–211.

———. 1993, April. Still learning to teach. Paper presented at the annual meeting of the American Educational Research Association, Atlanta, GA.

Clandinin, D. J., and Connelly, F. M. 1987. Teachers' personal knowledge: What counts as "personal" in studies of the personal. *Journal of Curriculum Studies, 19*(9), 487–500.

———. 1990. Narrative experience and the study of curriculum. *Cambridge Journal of Education, 20*(3), 241–253.

———. 1992. Teacher as curriculum maker. In P. W. Jackson (Ed.), *Handbook of research on curriculum* (pp. 363–401). Washington, D.C.: American Educational Research Association.

———. (1995). *Teachers' professional knowledge landscapes.* New York: Teachers College Press.

Clandinin, D. J.; Davies, A.; Hogan, P.; and Kennard, B. (Eds.). 1993. *Learning to teach, teaching to learn: Stories of collaboration in teacher education.* New York: Teachers College Press.

Clark, C. 1987. *The academic life: Small worlds, different worlds.* Princeton, NJ: Carnegie Foundation.

——. 1992. Teachers as designers in self-directed professional development. In A. Hargreaves & M. Fullan (Eds.), *Understanding teacher development* (pp. 75–84). New York: Teachers College Press.

Clark, R. W. 1986. *School-university relationships: Partnerships and networks* (Occasional Paper No. 2). Seattle: University of Washington, College of Education, Center for Educational Renewal.

——. 1988. School-university partnerships: An interpretive view. In K. A. Sirotnik & J. I. Goodlad (Eds.), *School university partnerships in action: Concepts, cases and concerns* (pp. 32–65). New York: Teachers College Press.

Clift, R. 1994. Conversations with collaborators, colleagues, and friends: Representing others and presenting ourselves. *Educational Researcher, 23*(6), 29–31.

Clift, R.; Johnson, M.; Holland, P.; and Veal, M. 1992. Developing the potential for collaborative school leadership. *American Educational Research Journal, 29*(4), 877–908.

Clift, R., and Say, M. 1988. Teacher education: Collaboration or conflict? *Journal of Teacher Education, 39*(3), 2–7.

Clift, R.; Veal, M. L.; Johnson, M.; and Holland, P. 1990. Restructuring teacher education through collaborative action research. *Journal of Teacher Education, 41*(2), 52–62.

Cochran-Smith, M., and Lytle, S. 1990. Research on teaching and teacher research: The issues that divide. *Educational Researcher, 19*(2), 2–11.

——. 1993. *Inside outside: Teacher research and knowledge.* New York: Teachers College Press.

Code, L. 1991. *What can she know? Feminist theory and the construction of knowledge.* Ithaca, NY: Cornell University Press.

Cole, A., and Knowles, J. G. 1993. Teacher development partnership research: A focus on methods and issues. *American Educational Research Journal, 30*(3), 473–495.

Cole, M. 1990. Cultural psychology: A once and future discipline. In J. Berman (Ed.), *Cultural perspectives: Nebraska Symposium on Motivation, 1989* (pp. 280–288). Lincoln, NE: University of Nebraska Press.

Coles, R. 1989. *The call of stories.* New York: Houghton Mifflin.

Connelly, F. M., and Clandinin, D. J. 1988. *Teachers as curriculum planners: Narratives of experience.* New York: Teachers College Press.

———. 1990. Stories of experience and narrative inquiry. *Educational Researcher, 19*(5), 2–14.

———. 1994. The promise of collaborative research in the political context. In S. Hollingsworth & H. Sockett (Eds.), *Teacher research and educational reform. Ninety-third Yearbook of the National Society for the Study of Education* (pp. 86–102). Chicago: University of Chicago Press.

———. (forthcoming). Narrative and education.

Craig, C. 1992. Coming to know in the professional knowledge context: Beginning teachers' experiences. Unpublished doctoral dissertation, University of Alberta, Edmonton, Canada.

Crites, S. 1971. The narrative quality of experience. *Journal of the American Academy of Religion, 39*(3), 292–311.

Crowe, G.; Levine, L.; and Nager, N. 1992. Are three heads better than one? Reflections on doing collaborative interdisciplinary research. *American Educational Research Journal, 29*(4), 737–753.

Csikszentmihalyi, M. 1975. *Beyond boredom and anxiety.* San Francisco: Jossey-Bass.

Cuban, L. 1990. Reforming again, again, and again. *Educational Researcher, 19*(1), 3– 13.

Deloria, V. 1991. Commentary: Research, redskins, and reality. *American Indian Quarterly, 15*(4), 457–468.

Denzin, N. K., and Lincoln, Y. S. (Eds.). 1994. *Handbook of qualitative research.* San Francisco: Sage.

Dewey, J. 1933. *How we think: A restatement of the relation of reflective thinking to the educative process.* Lexington, MA: D.C. Heath.

———. 1938. *Experience and education.* New York: Macmillan.

Dewey, J., and Bentley, A. F. 1949. *Knowing and the known.* Boston: Beacon Press.

Drake, S. 1993. *Planning an integrated curriculum: The call to adventure.* Alexandria, VA: Association for Supervision and Curriculum Development.

Drake, S.; Basaraba, J.; Castle, J.; Court-Lamond, M.; Parker, J.; Stewart, H.; Thomas, A.; White, S.; and Elliott, A. 1993, June. Exploring the role of the collective in developing school-university partnerships. Symposium conducted at the annual meeting of the Canadian Society for the Study of Education, Carleton University, Ottawa, Ontario.

Drake, S.; Basaraba, J.; Castle, J.; Shuttler, S.; Elliott, A.; Court-Lamond, M.; Thomas, A.; and White, S. 1993, June. School-university partnerships in action. Symposium conducted at the annual meeting of the

Canadian Society for the Study of Education, Carleton University, Ottawa, Ontario.

Drake, S.; Bebbington, J.; Laksman, S.; Mackie, P.; Maynes, N.; and Wayne, L. 1992. *Developing an integrated curriculum using the story model.* Toronto, ON: OISE Press.

Drake, S.; Elliott, A.; and Castle, J. 1993. Collaborative reflection through story: Towards a deeper understanding of ourselves as women researchers. *Qualitative Studies in Education, 6*(4), 291–301.

Eisner, E. W. 1988. The primacy of experience and the politics of method. *Educational Researcher, 17*(5), 15–20.

———. 1993. Forms of understanding and the future of educational research. *Educational Researcher, 22*(7), 5–11.

Elbaz, F. 1983. *Teacher thinking: A study of practical knowledge.* New York: Nichols.

Elliott, J. 1985. Facilitating action research in schools: Some dilemmas. In R. Burgess (Ed.), *Field methods in the study of education* (pp. 235–262). London: Falmer Press.

———. 1991. *Action research for educational change.* Milton Keynes, United Kingdom: Open University Press.

Ellis, N. E. 1993. Collegiality from the teacher's perspective: Social contexts for professional development. *Action in Teacher Education, 15*(1), 42–48.

Erickson, F. 1989. Research currents: Learning and collaboration in teaching. *Language Arts, 66*(4), 430–431.

Evertson, C. M. 1990. Bridging knowledge and action through clinical experiences. In D. D. Dill, *What teachers need to know* (pp. 94–109). San Francisco: Jossey-Bass.

Feldman, A. F. 1993. Promoting equitable collaboration between university researchers and school teachers. *International Journal of Qualitative Studies in Education, 6*(4), 341–358.

Fellows, M. R. 1991. Computer science and mathematics in the elementary schools. Report given to the Computer Science Department, University of Victoria, British Columbia, Canada.

Field, D., and Castle, J. 1992. Readers theatre: Collaborating in a primary classroom. *FWTAO Newsletter Curriculum Insert, 10*(4).

Fisher, R., and Brown, S. 1988. *Getting together: Building a relationship that gets to yes.* Boston, MA: Houghton Mifflin.

Florio-Ruane, S. 1991. Conversation and narrative in collaborative research: An ethnography of the Written Literacy Forum. In C. Witherell &

N. Noddings (Eds.), *Stories lives tell: Narrative and dialogue in education* (pp. 234–256). New York: Teachers College Press.

Fountain, C. E., and Evans, D. B. 1994. Beyond shared rhetoric: A collaborative model for integrating preservice and inservice urban educational delivery systems. *Journal of Teacher Education, 45*(3), 218–228.

Friesen, D. W. 1993. Internship possibilities in teacher education: An interpretive exploration of the action research pathway. University of Alberta, Edmonton, Canada.

———. 1994. The action research game: Recreating pedagogical relationships in the teaching internship. *Educational Action Research, 2*(2), 243–258.

Frye, N. 1963. *The educated imagination.* Toronto, ON: Canadian Broadcasting Corporation.

———. 1976. *The secular scripture: A study of the structure of romance.* Cambridge, MA: Harvard University Press.

———. 1981, Winter. The beginnning of the word. Ontario Council of Teachers of English (OCTE) Conference Keynote Address, 1980. In *Directions*, Ontario Council of Teachers of English.

Frymier, R.; Flynn, J.; and Flynn, R. B. 1992. *School-university collaboration.* Bloomington, IN: Phi Delta Kappa Educational Foundation.

Fullan, M. 1991. *The new meaning of educational change* (2nd ed.). New York: Teachers College Press.

———. 1992. Visions that blind. *Educational Leadership, 49*(5), 19–20.

———. 1993a. Why teachers must become change agents. *Educational Leadership, 50*(6), 12–17.

———. 1993b. *Change forces: Probing the depth of educational reform.* London: Falmer Press.

Fullan, M., and Connelly, F. M. 1987. *Teacher education in Ontario: Current practice and options for the future* (Position paper). Toronto, ON: OISE Press.

Fullan, M., and Miles, M. 1992. Getting reform right: What works and what doesn't. *Phi Delta Kappan, 73*(10), 745–752.

Gadamer, H. G. 1975. *Truth and method.* New York: Crossroad Publishing.

———. 1988. The hermeneutics of suspicion. In G. Shapiro & A. Sica (Eds.), *Hermeneutics: Questions and prospects* (pp. 54–65). Amherst, MA: University of Massachusetts Press.

———. 1989. *Truth and method* (Rev. ed., J. Weinsheimer & D. Marshall, Trans.). New York: Crossroad Publishing. (Original work published 1960)

Gallessich, J. 1982. *The profession and practice of consultation*. San Francisco: Jossey-Bass.

Gehrke, N. 1991. Explorations of teachers' development of integrative curriculums. *Journal of Curriculum and Supervision, 6*(2), 107–117.

Giroux, H. 1992. *Border crossings: Cultural workers and the politics of education*. New York: Routledge.

Gitlin, A. D. 1990. Educative research, voice, and school change. *Harvard Educational Review, 60*(4), 443–466.

Gitlin, A.; Bringhurst, K.; Burns, M.; Colley, V.; Myers, B.; Price, K.; Russell, R.; and Tiess, P. 1992. *Teachers' voices for school change*. New York: Teachers College Press.

Glaser, B. G., and Strauss, A. L. 1967. *The discovery of grounded theory*. London: Weidenfeld and Nicolson.

Gomez, M. N.; Bissell, J.; Danziger, L.; and Casselman, R. 1990. *To advance learning: A handbook on developing K–12 postsecondary partnerships*. Landham, MD: University Press of America.

Goodlad, J. 1988. School-university partnerships for educational renewal: Rationale and concepts. In K. A. Sirotnik & J. Goodlad (Eds.), *School-university partnerships in action: Concepts and concerns* (pp. 3–31). New York: Teachers College Press.

———. 1990a. *Teachers for our nation's schools*. San Francisco: Jossey-Bass.

———. 1990b. Foreword. In M. Gomez, J. Bissell, L. Danziger, & R. Casselman (Eds.), *To advance learning: A handbook on developing postsecondary partnerships* (pp. xii– xvi). Lanham, MD: University Press of America.

———. 1994. *Educational renewal*. San Francisco: Jossey-Bass.

Goodman, J. 1992. Theoretical and practical considerations for school-based research in a post-positivistic era. *International Journal of Qualitative Studies in Education, 5*(2), 117–133.

Goodson, I. F. 1988. *The making of curriculum: Collected essays*. Barcombe, Lewes, United Kingdom: Falmer Press.

———. 1991. Sponsoring the teacher's voice: Teachers' lives and teacher development. *Cambridge Journal of Education, 21*(2), 35–45.

Goodson, I. F., and Goodlad, J. 1994. *Educational renewal*. San Francisco: Jossey-Bass.

Gore, J. 1991. Practicing what we preach: Action research and the supervision of student teachers. In R. Tabachnich & K. Zeichner (Eds.), *Issues and practices in inquiry-oriented teacher education* (pp. 253–272). London: Falmer Press.

Goulet, K. 1986. Oral history as an authentic and credible research base for curriculum: The Cree of Sandy Bay and hydroelectric power development 1927–67, an example. University of Regina, Regina, Canada.

Goulet, L. 1996. Implementing Indian curriculum in Indian teacher education: The students' perspective. *Journal of Professional Studies, 3*(1), 11–20.

Goulet, L.; Beaudin, S.; Fietz, O.; Heit, M.; and Tarasoff, J. 1991, July. One turn of the circle: Faculty reflection and practice in implementing Indian teacher education. Paper presented at the Canadian Indian Teacher Education Conference, Fort Smith, North West Territories, Canada.

Grant, G. E. 1992. The sources of structural metaphors in teacher knowledge: Three cases. *Teaching and Teacher Education, 8*(95/96), 433–440.

Gray, B. 1989. *Collaborating: Finding common ground for multiparty problems.* San Francisco: Jossey-Bass.

Green, N.; Baldini, B.; and Stack, W. 1993. Spanning cultures: Teachers and professors in PDS's. *Action in Teacher Education, 15*(2), 18–24.

Greene, M. 1973. *Teacher as stranger.* Belmont, CA: Wadsworth Publishing.

———. 1988. Qualitative research and the uses of literature. In R. Sherman & R. B. Webb (Eds.), *Qualitative research in education: Focus and methods* (pp. 175–189). Philadelphia: Falmer Press.

Grimmett, P. 1994. Revisiting collaboration. *International Analysis of Teacher Education,* 195–203.

Guba, E. G., and Lincoln, Y. S. 1989. *Fourth generation evaluation.* San Francisco: Sage.

Haig-Brown, C. 1992. Choosing border work. *Canadian Journal of Native Education, 19*(1), 96–116.

Hamilton, D.; MacDonald, B.; King, C.; Jenkins, D.; and Parlett, M. (Eds.). 1977. *Beyond the numbers game: A reader in educational observation.* Berkeley, CA: McCutcheon Publishers.

Hargreaves, A. 1992. Cultures of teaching: A focus for change. In A. Hargreaves & M. Fullan, *Understanding teacher development* (pp. 216–240). New York: Teachers College Press.

Hart, P.; Robottom, I.; and Taylor, M. 1993. *Dilemmas of participatory enquiry: A case study of method-in-action.* Regina, SK: Saskatchewan Instructional Development & Research Unit, University of Regina.

Hattrup, R., and Bickel, W. 1993. Teacher-researcher collaboration: Resolving the tensions. *Educational Leadership, 50*(6), 38–41.

Heshusius, L. 1994. Freeing ourselves from objectivity: Managing subjectivity or turning toward a participatory mode of consciousness. *Educational Researcher*, *23*(3), 15–22.

Hollingsworth, S. 1992. Learning to teach through collaborative conversation: A feminist approach. *American Educational Research Journal*, *29*(2), 373–404.

Hollingsworth, S.; Cody, A.; Davis-Smallwood, J.; Dybdahl, M.; Gallagher, P.; Gallego, M.; Maestre, T.; Minarik, L. T.; Raffel, L.; Standerford, N. S.; and Teel, K. M. 1994. *Teacher research and urban literacy education: Lessons and conversations in a feminist key.* New York: Teachers College Press.

Hollingsworth, S.; Dybdahl, M.; and Minarik, L. T. 1993. By chart and chance and passion: The importance of relational knowing in learning to teach. *Curriculum Inquiry, 23*(1), 5–35.

Hollingsworth, S.; and Miller, J. L. 1994. Rewriting "gender equity" in teacher research. In S. Hollingsworth & H. Sockett (Eds.), *Teacher research and educational reform. Ninety-third Yearbook of the National Society for the Study of Education* (pp. 121–140). Chicago: University of Chicago Press.

Holmes Group. 1986. *Tomorrow's teachers.* East Lansing, MI: Author.

Hookey, P. M. R. 1985. Educational consultation: Reflections of teachers and resource personnel. University of Toronto, Ontario.

————. 1993. *Our hidden resources: A study of resource personnel.* Toronto, ON: Federation of Women Teachers Associations of Ontario.

————. 1994. Negotiating partnerships, negotiating collaborative research: Bringing the two together. In D.J. Clandinin et al., *Revisioning teacher education through collaborative research: Continuing the conversation* (pp. 57–61). Edmonton, AB: Among Teachers Community.

————. 1994/1995, Winter. Music education as a collaborative project: Insights from teacher research. *The Bulletin of the Council of Research in Music Education* (No. 122).

Hopkins, D. 1993. *A teacher's guide to classroom research.* Milton Keynes, United Kingdom: Open University Press.

Houser, N. 1990. Teacher-researcher: The synthesis of roles for teacher empowerment. *Action in Teacher Education, 12*(2), 55–60.

Huberman, M. 1990. Linkage between researchers and practitioners: A qualitative study. *American Educational Research Journal, 27*(2), 363–391.

Hunsaker, L., and Johnston, M. 1992. Teacher under construction: A collaborative case study of teacher change. *American Educational Research Journal, 29*(2), 350–372.

Irvin, J. L. 1990. *Reading and the middle school student*. Boston: Allyn and Bacon.

Jackson, P. 1992. Helping teachers develop. In A. Hargreaves & M. Fullan (Eds.), *Understanding teacher development* (pp. 62–74). New York: Teachers College Press.

Jardine, D. 1988. Play and hermeneutics: An exploration of the bi-polarities of mutual understanding. *Journal of Curriculum Theorizing, 8*(2), 23–41.

———. 1991, October. 'Healing the wounds': De-pathologizing the agonies of pedagogic interpretation. Paper presented at the Bergamo Conference of An Interdisciplinary Journal of Curriculum Studies, Dayton, Ohio.

Jones, B. L., and Maloy, C. W. 1988. *Partnerships in improving schools*. New York: Greenwood Press.

Kagan, S. 1985. *Cooperative learning: Resources for teachers*. Riverside, CA: University of California.

Keller, E. F. 1992. *Secrets of life, secrets of death: Essays on language, gender and science*. New York: Routledge.

Kemmis, S., and McTaggart, R. (Eds.). 1988. *The action research planner* (3rd ed.). Victoria, Australia: Deakin University.

Knight, S.; Wiseman, D.; and Smith, C. 1992. The reflectivity dilemma in school-university partnerships. *Journal of Teacher Education, 43*(3), 269–277.

Knoff, H. M. 1988. Clinical supervision, consultation and counselling: A comparative analysis for supervisors and other educational leaders. *Journal of Curriculum and Supervision, 3*(3), 240–252.

Knowles, J. G.; Cole, A.; and Presswood, C. 1994. *Through preservice teachers eyes: Exploring field experiences through narrative inquiry*. New York: Merrill.

Knowles, J. G., and Holt-Reynolds, D. 1991. Shaping pedagogies against personal histories in preservice teacher education. *Teachers College Record, 93*(1), 87–113.

Krentz, C., and Warkentin, B. 1994. *An evaluation of Project Child*. Regina, SK: University of Regina.

Kyle, D., and McCutcheon, G. 1984. Collaborative research: Development and issues. *Journal of Curriculum Studies, 16*(2), 173–179.

LaFramboise, T. D., and Plake, B. S. 1983. Toward meeting the research needs of American Indians. *Harvard Educational Review, 53*(1), 45–51.

LaRocque, L. 1995. Some thoughts on school-university collaboration. *Canadian Administrator, 34*(5), 1–7.

Lasley, T.; Matczynski, T.; and Williams, J. 1992. Collaborative and noncollaborative partnership structures in teacher education. *Journal of Teacher Education, 43*(4), 257–261.

Lather, P. 1991. *Getting smart.* New York: Routledge.

Lave, J., and Wenger, E. 1991. *Situated learning: Legitimate peripheral participation.* New York: Cambridge University Press.

Levine, M. 1992. *Professional practice schools: Linking teacher education and school reform.* New York: Teachers College Press.

Lewis, M. G. 1993. *Without a word: Teaching beyond women's silences.* New York: Routledge.

Lieberman, A. 1992, October. School-university collaboration: A view from the inside. *Phi Delta Kappan,* 147–157.

Lieberman, A., and Miller, L. 1990. Teacher development and professional practice. *Teachers College Record, 92*(1), 105–122.

Lincoln, Y. S., and Guba, E. G. 1985. *Naturalistic inquiry.* San Francisco: Sage.

Little, J. W. 1985. Teachers as teacher advisors: The delicacy of collegial leadership. *Educational Leadership, 43*(3), 34–36.

Luke, C., and Gore, J. (Eds.). 1992. *Feminisms and critical pedagogy.* New York: Routledge.

Maeers, M. 1992, June. How metaphors can guide instruction in a mathematics teacher education course. Paper presented at the annual meeting of the Canadian Association of Teachers of Education, Charlottetown, Prince Edward Island.

Maloy, R. W. 1985. The multiple realities of school-university collaboration. *The Educational Forum, 40,* 341–350.

Martin, W. B. W. 1976. *The negotiated order of the school.* Toronto, ON: MacMillan Company of Canada Limited.

Maudsley, D. 1992, March. Teacher education. Comments and closing remarks for session: Orientation for faculties of education on the restructuring initiatives. Toronto, ON: Ministry of Education.

May, P. A. 1989. That was yesterday, and (hopefully) yesterday is gone. *American Indian and Alaska Native Mental Health Research, 2*(3), 71–74.

McAlpine, L.; Cross, E.; Whiteduck, G.; and Wolforth, J. 1990. Defining Aboriginal teacher education programs through two pairs of eyes. *Canadian Journal of Native Education, 17*(2), 82–87.

McIntyre, A. 1981. *After virtue: A study in moral theory*. Notre Dame, IN: University of Notre Dame Press.

McKay, R. A. 1990. Children's construction of meaning in a thematic unit. University of Alberta, Edmonton, Canada.

McKernan, J. 1991. Action inquiry. In E. Short (Ed.), *Forms of curriculum inquiry* (pp. 309–326). Albany, NY: State University of New York Press.

Medicine, B. 1993, March. Prelude to research in an indigenous community in Canada. Paper presented at the meeting of the Royal Commission on Aboriginal Peoples, Montreal, Canada.

Miller, J. L. 1990. *Creating spaces and finding voices: Teachers collaborating for empowerment*. Albany, NY: State University of New York Press.

Miller, J. P. 1988. *The holistic curriculum*. Toronto, ON: OISE Press.

National Indian Brotherhood, Assembly of First Nations. 1988. *Tradition and education: Toward a vision of our future* (Vol. 1). Summerstown, ON:Author.

National Science Teachers Association. 1982. *Science-technology-society: Science education for the '80's. Position statement*. Washington, DC: Author.

Nias, J. 1987. Learning from difference: A collegial approach to change. In J. Smyth (Ed.), *Educating teachers: Changing the nature of pedagogical knowledge* (pp. 137–154). London: Falmer Press.

———. 1992. Introduction. In C. Biott & J. Nias (Eds.), *Working and learning together for change*. Bristol, PA: Open University Press.

Nias, J.; Southworth, G.; and Yeomans, R. 1989. *Staff relationships in the primary school*. London: Cassell.

Nieto, S. 1994. Lessons from students on creating a chance to dream. *Harvard Educational Review, 64*(4), 392–496.

Noddings, N. 1984. *Caring: A feminine approach to ethics and moral education*. Berkeley, CA: University of California Press.

———. 1986. Fidelity in teaching, teacher education, and research for teaching. *Harvard Educational Review, 56*(4), 496–510.

Noffke, S., and Brennan, M. 1991. Student teachers use action research: Issues and examples. In R. Tabachnich & K. Zeichner (Eds.), *Issues and practices in inquiry-oriented teacher education* (pp. 186–201). London: Falmer Press.

Nur, M. 1983. University-district collaboration for promoting change in curriculum and classroom practice. *Theory into Practice, 22*(3), 224–230.

Oakes, J.; Hare, S.; and Sirotnik, K. A. 1986. Collaborative inquiry: A congenial paradigm in a cantankerous world. *Teachers College Record, 87*(4), 545–561.

Oja, S. N., and Smulyan, L. 1989. *Collaborative action research: A developmental approach*. Philadelphia, PA: Falmer Press.

Olds, L. 1992. *Metaphors of interrelatedness*. Albany, NY: State University of New York Press.

Olesen, V. 1994. Feminisms and models of qualitative research. In N. K. Denzin & Y. S. Lincoln (Eds.), *Handbook of qualitative research* (pp. 158–174). San Francisco: Sage.

Olson, M. 1993. Narrative authority in (teacher) education. University of Alberta, Edmonton, Canada.

———. 1994. Interlocking narratives in teacher education. *Journal of Professional Studies, 1*(2), 26–34.

———. 1995a. Co-authoring professional re-creation. Paper presented at the Canadian Society for the Study of Education, Montreal, Canada.

———. 1995b. Conceptualizing narrative authority: Implications for teacher education. *Teaching and Teacher Education, 11*(2), 119–135.

O'Neill, M. 1990. *Women speaking, women listening*. Maryknoll, NY: Orbis Books.

Ontario Royal Commission. 1994. *For the love of learning. Report of the Royal Commission on Learning*. Ottawa, ON: Queen's Printer.

Paley, V. 1979. *White teacher*. Cambridge, MA: Harvard University Press.

———. 1986. On listening to what the children say. *Harvard Educational Review, 56*(2), 122–131.

Pallante, J. A. 1993. Selected perspectives on teacher reform efforts. *Action in Teacher Education, 15*(2), 25–34.

Pascale, P. 1990. *Managing on the edge*. New York, NY: Touchstone.

Patterson, L., and Stansell, J. 1987. Teachers and researchers: A new mutualism. *Language Arts, 64*(7), 717–721.

Patterson, R. S. 1983. Go, grit and gumption: A normal school perspective on teacher education. Paper presented at the McCalla Lecture, Faculty of Education, University of Alberta, Edmonton, Canada.

Polkinghorne, D. 1988. *Narrative knowing in the human sciences*. Albany, NY: State University of New York Press.

Raths, J.; McAninch, A.; and Katz, L. 1991. A plight of teacher education: Clinical mentalities in a scientific culture. *Advances in Teacher Education, 4*, 37–48.

Rizvi, F., and Kemmis, S. 1987. *Dilemmas of reform: The participation and equity program in schools.* Geelong, Australia: Deakin Institute for Studies in Education.

Rogoff, B. 1994. Developing understanding of the idea of communities of learners. *Mind, Culture, and Activity, 1*(4), 209–229.

Rorty, R. 1989. *Contingency, irony, and solidarity.* Cambridge, MA: Cambridge University Press.

———. 1991. *Objectivity, relativism and truth: Philosophical papers* (Vol. 1). Cambridge, MA: Cambridge University Press.

Rothe, J. P. 1982. Researching Native education: An ethnomethodological perspective. *Canadian Journal of Native Education, 9*(4), 1–11.

Royal Commission on Aboriginal Peoples. 1993. *Ethical guidelines for research.* Ottawa, ON: Author.

Rushcamp, S., and Roehler, L. R. 1992. Characteristics supporting change in a professional development school. *Journal of Teacher Education, 43*(1), 19–27.

Russell, T., and Munby, H. 1991. Reframing: The role of experience in developing teachers' professional knowledge. In D. Schön (Ed.), *The reflective turn* (pp. 164–187). New York: Teachers College Press.

Ryan, J. R., and Robinson, M. P. 1992. Participatory action research: An examination of two northern case studies. University of Calgary, Arctic Institute of North America, Calgary, Canada.

Saskatchewan Education. 1992. *Mathematics: A curriculum guide for the elementary level.* Regina, SK: Author.

———. 1993. *Science: A curriculum guide for the middle level.* Regina, SK: Author.

Schön, D. A. 1979. Generative metaphor: A perspective on problem-setting in social policy. In A. Ortony (Ed.), *Metaphor and thought* (pp. 254–283). Cambridge, MA: Cambridge University Press.

———. 1983. *The reflective practitioner.* New York: Basic Books.

———. 1987. *Educating the reflective practitioner: Toward a new design for teaching and learning in the professions.* San Francisco: Jossey-Bass.

Schubert, W., and Ayers, W. (Eds.). 1992. *Teacher lore: Learning from our own experience.* New York: Longman.

Schulz, R. 1994, January. Coming to know about teachers' lives and teaching: Methods and issues. University of Alberta, The Centre for Research for Teacher Education and Development, Edmonton, Canada.

Schutz, A. 1970. On phenomenology and social relations: Selected writings. Chicago: University of Chicago Press.

Schutz, A.; Abbey, S.; Drake, S.; Reynolds, C.; Elliott, A.; Castle, J.; Richards, M.; and Woloshyn, V. 1992, November. Collaborative reflection through story: The graduate educational experience. Paper presented at the American Education Research Association Conference, Pennsylvania State University.

Senge, P. 1990. *The fifth discipline. The art and practice of the learning organization.* New York: Currency/Doubleday.

Sherman. R., and Webb, R. B. 1988. Qualitative research in education: A focus. In R. Sherman & R. B. Webb (Eds.), *Qualitative research in education: Focus and methods* (pp. 2–21). Barcombe, Lewes, UK: Falmer Press.

Shulha, L., and Wilson, R. 1993, June. When teachers are collaborators: The invitation to collaborative research. Paper presented at the annual meeting of the Canadian Society for the Study of Education, Ottawa, ON.

Sirotnik, K. A. 1988. The meaning and conduct of inquiry in school-university partnerships. In K. A. Sirotnik & J. Goodlad (Eds.), *School-university partnerships in action: Concepts, cases, and concerns* (pp. 169–190). New York: Teachers College Press.

Sirotnik, K. A., and Goodlad, J. I. (Eds.). 1988. *School-university partnerships in action: Concepts, cases, and concerns.* New York: Teachers College Press.

Skau, K. 1987. Collaborative research in education: A useful approach. *Education Canada, 27*(2), 14–19.

Skemp, R. R. 1989. *Mathematics in the primary school.* London: Routledge.

————. 1993a. *Sail through mathematics. Structured activities for intelligent learning* (Vol. 1). Calgary, AB: EEC Ltd.

————. 1993b. *Sail through mathematics. Structured activities for intelligent learning* (Vol. 2). Calgary, AB: EEC Ltd.

Smith, S. L. 1991. *Report of the Commisson of Inquiry on Canadian University Education.* Ottawa, ON: Association of Universities and Colleges of Canada.

Social Sciences and Humanities Research Council of Canada. 1983. *SSHRC granting programs.* Ottawa, Canada: Author.

Somekh, B. 1991. Collaborative action research: Working together towards professional development. In C. Biott (Ed.), *Semi-detached teachers: Building support and advisory relationships in classrooms,* (pp. 67–84). London: Falmer Press.

————. 1994, April. Inhabiting each other's castles: Towards knowledge and mutual growth through collaboration. Paper presented at the symposium, The Many Faces of School/University Collaboration, at the annual meeting of the American Educational Research Association, New Orleans, LA.

Spradley, J. 1979. *The ethnographic interview.* New York: Holt, Rinehart and Winston.

St. Denis, V. 1992. Community-based participatory research: Aspects of the concept relevant for practice. *Native Studies Review, 8*(2), 51–74.

Stacey, R. 1992. *Managing the unknowable.* San Francisco: Jossey-Bass.

Stairs, A. 1994, April. Human development as cultural negotiation: Indigenous lessons on becoming a teacher. Paper presented at the annual meeting of the American Educational Research Association, New Orleans, LA.

Stewart, H. J. 1992. English plus: An innovative honors English program. *Brock Education, 2*(1), 16–19.

―――. 1993. A Search for identity: A retrospective view of the processes of formation of the Brock Faculty of Education Centre on Collaborative Research. In D. J. Clandinin (Ed.), *Searching for connections: Struggling for community* (pp. 14–21). Edmonton AB: Among Teachers Community, Research for Teacher Education and Development, University of Alberta.

Stewart, H. J.; Abbey, S.; Castle, J.; Elliott, A.; Reynolds, C.; and Schutz, A. 1994, April. Exploring collaborative research: Grounded theory in process—metaphor: Heuristic for examining processes of collaboration. Paper presented at the annual meeting of the American Educational Research Association Conference, New Orleans, LA.

Tabachnich, B. R., and Zeichner, K. (Eds.). 1991. *Issues and practices in inquiry-oriented teacher education.* London: Falmer Press.

Tafoya, T. 1982. Coyotes eyes: Native cognition styles. *Journal of American Indian Education, 2,* 21–33.

Taylor, M.; Goulet, L.; Hart, P.; Robottom, I.; and Sykes, H. 1993. *Yukon Native Teacher Education Program: Beginning the story.* Regina, SK: University of Regina, Saskatchewan Instructional Development and Research Unit.

Thompkins, G. E., and McGee, L. M. 1993. *Teaching reading with literature.* New York: Merrill.

Tikunoff, W. J., and Ward, B. A. 1983. Collaborative research on teaching. *The Elementary School Journal, 83*(4), 453–468.

Tikunoff, W. J.; Ward, B. A.; and Griffin, G. A. 1979. *Interactive research and development on teaching: Final report* (Report 1R & DT-79-11). San Francisco: Far West Laboratory for Educational Research and Development.

Tripp, D. H. 1987. Teachers, journals and collaborative research. In J. Smyth (Ed.), *Educating teachers: Changing the nature of pedagogical knowledge* (pp. 179–191). New York: Falmer Press.

University of Alberta. 1995/6. *University of Alberta Calendar.* Edmonton, AB: Author.

Urban, W. J. 1990. Historical studies of teacher education. In W. R. Houston (Ed.), *Handbook of research on teacher education* (pp. 59–71). New York: Macmillan.

Valli, L. 1994, April. Professional development schools: Reconceptualizing schooling and teacher education as learning communities. Paper presented at the 14th Annual Conference of the International Society of Teacher Educators, Maastricht, Netherlands.

Van Manen, M. 1990. *Researching lived experience: Human science for an action sensitive pedagogy.* London, ON: Althouse Press.

Vare, J. W. 1994. Partnership contrasts: Microteaching activity as two apprenticeships in thinking. *Journal of Teacher Education, 45*(3), 209–217.

Varela, F.J. 1987. Laying down a path in walking. In W.I. Thompson (Ed.), *GAIA: A way of knowing: Political implications of the new biology* (pp. 48–64). Hudson, NY: Lindisfarne Press.

Vygotsky, L. S. 1962. *Thought and language.* Cambridge, MA: Massachusetts Institute of Technology Press.

Wallace, J., and Louden, W. 1991, April. Qualities of collaboration and the growth of teachers' knowledge. Paper presented at the meeting of the American Educational Research Association, Chicago, IL.

Watson, N., and Allison, P. 1992, April. Ontario faculties of education responding to change. A report prepared for the Ontario Association of Deans of Education, Queen's Park, Toronto, Ontario.

———. 1993. Responding to change. *Brock Education, 2*(3), 1–3.

Watson, N., and Fullan, M. G. 1992. Beyond school district-university partnerships. In M. Fullan & A. Hargreaves (Eds.), *Teacher development and educational change* (pp. 213–242). London: Falmer Press.

Wax, M. L. 1991. The ethics of research in American Indian communities. *American Indian Quarterly, 15*(4), 431–456.

Webb, K. M. 1994. The parent-visitor story. *Among Teachers, 14,* 5–9.

Webb, K. M., and Blond, J. M. 1994, April. Teacher as curriculum maker: Researcher and practitioner perspectives. Paper presented at the annual meeting of the American Educational Research Association, New Orleans, LA.

————. 1995. Teacher knowledge: The relationship between caring and knowing. *Teaching and Teacher Education, 11*(6), 611–626.

Webb, K. M.; Schulz, R.; Schroeder, D.; and Brody, C. 1994, April. Collaborative narrative inquiry: Fidelity and the ethics of caring in teacher research. Paper presented at the annual meeting of the American Educational Research Association, New Orleans, LA.

Weinsheimer, J. 1985. *Gadamer's hermeneutics: A reading of truth and method.* New Haven, CT: Yale University Press.

————— 1991. Gadamer's metaphorical hermeneutics. In H. Silverman (Ed.), *Gadamer and hermeneutics* (pp. 181–201). New York: Routledge.

Witherell, C., and Noddings, N. (Eds.). 1991. *Stories lives tell: Narrative and dialogue in education.* New York: Teachers College Press.

Wittrock, M. C. (Ed.). 1986. *Handbook of research on teaching* (3rd ed.). New York: Macmillan.

Woods, P. 1988. Educational ethnography in Britain. In R. Sherman & R. B. Webb (Eds.), *Qualitative research in education: Focus and methods* (pp. 90–109). Philadelphia: Falmer Press.

Yonge, G. 1985. Andragogy and pedagogy: Two ways of accompaniment. *Adult Education Quarterly, 38*, 160–172.

Yopp, H. K.; Guillaume, A. M.; and Savage, T. V. 1993–94. Collaboration at the grassroots: Implementing the professional development school concept. *Action in Teacher Education, 15*(4), 29–35.

Zajano, N. C., and Edelsberg, C. M. 1993. Living and writing the researcher-researched relationship. *International Journal of Qualitative Studies in Education, 6*(2), 143–157.

Zeichner, K. M. 1990. Changing directions in the practicum: Looking ahead to the 1990s. *Journal of Education for Teaching, 16*(2), 105–132.

Zukav, G. 1986. *The dancing wu li masters: An overview of the new physics* (8th ed.). Toronto, ON: Bantam.

ABOUT THE CONTRIBUTORS

Brian Aubichon has worked 16 years in affirmative action adult education. He is a Native educator and the Executive Director of the Yukon Native Teacher Education Program (YNTEP).

Penelope Bailey was a lecturer and the Elementary Program Manager in the Faculty of Education at the University of Regina, Saskatchewan.

Jan Basaraba is an assistant department head of English with the Lincoln County School Board, St. Catharines, Ontario. She became increasingly interested in the research process and curriculum innovations during the collaborative project with Susan.

Mary Beattie is an associate professor in the Department of Educational Policy and Foundational Studies in the Faculty of Education, University of Toronto. Her interests lie in teacher development, teacher education at the pre-service level, and narrative inquiry.

Sandra Blenkinsop is an associate professor of language arts education in the Faculty of Education, University of Regina. She has worked collaboratively both in the development of workshops for in-service teachers and in the integration of science and language arts methods courses in a teacher education program.

313

Janet Blond, in teaching and in life, views connectedness and being connected as important. She has taught school for many years with the Edmonton Public School Board.

Joyce Castle teaches pre-service and in-service courses in the Faculty of Education at Brock University, where she is an associate professor and Coordinator of Field Experiences.

Helen Christiansen has a long standing interest in working collaboratively with teachers, student teachers, and teacher educators. She is an associate professor in the Faculty of Education, University of Regina, specializing in secondary and French immersion teacher education.

D. Jean Clandinin is currently a professor and Director of the Centre for Research for Teacher Education and Development at the University of Alberta. She is recognized as an international scholar in the areas of personal practical knowledge and narrative as process and product of inquiry. Throughout her professional career, she has promoted collaborative research between teachers and teacher educators.

Martha B. Crago is an associate professor in the School of Human Communication Disorders at McGill University, Quebec. She has conducted cross-linguistic research on family aggregations with specific-language impairment in a series of language-socialization studies within the homes and schools of the Inuit, Cree, Mohawk, and Algonquin communities.

Janet Devitt is a teacher on secondment from the Regina Public School Board. A long-time cooperating teacher, she specializes in early childhood and elementary teacher education in French immersion at the University of Regina.

Zoe Donoahue has taught with the Etobicoke Board of Education in North Bay, Ontario, for the past nine years. She is currently completing her M.Ed. degree.

Susan Drake is an associate professor in the Graduate Education Department of the Faculty of Education at Brock University and is on the steering committee of the Brock Centre on Collaborative Research (CCR).

David Friesen is an associate professor in the Faculty of Education, University of Regina. He teaches in the Educational Professional Studies area and is interested in collaborative and hermeneutic inquiry.

Linda Goulet is an assistant professor in the Department of Indian Education at the Saskatchewan Indian Federated College (SIFC) at the University of Regina. She has been associated with

First Nations teacher education programs for many years and participated in several collaborative research projects in education.

Mary Hookey is an associate professor in the Faculty of Education, at Nipissing University, North Bay, Ontario. Her research interests include working in collaborative endeavors with teachers in the development of classroom music programs.

R. H. (Bert) Horwood was a science teacher, department head, and school inspector, before his twenty-five years as a professor of education at Queen's University. He has been involved in experiential education research and is author of a number of natural science textbooks.

Phyllis Kapuscinski was a science education professor in the Faculty of Education at the University of Regina. She worked collaboratively with faculty on several research projects.

Karne Kozolanka taught at the University of Regina in the Vocational and Technology Education Department. He is interested in research that focuses on engaging students in the teaching of technology in social contexts.

Caroline Krentz is a professor in the Elementary Education and Graduate Studies programs in the Faculty of Education at the University of Regina. As Director of the Saskatchewan Instructional Development and Research Unit (SIDRU), she collaborates on an ongoing basis with researchers and writers.

Mhairi (Vi) Maeers is an assistant professor of mathematics education at the University of Regina. Vi is presently working on two collaborative action research projects with elementary teachers and enjoys working collaboratively with colleagues and pre-service students.

Lynn McAlpine is the Associate Director at the Office of Native and Northern Education in the Faculty of Education at McGill University. Her research pursuits include classroom interaction and local control of field-based aboriginal education, especially as it applies to culturally sensitive teacher education.

Shelley Neal, a teacher of thirteen years, is presently on staff with the Etobicoke Board of Education in North Bay, Ontario, and working on her M.Ed. in the area of curriculum development.

Margaret Olson is an assistant professor in teacher education at St. Francis Xavier University in Nova Scotia.

Jeff Orr is an assistant professor in social studies and cross-cultural education at St. Francis Xavier University in Nova Scotia.

Lorri Robison, as an elementary teacher in the Regina Public School Division, has worked collaboratively on projects that involved the implementation of new curriculum in Saskatchewan schools.

Debra Schroeder is an early childhood classroom teacher in Lacombe, Alberta, working on her Ph.D. in teacher education.

Helen J. Stewart was an assistant professor in the Faculty of Education at Brock University and a founding member of the Centre on Collaborative Research (CCR). She published extensively for the Ministry of Education in Ontario. Her untimely death has saddened all who knew her and she will be greatly missed by her friends and colleagues across the country.

Kathie Webb was a Commonwealth Scholar in the Department of Educational Administration at the University of Alberta. Her doctoral research focused on teachers' personal practical knowledge and its implications for curriculum change and teacher development.

Beth Warkentin, as a sessional lecturer and Elementary Program Manager, has been extensively involved in the collaborative planning and implementation of curriculum in the Educational Professional Studies courses in the Faculty of Education at the University of Regina. Currently, she is working on collaborative action research in the teaching and assessing of experiential learning.

INDEX

317